OUR OWN WORST ENEMY

The Assault from within on Modern Democracy

Tom Nichols

OXFORD
UNIVERSITY PRESS

OXFORD
UNIVERSITY PRESS

Oxford University Press is a department of the University of Oxford. It furthers
the University's objective of excellence in research, scholarship, and education
by publishing worldwide. Oxford is a registered trade mark of Oxford University
Press in the UK and certain other countries.

Published in the United States of America by Oxford University Press
198 Madison Avenue, New York, NY 10016, United States of America.

Library of Congress Control Number: 2021939765
ISBN 978-0-19-751887-8

3 5 7 9 8 6 4 2

Printed by LSC Communications, United States of America

For Lynn
Who makes everything possible

TABLE OF CONTENTS

PREFACE

Sometimes, when you present an argument in writing and then talk about it with the public, you come to realize there's an even larger argument lurking beneath it. It comes up even when you think you might be talking about something else. It might not be an argument you wanted to make, and it is often uncomfortable to confront it, but it's there. That's how the book you're now reading came about.

In 2013 I wrote an essay called "The Death of Expertise," which a few years later became a popular book with that same title. It was about the disturbing ways in which people reject established knowledge and argue with experts as if they know what they're talking about. Some of it was, of course, just the usual complaining from intellectuals like me about how people should listen to intellectuals like me. Even as I wrote it, I had the sense that something even more chilling was taking place, and I could tell from the comments from readers and at public discussions and lectures over the years that others had the same fear. Maybe the rejection of knowledge wasn't just about people not knowing very much. Maybe it was just one of many arenas of social conflict threatening to undermine the foundations of civic life in democracies. Maybe it was one of the many accumulating symptoms of the decline of liberal democracy itself.

Everywhere I went, in the United States or abroad, discussions about knowledge and science turned to darker concerns about the survival of democracy, and I was almost always asked the same question: How long can we go on like this? Usually, I answered with what now seems in retrospect to be unwarranted optimism. I told audiences that I was confident that when faced with a major disaster, such as a war, or a depression, or perhaps even a pandemic—a possibility I raised often while still thinking it unlikely—Americans would rise to the challenge. This was before COVID-19 had a name.

And while some of these concerns were directly related to the rise of Donald Trump, even there (despite my early and consistent opposition to Trump and his authoritarian political movement), I argued for a calm approach. I reassured audiences and told them to trust in the culture of constitutionalism and the resilience of democratic institutions. I could see that illiberalism was on the rise in other nations, but I held out the hope—the exceptionalist belief, really—that the United States would hold firm even if other nations wavered.

These assurances about the durability of Western democracy were sincere, but beneath them I also harbored worries that had been growing for some time, many of them before the new wave of authoritarianism in Europe, before the COVID pandemic, before Trump's multiple attacks on democracy and the rule of law, and before his fight to stay in power that culminated in the first successful breach of the U.S. Capitol by hostile forces since 1814. In *The Death of Expertise*, I wrote that when voters abdicate their responsibilities as citizens, they "lose control of important decisions and risk the hijacking of their democracy by ignorant demagogues, or the more quiet and gradual decay of their democratic institutions into authoritarian technocracy." I did not, at the moment I wrote those words, foresee the emergence of any one leader, whether Viktor Orbán in Hungary,

Recep Erdoğan in Turkey, Narendra Modi in India, Jair Bolsonaro in Brazil, or Trump in the United States. But I had long been worried about the appearance of someone, or something, like all of them.

Some of this anxiety was perhaps just the natural extension of spending too much time observing authoritarian regimes. In my early career, I was a scholar of the old Soviet Union. When you study (and visit) repressive countries, you think hard about what makes your own nation different. You wonder whether the freedoms you cherish—the ability to move about freely, to say what you please, to associate with others at will, to worship if you so choose—are fragile and transitory. It's a fear inherent in every open society, I suppose. This is why we carve inspirational odes to democracy in the stone walls of memorials to Jefferson and Lincoln: they are a tribute to our own doubts, a hope that marble and granite will give permanence to those words and ideals even if we ourselves might not always defend them.

The blossoming of newly free societies at the end of the twentieth century also encouraged me to put away some of my doubts. The collapse of the USSR and the great wave of democratization that followed it in the 1990s was supposedly the "third" wave of human liberation, after the great social revolutions of the eighteenth century and then the defeat of fascism in the 1940s. Heading into the new century, it seemed that the only question was how fast democracy, in its various iterations, could now spread across the globe. I did not believe that we had solved all of life's problems—just one of the biggest facing us at the time. There will always be authoritarian governments as long as there are corrupt and evil human beings, but absent a nightmare like a nuclear war or mass starvation, I was confident that in the postindustrial world, we were no longer arguing over whether liberal democracy—the kind based on tolerance, trust, and inalienable human rights—was here to stay. The fall of the authoritarians and the surge of liberal democracy might not be Francis Fukuyama's "end of history," but it was progress and it was in the right direction. Maybe we'd finally learned our lesson as a species.

Or so I thought. I watched with sadness as the brief Russian experiment with democracy hardened back into Vladimir Putin's dictatorship, but I hoped that Russia was the exception. The idea that democratization, particularly where it was already well established, could start to unwind still seemed to me to be unnatural. And yet, here we are. (The condition of global democracy is now so precarious that one group of Swedish scholars at the University of Gothenburg has called the early twenty-first century a new "wave of *autocratization*.") My particular assumption that the United States would always look like the United States turned out—painfully—to be more a matter of pride than evidence.

In the 1990s, my Russian friends used to scoff at my advice as an American about their constitutional issues, telling me that America was just too young a country to give anyone pointers about democracy. Yes, I would always answer, Russia is an ancient *country*, but a young *state*, while America was a young country but governed by a constitution that was established while Russia was still a land of tsars and serfs. I was confident enough in this fact that I did not hesitate to lecture my Russian colleagues on the virtues of liberal democracy.

I am more reticent to deliver such sermons these days.

There are signs of hope, even if they are small and inconstant. Illiberal populists, as it turns out, are pretty lousy at governing, especially during a crisis that demands a steady and stoic engagement with science. In the United States, in particular, voters saw a mismanaged pandemic become a politicized catastrophe that eventually inflicted a 9/11-level death toll almost every day, and as of this writing has killed more Americans than combat in World War I, World War II, the Korean War, and Vietnam combined. Partly as a consequence of this disaster, Donald Trump was driven from office with a record voter turnout. His party, however, gained ground, and if some forty or fifty thousand voters spread across just four or five American states changed their votes, Trump would still be leading the charge against liberal democracy from behind the Resolute Desk in the Oval Office.

Even if voters in the United States and elsewhere who once preferred such regimes are rethinking their choices, the damage is already done. The citizens of the world's democracies now must live with the undeniable knowledge that they are capable of embracing illiberal movements and attacking their own liberties as a matter of their own free will rather than as the result of disaster or foreign conquest. Worse, the budding authoritarians who live among us now know it too. They have seen a demonstrated market for what they are selling. They will be back, and the next time they will bring glossier and better-packaged versions of dictatorship than the ragged prototypes this first wave of loud and pushy salesmen offered.

* * *

This book covers a wide range of subjects and disciplines, and I am grateful to the many people who offered insights and feedback on several topics. This list is incomplete, but I would like to thank Chris Arnade, Ellen Braaten, Ian Bremmer, Jonathan Cristol, Dennis Herring, Toomas Ilves, Steve Knott, Scott Lincicome, Brink Lindsey, Edward Luce, Jennifer Taub, Steve Van Anglen, and Gary Winslet, as well as the anonymous reviewers at Oxford University Press. I was able to explore some of the concepts in the book in my writing as a columnist for *USA Today* and as a contributing writer at *The Atlantic*, and I am grateful to the editors at both publications, and especially Jill Lawrence and Whitney Dangerfield, respectively.

I owe special thanks to three friends and colleagues who rendered assistance beyond the call of professional duty. Nick Gvosdev walked me through many discussions as I tried to clarify my own thinking on the key propositions in this study. Geoff Kabaservice returned detailed comments on several drafts, an arduous service that made significant improvements to the final version. Windsor Mann reminded me to revisit classic works on populism and authoritarianism, and he pointed me toward important sources at each stage of the project. And, of course, my editor at Oxford, David McBride, provided important insights and honest criticism while allowing me to benefit from his patience as he guided me along the path from the project's inception to its final version. These friends and colleagues all helped to create some of the best moments in this book, but the flaws, errors, and arguments are mine alone.

I am fortunate to work for two institutions that actively support faculty research. The Harvard Extension School encourages student involvement with faculty research and made it possible for me to work with excellent students there as research assistants, and I would like to thank Madelyn McGlynn, Meredith McKinney, and Kathryn Kennedy for their help. I also would like to thank my colleagues at the Naval War College and my department chairman, Derek Reveron, for the supportive and intellectually invigorating environment at the College, but, as always, the views in this book are mine and do not reflect the views of the Naval War College, the Defense Department, or any agency of the U.S. government.

Finally, I owe the greatest thanks to my wife, Lynn. I am difficult to live with on my best days, but when I'm trying to write, only my cat, Carla, should have to put up with me. Lynn listened with great patience as I tried to unravel the various ideas in these pages, and then she offered wise reflections and advice that made me a better writer and a better person for listening to her. She also provided detailed editorial assistance on more drafts than I could count. She made this book—and so much else in my life—possible, and so it is dedicated to her with love and gratitude.

* * *

I am asking you, the reader, to join me in a difficult look at ourselves as voters and citizens, and so before we begin, I'll add one more story here that I hope encourages you to continue on through the coming pages.

In the summer of 2012, my father was ninety-four years old. My mother had passed away many years earlier, and his health was rapidly deteriorating. An election was coming, and despite his fading vitality, Dad was as alert and as interested in politics as he had been when he cast his first presidential vote for Franklin Roosevelt. Both of my parents were the children of immigrants, high-school dropouts from impoverished childhoods during the Great Depression, and they were natural members of the twentieth-century Democratic Party well into middle age. And like many in the white working class, they abandoned the Democrats after the upheavals of the late 1960s.

Still, my father would brook no criticism of FDR. Likewise, my Irish American mother when she was alive never allowed a harsh word to be spoken against John F. Kennedy, whom she routinely called "Jack." Our house in a factory town in Massachusetts reflected our mixed political history: Mom hung a portrait of JFK in our dining room shortly after the assassination, and my father tacked up a picture of Ronald Reagan near his desk sometime in the 1990s after Reagan's announcement of his Alzheimer's diagnosis and his retreat from public life. Both pictures were still there when I sold the house after my parents were both gone.

My father was a diligent voter who never missed an election. Even after he moved to the right, he often split his tickets between Democrats (at least at the state and local level) and the national Republicans. Despite this occasional bipartisan voting, he was the personification of the old "Archie Bunker" stereotype. Perhaps even that is too kind. I could say that he was "a man of his time and place," but that is just a gentle way of saying that my father was a bigot. But he also had an old-school reverence for American political institutions, and especially for the presidency, that restrained him from speaking too viciously of candidates and sitting presidents—even when Barack Obama became the first African American president. And despite being poor for a good part of his life, my father had no interest in populism. He rejected fringe candidates like George Wallace in 1968 or Ross Perot in 1992. When Donald Trump opened a 1999 exploration for the presidency, I recall my father reacting with open ridicule.

One afternoon during that last summer of his life, we were sitting in his room in an assisted care facility. He had trouble getting around, and so we spent a lot of time just watching television together. President Obama was giving a campaign speech that day, and looking ahead to the election, I said, "I think he's got this one, Dad." Obama's opponent, Mitt Romney, had been our governor in Massachusetts, and we both thought well of him, but we knew he had little chance against Obama. My father nodded, and then he said something I did not expect to hear from him after a lifetime of bigotry and right-wing views.

"They're both good men," Dad said. "We'll be fine no matter who wins."

My father died peacefully a few weeks later and never cast his final vote. I am still struck, however, by how remarkable it now seems that a man like my father would look at Barack Obama and Mitt Romney and feel that the country would be just fine no matter who won.

And yet this kind of equanimity was once normal in American life. Although it may seem like we've been living with it forever, the dramatic and silly hysteria that every election is the last, that civilization hangs in the balance, and that our fellow citizens are an intolerable threat to our own safety, is in fact a relatively new phenomenon. There was once a time when no one was really voting for Jimmy Carter or Bob Dole because they thought Gerald Ford or Bill Clinton was the end of the world. We were once a nation too sensible and serious to believe such nonsense. And if my father—a man hobbled by a childhood of poverty and a lifetime of sexism and racism—could still believe in 2012 that the political system would endure, that both of the candidates were good people, and that America could prosper no matter who was elected, then perhaps the rest of us can believe it too.

Sometimes, when I think about that afternoon with my father, I wonder if things will ever be fine again. Some days I am more pessimistic than others. But if I am certain of anything, it is that it is well within our power as citizens to return to a more civic and more confident democratic life, if we so choose. We do not have to remain slaves to our anger and our fears. We do not have destroy our own traditions and institutions out of rage and resentment. We do not have to live this way. That is why I wrote this book.

Introduction

Our Own Worst Enemy

Open societies across the democratic world—some so-called new, others old established ones—are one by one turning toward what they themselves proudly proclaim as "illiberal democracy," characterized by restrictions of freedom, by corruption, arbitrariness, and sometimes even by fear and repressions of the sort we in the formerly communist East strived so hard to leave behind us. The various putative causes for this have been weighed and discussed enough, but to little avail: "Globalism," "the revolt of ones left behind," the "failure of the elites."

This is nonsense.

—Former Estonian President Toomas Ilves

Each age suffers moments of bitter disappointment, and so it was at the beginning of the new century, when hopes faded for that thing everybody called democracy.

—John Keane

BURN IT ALL DOWN

You can hear it everywhere. These are just the worst times ever, and we all know it. We're awash in crime and drugs and joblessness. We're killing ourselves, intentionally and accidentally. Maybe we're even on the verge of another civil war. Even before COVID-19 arrived and sank us all into a new misery that made us think of the time before the pandemic as the Good Old Days, Americans and other citizens of the world's democracies were worn out, fed up, angry. Freedom, prosperity, peace—these were just the slogans of regimes that had promised these benefits and then provided nothing but stagnation and endless war. Perhaps the Constitution has run its course, or maybe liberal democracy itself was just a bad idea, a blip on the historical radar, and now it's time to move on. Either way, "the system" has failed, and so perhaps we ourselves should destroy it.

This is all nonsense, as Toomas Ilves, a former president of Estonia, noted in 2019. (The Estonians, having lived through decades in a Soviet republic, are a people who know a thing or two about repression and deprivation.) The citizens of the world's democracies are living in a time of peace and plenty that was unimaginable a half century ago. The increases in living standards even in my own adult lifetime are stunning—and I'd like to think I'm not *that* old. Had anyone said forty or fifty years ago that everything from energy to clothing would be cheaper and better, that food would be so plentiful that we wouldn't know what to do with most of it, that the Soviet Union would vanish peacefully and that we would dismantle tens of thousands of nuclear weapons, or that diseases that once struck fear into us were curable, most people would have burst out laughing at such utopianism. This is the twenty-first century. We were supposed to be choking on overpopulation, eating Soylent Green, and joining gangs in the wasteland to protect our supplies of water and gasoline. Instead, we're put out when the Wi-Fi goes down on our flight to Orlando.

This all sounds, I realize, like the huffy sniffing of British prime minister Harold Macmillan in 1957, when he declared that "most of our people have never had it so good." It was true when Macmillan said it, of course, because it's true in almost *any* given year that life is generally better than in the past. We can always look back a few decades and say that things are better than they were, and to insist that people settle for things being better than the absolute misery of some earlier era is to be the annoying grandfather at the Thanksgiving table droning on about tying cardboard to his feet for shoes during the Great Depression. We can be grateful for improvements while remaining aware of the problems we face, even in a time of relative well-being.

But we also cannot completely ignore the reality around us. The world isn't perfect, but perfection is not a true measure of government, much less of an entire era. The question, rather, is whether liberal democracy has somehow failed us on its own terms, and made life less free, less prosperous, and even less worth living, in ways that justify retracting our consent to be governed by such arrangements.

Millions of people in the United States and the other established democracies seem to think so. Even before a mob overran the U.S. Capitol in January 2021—some of whom were intent on murdering members of the House and Senate and lynching the vice president—liberal democracy, by any number of measures, was in trouble. When nearly a fifth of the voters in America, Italy, and France (and a third of younger Europeans in general) think military rule would be a good idea, that's trouble.[1] When most people around the world, including four in ten Americans and Canadians, think a governing system in which someone "other than elected officials" made national decisions would be a good alternative to democracy, that's trouble. When fully a third of Americans, just a week before an election, think it is justified to "use violence to advance political goals," that's very serious trouble.[2] And when successive generations in democracies across the world think it is less and less "essential to live in a democracy," with the youngest citizens among us the least interested in democracy, that's not just trouble, but trouble for the foreseeable future.[3]

From the faltering democratic restorations in Poland and Hungary to the venerable "Mother of Parliaments" in the United Kingdom and her most populous and powerful offspring in India and the United States of America, liberal democratic government, with its notions of equality, tolerance, and compromise, is under assault from political movements and ordinary citizens who believe their interests and their futures are being subverted by malign forces at home and abroad. These citizens are turning to illiberal and anti-democratic alternatives, including a gamut of aspiring demagogues whose appeals run from know-nothing populism to blood-and-soil nationalism.

Who's to blame? Enraged populists of the right and would-be revolutionaries of the left (whose views on government are sometimes indistinguishable) have offered up a whole cast of villains, all of them in some form the hated "elites" who ostensibly run the lives of the innocent billions who just want to work at good jobs and be left alone. This, as the writer Dalibor Rohac has noted, is the essence of populism. It is a Manichean view that "pits good and pure-hearted 'ordinary people' against a self-serving, out-of-touch 'elite.' As such, populism is inherently divisive as it singles out specific groups as distinct from the people (elites, immigrants, bankers, journalists)."[4] To these groups standing in opposition to "The People," we could add globalists, military officers, bureaucrats, lawyers, experts, intellectuals, and anyone who might seem politically connected or economically privileged. They're all in on the same scam, we're told, and they all use "democracy" and "freedom" as meaningless incantations to cover up their complicity in the same conspiracy to squeeze the last few ounces of cheap labor from a victimized working class.

If you are one of the people who has lost a job, or seen your community collapse into a ghost town, or lost a loved one in a faraway war, this is a story that feels true at the most visceral level. It is what writers and ad-makers would call a "compelling" narrative, and like all compelling narratives, it has some elements of reality in it. It is also a narrative that is irresistible to political leaders. As the political scientist Ian Bremmer wrote in the run-up to the U.S. elections of 2020, victims seek saviors, and there is never a shortage of volunteers.

> Then the call for help is answered. Donald Trump tells an excited overflow crowd that he sees them, that he sees their enemies, and that only he can take them (back) to the promised land. Senators Elizabeth Warren and Bernie Sanders tell cheering fans that big corporations and Wall Street banks are robbing them blind. Champions of Brexit tell voters they must reclaim Britain's borders and reject laws and rules imposed by Europeans. European populists tell followers they will lead the charge of patriots against foreigners and globalists.[5]

It is perhaps even an understatement to call this "compelling." It is restorative, heroic, and hopeful. It is also dark, nostalgic, and vengeful. It is a promise to make us whole, but at the expense of others, to return us to the past or propel us forward into future, both places where we will be better off than today.

Whether rooted in sincere beliefs or merely the product of opportunism and lies, all of these appeals share the same jaundiced view of life in the early twenty-first century. This is especially the case for the populist right, a movement mired in nostalgia and social revenge that has emerged as the main threat to liberal democracy over the past twenty years. The writer Anne Applebaum notes that this new illiberalism is rooted in parties once called "rightist" but that have now become "a specific kind of right," one that is "more Bolshevik than Burkean" and seeks not to preserve but to destroy in order to "redefine their nations, to rewrite social contracts, and, sometimes, to alter the rules of democracy so that they never lose power." Alexander

Hamilton, she says ruefully, "warned against them, Cicero fought against them. Some of them used to be my friends."[6]

Indeed, these are the voices not of rebels but of those who are already in power, and their rhetoric is remarkably similar. In his inaugural speech in 2017, President Donald Trump depicted the United States as something like a failed state:

> Mothers and children trapped in poverty in our inner cities; rusted-out factories scattered like tombstones across the landscape of our nation; an education system, flush with cash, but which leaves our young and beautiful students deprived of knowledge; and the crime and gangs and drugs that have stolen too many lives and robbed our country of so much unrealized potential.[7]

Trump promised to stop this "American carnage," but his imagery was not much different from that of his right-populist counterparts around the world. "Liberal democracy," the Hungarian prime minister Viktor Orbán said in 2018, "is no longer able to protect people's dignity, provide freedom, guarantee physical security or maintain Christian culture," and he insisted that he would never allow Hungarians to be a "slave-like nation."[8] A hemisphere away, the Brazilian president Jair Bolsonaro promised to "unite the people" and "combat gender ideology"—meaning, apparently, the pernicious growth of equal rights for Brazilian women and sexual minorities.[9]

This is normally the kind of talk one hears from national leaders in the wake of a military defeat or a devastating economic collapse. Instead, these are leading figures in advanced nations who are promising to rescue their people from a world that is more prosperous, more peaceful, and—yes, even in the middle of a pandemic—healthier than it has ever been in history.

And this is why it is important to distinguish between smug political assertions about progress and a sensible recognition of the dramatic advances made by human society in the past century—because the state of the planet is itself a rebuke to such brutal and illiberal appeals. Indeed, modern standards of living are why populist leaders have to ramp up white-hot rhetoric about "carnage" or "gender ideology," lest the public doubt for a moment whether they should believe what they're hearing or seeing with their own lying eyes. These appeals have found an audience with millions of citizens of the advanced democracies. Political entrepreneurs have taken a dangerous mixture of entitlement, social resentment, and the natural human fear of change and fanned these emotions into ever larger flames of anger and dissatisfaction. After surviving multiple global conflicts (including the Cold War), after defeating oppressive institutions like slavery at home and totalitarianism overseas, after weathering multiple depressions and recessions, it seems that the only challenges democracies cannot overcome are peace and prosperity.

There's plenty of trouble on the planet, and more than enough of it in the United States, from economic stresses to climate change to the eternal struggle for political equality. All of these problems, however, are within the power of a democracy to solve, and none of them, no matter how awful, can explain millions of people voting to put gigantic economies, powerful militaries, and, in some cases, actual nuclear weapons in the hands of populist charlatans, outright racists, confused New Age mystics, or wealthy political tourists on an ego trip. Failures of government cannot explain the sympathy of a growing number of people in a liberal democracy like the United States with foreign dictators or domestic anarchists.

Some troubles (including the disastrous initial American response to the coronavirus) really are the result of bad policies and incompetent leadership. Even without the added challenges of natural disasters, there are millions of people around the world in economic and physical pain. No system of government produces perfect equality, and no economy prevents poverty. Citizens of a democracy can always do better, especially if voters take seriously the idea that they are the stewards of their government, their nation's resources, and their own rights. Instead, those same citizens have embarked on searches for scapegoats, enabled and encouraged by intellectuals and opportunists who labor mightily on rationalizations for the public's illiberal attitudes and behavior. Such rationalizations amount to little more than infantilizing the public, treating adult citizens as no better than children who cannot control their impulse to smash anything that immediately frustrates them.

In a liberal democracy, citizens are the masters of their fate. If we believe democracy has failed us, we should first ask ourselves whether we have failed the test of democracy. It is an uncomfortable question, and it is the subject of this book.

This is not an invitation to self-justification or to self-incrimination, but to introspection, a process that can be uncomfortable if we're being prodded to it as part of understanding our own unhappiness during tough times. I've had to do plenty of it while writing this book, and it wasn't pleasant. Social scientists pride themselves on their detachment and their dispassionate review of evidence, but I found such distance more difficult to achieve when writing about both the ordinary working voters of the United States and the pampered and better-off elites—and then realizing that I've been a member of both classes, which then made me wonder if I've managed to be part of America's problems at both stages of my own life.

In any case, civic introspection is an indispensable duty for voters in a democracy, even in good times. It may be even more important during the *best* of times; if we think things are going well, we should ask what we're doing right, and especially whether our happiness is shared by enough of our fellow citizens. And if we are on the verge of considering withdrawing our support from our own form of government, it is absolutely crucial to look inward, and to ask if the problems we face are injustices inflicted on us from without, or the manifestation of failings from within. When Thomas Jefferson wrote the Declaration of Independence and asserted the right of Americans to cease observing the authority of the British Crown, he acknowledged that "a decent respect to the opinions of mankind requires that they should declare the causes which impel them to the separation." We ought to do the same before we do any further damage to the institutions and norms by which we govern ourselves.

In a democracy, the people are responsible for their own happiness and for the safety of their own freedoms, but they are also often the source of their own problems. Back in the mid-twentieth century, the cartoonist Walt Kelly drew a popular comic strip called "Pogo" that featured the furry creatures of a remote southeastern American swamp who, despite lazing about and drawling in a down-home style, were also savvy political observers. In 1953, Kelly wrote a forward to a book of his strips in which he warned his readers that Americans needed to see in themselves the foundations of the anti-communist hysteria whipped up by Senator Joseph McCarthy, and in doing so he created a line that became a part of American political culture. Kelly borrowed the famous message from Admiral Oliver Hazard Perry of the U.S. Navy as he went into battle against the British—"We have met the enemy, and they are ours"—and turned it into a challenge to his fellow Americans: "Resolve then, that on this very ground, with small flags waving, and tinny blasts on tiny trumpets, we shall meet the enemy, and not only may he be ours, he may be us."

In 1971, as Pogo and his friends contemplated the damage done to the planet after the first celebration of Earth Day, Kelly reduced his saying to the pithier version that is still with us: "We have met the enemy, and he is us."[10]

Over a half-century later, Pogo is still right. We face the consequences of our own behavior yet again. Rather than accept their responsibilities as citizens, however, a significant number of people in the democracies around the world have instead laid blame for the decay of their democratic governments on baleful and mysterious forces in every direction, choosing the doomed course that could take us, without our even realizing it, away from the freedom and security we have gained over nearly three centuries and toward the darkness of violence and authoritarianism. The democracies face no serious external threat to their existence; today, the greatest dangers lie within. We are, for now, our own worst enemy. It is time to think about how we got this way, and what we can do about it.

IS IT TIME TO WORRY?

Am I worrying too much? One of the problems with talking about the state of democracy, in the United States or anywhere else, is that it is easy to reach the conclusion that the system is failing while ignoring the reality that the system seems pretty resilient. Democracies, even when they work well, are always places where people argue and disagree in public—often at high volume and with considerable invective.

Besides, worrying about the state of democracy is what people in democracies do. Predicting the demise of the American republic is a regular feature of life in the United States. Donald Trump's victory in 2016 produced only the most recent example of these cyclical concerns about populist anger. As Trump was heading for what looked to be an electoral disaster in the summer of 2020, for example, the former Ronald Reagan speechwriter Peggy Noonan retrofitted Trump's election as a reaction by ordinary voters to "bad policy and bad stands on crucial issues," including "two unwon wars." There was no evidence that ordinary Americans who supported or opposed Trump were basing their votes on Noonan's issues, but that did not stop her from arguing—because *this time*, of course, was different—that it was all due to "a spirit of nihilism" that "no one is sure how [to repair]."[11] Mostly, this was Noonan trying to explain away how her beloved Republican Party had fallen under Trump's spell—it was the fault of bad policies, you see. Six months later, in the wake of the Capitol attack, Noonan was calling for Trump's immediate removal from office; the rioters had proven her point about the growing "burn it down" nihilism of American politics in a way that she had perhaps not expected.[12]

Perhaps *this* time—that is, in the early twenty-first century—things really are different. Both Americans and citizens in other democratic nations seem finally to believe all the tiresome obituaries written for liberal democracy over the years and now see their only role as adding one more shovel of dirt to the burial mound. Decades of constant complaint and grievance, regularly aired in the midst of continual improvement in living standards by almost every measure, have finally taken their toll. Where Noonan and other apologists of populism err, however, is to believe that any of this is about policy. There is no coherent "revolt" among the public, no broad agreement on reform, no evidence of sustained citizen involvement, no sudden movement to candidates who represent real change. Indeed, an actual social awakening, with all of the turbulence it might bring, might even be preferable to the sullen resentfulness of the masses who now see voting primarily as an act of hostility against their neighbors, a way to vent social grievances that are beyond the reach of governments or other institutions.

Today, the very character of the world's democracies has changed for the worse. Their peoples are short-tempered—with government and with each other—and more prone to extreme and self-centered fantasies about politics that are far removed from the routine and boring grind of keeping large nations functioning every day. These are not disagreements over substance or process; rather, these citizens are rejecting the attitudes and behaviors that are the under-pinnings of the democratic form of government. This abandonment is manifested in ways large and small, from inexcusably low voter turnout rates to a political discourse increasingly phrased in terms of revenge rather than cooperation. It is visible in the immediate physical destruction levied by anarchists on the left and in the anti-constitutional broadsides launched by theocratic intellectuals and scheming lawyers on the right.

It would be a comfort to ascribe all of this concern to my per-sonal objection to the outcome of one election in one country—my own, in 2016—especially since I voted for the losing side. It would be easier to look away from the events of the past several years and con-vince myself that democracies will from time to time produce odd outcomes. Normal but fallible human beings are involved in the pro-cess, and one need not be a political scientist to know that free people will often vote for idiosyncratic or even logically contradictory rea-sons, especially when given the choice between relative strangers and known celebrities. To this day, many voters in the United States bristle at the 1980 election of Ronald Reagan, attributing his success to his genial television presence—and they have a point. Decades later, it is easy to forget that Reagan, a two-term governor of America's largest state, seemed almost overqualified for the job compared to two other action stars, Jesse Ventura and Arnold Schwarzenegger (who actu-ally battled each other on-screen in the cheesy 1987 sci-fi movie *The Running Man*), each of whom went on to win elections in 1999 and 2003 as the governors of Minnesota and California, respectively. In a democracy, stars can shine brightly and suddenly, and unexpected things can happen.

Unfortunately, the ascendance of the illiberal streak in modern democratic societies is more than the temporary elevation of flam-boyant showmen like Trump or Brazil's Bolsonaro or Britain's Boris Johnson. To be perfectly honest, the fact that I was later able to vote for the winning side in 2020 is of almost no consolation to me at all. In the United States and around the world, citizens of free countries are still gravitating to showboating political entrepreneurs and crackpot conspiracy theories as a way of lashing out and undermining the democratic foundations of their own systems of government. Even as Trump went down to defeat in 2020, for example, Congress saw the first adherents of the deranged QAnon internet cult seated in the House of Representatives, as well as multiple attempts by elected U.S. lawmakers to walk onto the floor of the House carrying weapons.[13] These are not merely oddball moments in an otherwise healthy polity, but signs of a growing irrational and illiberal self-indulgence among an increasing number of voters and their elected representatives.

Citizens of the United States have in the past managed to resist such appeals, and throughout American history, the stories of figures like Huey Long, Father Coughlin, Joseph McCarthy, and George Wallace have always ended with their eventual repudiation by the public. (In the case of Wallace, his presidential bid in 1972 was cut short by a would-be assassin; he tried once more in 1976, and then repudiated his previous racist views before winning re-election for one final term as Alabama's governor in 1982.) Such men entranced millions, even if only briefly, and it has always been a reassuring theme in the American story that most voters somehow realized the importance of denying them the power they sought.

Today, however, Americans are deeply divided, their elections rocked by scandals, recriminations, division, and even violence that represent the greatest threats to the U.S. constitutional order since the Civil War. Never in American history, for example, has a U.S. president tried to sow discord and doubt about the electoral process itself, as Donald Trump did in 2020 and 2021. During a series of outlandish legal challenges to his loss, Trump used incendiary rhetoric to claim that secret cabals had stolen the election. In some cases, state and local officials, many of them Trump's fellow Republicans, had to endure death threats for doing their duty to count the votes of their own citizens because of the U.S. president's unhinged charges and accusations. When Trump's loyalists stormed Congress, it was the first breach of the U.S. Capitol since the invasion of British troops in 1814. The damage to the edifice can be repaired, but as the writer George Packer warned, Trump's entire "stab-in-the-back narrative" will "linger for years, poisoning the atmosphere like radioactive dust," burning away in the minds of millions of Americans and "consuming whatever is left of their trust in democratic institutions and values."[14]

The 2016 U.S. presidential election foreshadowed this chaos when it turned into a made-for-television carnival between two candidates, Trump and Hillary Clinton, who were beloved to their base and widely disliked by everyone else. Clinton won the popular vote, but in a handful of states the election was so close that for the second time in five national elections the American electoral system produced a winner who ascended to the presidency with fewer votes than his opponent. Many of Clinton's supporters refused to accept Trump's legitimate 2016 victory because they believed it was due to Russian manipulation of social media (which U.S. intelligence agencies confirmed occurred), as well as to actual Russian hacking of vote totals (which did not happen). Trump, predictably, was impeached in 2019, both for his own stunningly lawless actions as well as because his political enemies were seeking to impeach him *even before he took office*. He was acquitted in a sham of a Senate "trial" in which the members of Trump's party defended him by voting against hearing any evidence, and then he was impeached *again* in 2021 for inciting insurrection. Once again, Trump's partisans vowed to acquit him even before the trial began, and they were as good as their word. Trump's initial impeachment was only the third such political trauma in the U.S. system in over two centuries—but the second within just twenty-five years. His repeated impeachment only a year later has no comparison in American history.

Other democracies are enduring their own upheavals. Across the Atlantic, British politics over the past decade have turned into a circus after a narrow up-or-down referendum on whether to leave the European Union, a move that the "Leavers" who supported a "Brexit" didn't seem to understand, and that British leaders could not figure out how to implement.[15] The question of whether the European Union was a good idea when it was created in 1992 or whether it was in Britain's interest to remain in it decades later was lost in a debate that was often overwhelmed by cheap nationalism and silly nostalgia. Some British voters believed, incorrectly, that Brexit would force immigrants to leave the UK, while others believed that money was flowing from Britain to Europe when in fact it was the other way around. Some, apparently, just wanted to sing "Rule Britannia" and magically restore the country of their childhood. "I want Britain post-Brexit to be what it was in the Swinging 60s," the British political provocateur George Galloway said in 2019, "when we were the cultural capital of the world. When we had a steel industry, when we had a coal industry—when we were something!"[16]

Younger Britons, of course, did not seem eager to mine coal or forge steel in exchange for the pride of seeing Sean Connery and Twiggy zipping through Piccadilly in an Aston Martin. Galloway is merely an odious gadfly, but much of the Brexit debate reflected a theme underlying anti-democratic surges elsewhere in the world: dark forces now control the lives of ordinary people, the elites are living it up at everyone else's expense, and the past is better than the present. As the scholar Steven Pinker has noted, populism tends to be an old man's movement, and the Brexit debate was one of many in which political entrepreneurs convinced Britons (as similar figures have done with Poles, Italians, and others) that a better life awaits them in the past.[17]

At least the early twenty-first century has been a good era for comedy, if not for democracy. The Italians in 2018 voted a party into power, the Five Star Movement, founded by an actual professional comedian named Beppe Grillo. One of Grillo's earliest initiatives was *Vaffanculo* Day (literally, F***-off Day) in Bologna in 2007, a drive to collect signatures demanding reforms. The joke, as is so often the case with populist superstars, was on the public: this "middle-finger to the establishment," as *Wired* described it, was actually the brainchild of one of Grillo's partners, Gianroberto Casaleggio, a wealthy tech executive who had been forced out of his job as a CEO after his company took huge losses under his leadership a few years earlier.[18]

Meanwhile, in Ukraine, voters decided that life should imitate art. In 2019, Ukrainians elected as president a comedian named Volodymyr Zelensky, who starred in a television show about a comedian who was elected president. Zelensky entered office as a completely inexperienced newcomer who made nearly impossible promises to end his country's war with Russia and to strike a blow against Ukraine's legendary corruption problems. Instead, he was instantly dragged into the U.S. impeachment drama of 2019–2020. Less than a year into his term, Zelensky soon fired his nation's chief prosecutor and pushed the Ukrainian legislature to replace him with a political loyalist, who immediately began investigating Zelensky's predecessor as president. "Shame is the only word I can use to describe what has happened," the Ukrainian journalist Kristina Berdynskykh said in early 2020.[19]

The world's largest democracy, India, also seems to have fallen to the illiberal temptation. In 2014, Narendra Modi, a Hindu nationalist, became Indian's prime minister. His party has won consecutive majorities, and now uses its popularity to intimidate Modi's critics, the Indian media, and even the Indian Supreme Court. Much like the United States, India's federal system is a check on national power, but a former Modi supporter, the Indian writer Tavleen Singh, said in 2020 that "a palpable menace has crept into India's political atmosphere," and in a reference to Nazi Germany's race laws, she described the Modi government's 2020 amendment to India's citizenship requirements as "India's first Nuremberg law."

There are notable exceptions to these trends in peaceable and relatively calm democracies, from Canada to Switzerland. But are such quiet places the face of the future, or have they only so far managed to avoid being struck by the stray neutrons given off by the fissioning of democracies elsewhere? The Swiss, for example, are starting to wonder if their practice of direct democracy is suitable for the twenty-first century. In conversations in 2018 and 2019, Swiss journalists and political analysts told me that they wonder if even a public as engaged and educated as theirs is capable of understanding the complexities of the state budget and other issues presented to a national vote.[20]

And even Canada has had its moments. Toronto mayor Rob Ford, a bizarre figure whose various addictions and scandals mesmerized a fair number of Canadians, might have become a more dominant presence in Canadian politics were it not for his personal troubles and then his untimely death in 2016. Toronto's voters duly replaced him with his own brother. In 2020, a majority of Canadians agreed with the statement that "Canada is broken," a remarkable finding in a country that on occasion has weathered doubts about its own national identity—including a secession crisis in 1995—and has long seemed to be a redoubt of stability compared to its southern neighbor.[21]

The areas in Europe formerly controlled by the old Soviet empire were once bright spots in the story of democratic progress, but they too have now experienced various degrees of illiberal reversal. New democracies in Poland, Hungary, and the Czech Republic have struggled since their liberation with the emergence of forces in their own society that are not only anti-democratic but pro-Russian, often with open admiration of the Kremlin strongman Putin and a selective nostalgia for the days of the Warsaw Pact that consigns the rest of the Soviet experience to the memory hole. The international democracy watchdog Freedom House called this a "stunning democratic breakdown" in the "the region stretching from Central Europe to Central Asia":

> [T]his shift has accelerated assaults on judicial independence, threats against civil society and the media, the manipulation of electoral frameworks, and the hollowing out of parliaments, which no longer fulfill their role as centers of political debate and oversight of the executive. Antidemocratic leaders in the region continue to pay lip service to the skeletal, majoritarian element of democracy—claiming that they act according to the will of the people—but they do so only to justify their concentration of power and escalating violations of political rights and civil liberties.[22]

This assault on liberty, often rationalized as protection against dangerous foreign ideas and threats ranging from homosexuality to immigration, has left citizens of the former Soviet empire "especially vulnerable to further rights abuses and power grabs associated with the coronavirus pandemic."

The United States and other established democracies are not yet on the verge of collapse. Their institutions still function. The lights are still on and the mail—despite Donald Trump's efforts in 2020—is getting delivered.[23] In the United States, there is still a Congress—despite the mob attack in 2021—a White House, and a Supreme Court. In the new century, however, too many citizens measure these institutions not by the rights they protect, but by whether they deliver material benefits to friends and punish political enemies both real and imagined.

More important, if our only concerns for democracy are the sudden appearance of a strongman or the rumble of tanks in the streets, then we are taking too narrow a view of the threat. Democratic decline today is more subtle and gradual. It also more dangerous, because it comes from within and from our own choices rather than being imposed by force from the outside. As the scholars Steven Levitsky and Daniel Ziblatt wrote in 2018:

> Blatant dictatorship—in the form of fascism, communism, or military rule—has disappeared across much of the world. Military coups and other violent seizures of power are rare. Most countries hold regular elections. Democracies still die, but by different means. Since the end of the Cold War, most democratic breakdowns have been caused not by generals and soldiers but by elected governments themselves. Like Chávez in Venezuela, elected leaders have subverted democratic institutions in Georgia, Hungary, Nicaragua, Peru, the Philippines, Poland, Russia, Sri Lanka, Turkey, and Ukraine. Democratic backsliding today begins at the ballot box.[24]

This internal danger is far more difficult to thwart because in such circumstances the voters see their own actions not as a problem but as a solution. Illiberal citizens do not think of themselves as illiberal; they think of themselves as populist or ultra-democratic (at least where their own preferred groups are concerned). When the rest of us are vigilantly scanning the horizon for the "man on horseback" or for the shock troops of a mass movement, it is easy to underestimate the impact of millions of people exchanging paranoid memes on Facebook who are already immune both to reason and to the basic requirements of anything like informed participation in democratic politics.

Analogies to the 1930s and the rise of fascism have become popular in the 2000s, but these concerns are too ahistorical. The world has not faced a global depression or a major interstate war for the better part of a century. (We have been immersed in a pandemic, but the rise of illiberalism in the democracies predates the first case of the coronavirus.) There are no totalitarian regimes or other challengers to the democracies creating alliances among themselves while building up mountains of arms to reshape the planetary order. These better conditions, however, create dangers that are in some aspects *worse* than the 1930s, because democracy is now under siege not from declared enemies but from the daily abandonment of the habits and virtues that strengthen the liberal foundations of democratic regimes. This all means that authoritarianism could arrive, like Carl Sandburg's fog, on little cat feet, quietly establishing itself while the rest of us are busy watching television, staring at our phones, and speaking to our friends and family through emojis.

These assaults on democratic norms, as we will see, are coming from populations whose anger is rooted far more in notional injustices and imagined dangers than in actual harms. The dissatisfied, illiberal citizens of the early twenty-first century are not the armies of unemployed men marching on Washington during the Great Depression because their families were on the verge of starving. They are not the disenfranchised African Americans of the 1950s seeking to attend school without being murdered. They are not the poor of Appalachia sleeping on dirt floors in the 1960s while men orbited the planet in space. They are not the women of the 1970s who still needed their husband's permission to get a credit card—or a divorce. They are not the gay and lesbian Americans of the 1980s who were told they could not marry. Instead, the threat to democracy now in America and elsewhere comes from the working and middle classes—the people among whom I was born and raised—whose rage comes overwhelmingly from cultural insecurity, inflated expectations, tribal partisan alliances, obsessions about ethnicity and identity, blunted ambition, and a childlike understanding of the limits of government.

Authoritarian systems are the authors of their own troubles and deserve every molecule of the opposition they face from within. But why are people who are already free, and who are by any relative measure materially and politically better off than those in more repressive states, attacking their own systems of government? The answers are as disturbing as they are counterintuitive: We are losing because we won. We are suffering because we are successful. We are unhappy because we have what we want.

WHAT'S AHEAD

Affluence and plenty can be a curse, especially in a society without discipline or self-control, and most Americans, in their hearts, have always known that this is a danger lurking in their own character. Consider a delightful parable written in 1957 by the celebrated science fiction writer Damon Knight titled "An Eye for a What?" Knight described a race of spherical, rubbery beings who are impervious to pain and whose only apparent weakness is their inability to control their own appetites. When one of these aliens, "George," offends a newly arrived Earth delegation in a diplomatic incident, the alien leaders insist that the human visitors, as the injured party, must devise and administer George's punishment.

After every possible torture fails to impress them, the human mission commander has a flash of inspiration. He turns to George and says: "Here are my orders to you. *Do as you please.*" After a stunned moment, the offending alien rapidly eats everything in sight, from the flowers on the table to the carpeting in the room. George rolls about in compulsive misery and is literally on the verge of exploding when the humans finally stop him. The alien leaders are aghast. They tell the Earth delegates that the punishment was not only acceptable, but "more severe than any they ever thought of, in twenty thousand years."

In Chapter 1, I suggest that we think about whether Americans and other citizens of the advanced democracies have become victims of the command—this time issued from within ourselves, rather than by an alien commander—to "Do as you please." The past forty years in most of the developed world have been decades of unequaled peace and prosperity. In the twenty-first century, income inequality has skyrocketed, but arguments about income differences are arguments primarily about *justice*, not standards of living; modern Americans of all classes and other citizens of the wealthy democracies are now plagued by self-destructive consumption and sky-high levels of expectation. Do we even realize it?

The course of political and social development since the end of World War II has been marked by a greater division of labor, better living standards, higher levels of education, and more interaction across borders, cultures, and classes—all of which have helped to deepen democratic institutions and the behaviors that support them. And yet these achievements have begun to sour, and many communities in highly developed democracies have regressed to the point where their social environment now resembles those found in the impoverished villages of an earlier time. In Chapter 2, we will visit one of those villages. In the 1950s, an American professor named Edward Banfield lived in a small, rural Italian community and tried to unlock the secret of its apparently immutable poverty. Banfield thought he was investigating economic development, but he ended up uncovering larger problems about the relationship between civic involvement and democracy itself. His depiction of a dysfunctional society where otherwise good people care only about themselves and their immediate family is uncomfortably close to describing life in the United States in the twenty-first century, and his conclusions have turned out to be important warnings for the United States and other democracies whose citizens might have thought that their political advancement was irreversible.

Democracies have survived stresses from civil war to economic collapse because they embody basic beliefs and values that allow the broken bones of a democratic polity to knit themselves back to sturdy health. But what happens if those underlying beliefs and values have been drained away by disuse and ignorance? What if those bones, after years of neglect, have become so brittle and so weak that they cannot be restored? In Chapter 3, I argue that the citizens of the democracies, and especially the Americans, have discarded many of the foundational virtues of democracy and instead have descended into the grip of narcissism, anger, and resentment.

These emotions are more destructive than mere bad citizenship. It is one thing to be lazy about voting, or happily uninformed about issues that are undeniably boring and complicated. (I consider myself a deeply involved citizen, but if I claimed fully to understand every bond issue I ever voted on here in my small town in Rhode Island, I would be lying.) It is another thing entirely, and far worse, to view democracy as a game for suckers, to treat votes as weapons, to believe that laws exist only to protect one favored group and to punish everyone else. Not only are these attitudes dangerously toxic to civic virtue, but they also have a long half-life, and once they become fused to the political identity of the ordinary citizen, it is almost impossible to overcome them. When enough citizens exhibit these attitudes and behaviors, liberal democracy sheds its liberalism and becomes "democracy" only as a demagogic, majoritarian nightmare.

The obvious rejoinder to any criticism of civic disengagement and illiberal behavior in the democracies is to note that life is not lived by abstract numbers and statistics, and that there are plenty of citizens in the democracies who are angry because they have every *right* to be angry. Democratic decline, in this view, is the result of bad policy choices made by an elite who, either by design or incompetence, have enriched themselves at the expense of ordinary citizens. Democracy is in danger not because its citizens have become less virtuous, but because elected leaders—and even more important, unelected elites—have betrayed their responsibilities, and the public knows it.

Any defense of liberal democracy has to take these objections seriously. In Chapter 4, I will engage these charges, but before we get there, I will admit right now that some of them are forceful and right. The real question is not whether elites have screwed up some important decisions—they have, and they will again—but rather whether such failures of policy are failures of *democracy*. Has the concept of liberal democracy run its course and failed us, or have we convinced ourselves, in regular cycles of self-pity, not only that we have a right to a relatively painless life, but also that anyone who denies us that life is part of some sort of plot against the average citizen? How much of what ails us is the result of incompetence or mendacity or even outright evil, and how much of it is the consequence of natural change?

I realize that this now sounds more like *The Princess Bride* than Harold Macmillan. ("You mock my pain!" Princess Buttercup says to her abductor. "Life is pain, Highness," the pirate responds, "and anyone who says differently is selling something.") Life is never easy, and a decent society tries to spread the benefits and burdens of daily existence among its citizens as they see fit and with their consent. But life in the democracies is not the impoverished, crime-ridden hellscape that populists of both the right and the left argue that it is. Critics of liberal democracy from the right and the left now have a vested interest in citizens reaching such conclusions, because the road away from democracy leads to their preferred solution, which is invariably to destroy the democratic order and replace it with themselves as the leaders of a new (and preferably unalterable) regime.

Much of the narcissism and resentment destroying the modern democracies is, ironically, fueled and exploited by the greater connectedness of human beings with each other. But this connectedness has turned to chaos, and in Chapter 5 we will confront the possibility that new technologies and platforms have eaten away at the foundations of democracy by spreading misinformation, generating a sense of massive relative deprivation, and rewarding negative social interaction. Better communications and the spread of information once helped to bring people together, and the internet is still among the most potent weapons possible against dictatorships and authoritarian systems, but these same advances now feed political cults of celebrity and offer the opportunity to influence—for good or ill—large movements of people more easily than ever before. Global connectedness also presents the democracies with qualitatively new challenges from authoritarian systems. Russia, China, North Korea, Iran, and other nations have seen the opportunities afforded by an open society, its lax approach to information security, and a credulous, underinformed democratic populace. (I take this threat rather personally, since all of my records as a government employee, including my security clearance, were stolen in a Chinese hack of the U.S. Office of Personnel Management in 2015.) But, in the end, we are victims of disinformation because we have chosen that role for ourselves. We seek information that confirms our tribalism, inflames our petty and narcissistic beliefs, and comforts us in our biases and prejudices.

In the concluding chapter, I will present what I hope are at least the outlines of some solutions. Some of what I advocate will boil down to moral scolding—not only do I think there is actually a role for that in any democracy, but it is usually my core skill set—but I admit it is also time to think more creatively about major policy and institutional solutions. Some of these solutions will represent ground we have all plowed before. Yes, we have to talk about creating an ethos of national service; yes, we need a serious and just plan for the redistribution of income; and yes, Americans in particular must come to grips with a Constitution whose mechanisms of representation are dividing, rather than aggregating, the interests of a gigantic and diverse federal state.

But we also have to think about innovative ways to reconsider how to implement such solutions, with the goal of encouraging civic virtue rather than checking meaningless boxes about tax plans, new constitutional conventions, and old-style universal military drafts that will never happen. This is a problem that requires solutions at the source of the problem: in communities and among people, rather than top-down mandates or quick fixes such as a teaching more civics classes in high school. Some solutions might make civil libertarians (myself among them) uncomfortable because they involve measures to stem the flow of sewage from the internet; other ideas, such as changing the structure of elections, will aggravate entrenched political interests who have benefitted from those arrangements.

I cannot promise to end this book with unalloyed optimism. (If I were that confident, after all, about the future of democracy in the United States or anywhere else, I would not have written it at all.) But I have great faith in the durability of liberal democracy. I believe it is the system of government that most accords with what is best in human nature. The challenge now is whether we can face down the threat we present to our own freedoms from what is worst in our nature, and whether we can allow Abraham Lincoln's "better angels" to guide us rather than be overwhelmed by more atavistic and inhumane impulses. All of this begins by taking stock of ourselves as citizens and the world we have created.

A Hunger for Apocalypse

The Perils of Peace and Plenty

What a beautiful fix we are in now; peace has been declared.

—Napoleon

The problem with modernity is not that it is too hard, but that it is too easy.

—Janan Ganesh

BOREDOM AMID PLENTY

Toward the end of his time in office in 2016, U.S. president Barack Obama said to an audience of young Europeans that people alive in the twenty-first century are more fortunate than they realize. "It may seem improbable," Obama said, "but it's true." He went on:

We are fortunate to be living in the most peaceful, most prosperous, most progressive era in human history. That may surprise young people who are watching TV or looking at your phones and it seems like only bad news comes through every day. But consider that it's been decades since the last war between major powers.

More people live in democracies. We're wealthier and healthier and better educated, with a global economy that has lifted up more than a billion people from extreme poverty and created new middle classes from the Americas to Africa to Asia. Think about the health of the average person in the world—tens of millions of lives that we now save from disease and infant mortality, and people now living longer lives.

If you had to choose a moment in time to be born, any time in human history, and you didn't know ahead of time what nationality you were or what gender or what your economic status might be, you'd choose today—which isn't to say that there is not still enormous suffering and enormous tragedy and so much work for us to do.[1]

Obama was criticized by some of his opponents as a disconnected optimist, but even some conservative economists and policy experts who could never be mistaken for fans of the forty-fourth president agreed with him.[2]

I, too, agreed with him, because the facts allow no other conclusion. Still, I can imagine someone reading this chapter years from now—if I can flatter myself that anyone will read it at all in the future—and wondering how I could reach the ridiculous conclusion that the early twenty-first century was anything but an arduous time. This is, after all, a book whose pages are still made from trees, written by an aging man soon to suffer any number of things that might one day be curable, tapping away on keys made of toxic and eternal plastic, straining his eyes while staring at a screen powered by fossil fuels, and hunkered down in his home during a pandemic that will one day be only a memory.

Such critics might also snort (even now) that I had no business lecturing anyone about whether times are good or bad. For people like me—at least as I have lived most of my adult life—times are always good. Hunger, other than as a fleeting inconvenience, has no real meaning to me. My home is warm and comfortable. My office is cluttered with an array of gadgets, many devoted to leisure, including a computer that has a glass door on it for no good reason other than so that I can see its expensive components glow in the dark. I complain about the parlous state of democracy while being in absolutely no danger myself while exercising my right to speak, to worship, to vote, or to write the very words you're reading now. Add the shocking fact that my *cat* has better access to health care than billions of my fellow human beings and millions of my fellow citizens, and all of this must seem like the very happy pronouncement of a very happy man that liberal democracy worked out just fine—for me.

It does little good, I suppose, to argue that the happiness or misery of any one person is no way to judge a society. And yet unless we are to adopt the position of dedicated revolutionaries—that is, to say that democracy itself is always a sham—then we need to think about whether less categorical criticisms are rooted in some kind of real and shared experience as citizens. It is not enough to say, as the British writer William Davies has, that "if people don't *feel* safe, it doesn't matter whether they are objectively safe or not," and that we must therefore "take people's feelings seriously as political issues, and not simply dismiss them as irrational."[3] Feelings matter, especially as a kind of general barometer of the public mood. But feelings are an unreliable way to know if our institutions are making life better or worse. It is never uniformly the best of times or the worst of times, and we have to find something in between Pangloss and panic.

Political leaders, of course, rarely have any interest in nuance or incrementalism, because "things could be better" or "overall, we're doing pretty well" are not particularly inspiring slogans. Even Obama, who was later such an optimist, argued for "Hope and Change" because we were losing hope and things needed changing; Donald Trump (and Ronald Reagan before him) promised to "Make America Great Again," because greatness is great and whatever situation we're in at any given moment, it's not great. Occasionally, there is the low-wattage duel such as the 1996 contest between Bob Dole, who was a "A Better Man for a Better America," and Bill Clinton, who was "Building a Bridge to the 21st Century," whatever that means. Usually, however, the incumbents tell us how good life is, and the challengers try to explain that we're really quite unhappy, no matter how we might feel about things at the moment.

The fact that so many free citizens nonetheless believe that they are on the edge of disaster is an indication of how much has changed, and how much has been forgotten, in the space of just a few decades. Until COVID-19, the world had been spared a serious pandemic for a full century. America and its allies have not faced a global war—the kind requiring national mobilization and a draft—for over three-quarters of a century. The Great Recession of 2008 was a recession, not a depression; not only was it overcome relatively quickly, but American consumers went right back to their bad credit habits within a decade. (Nor did the pandemic-induced recession of 2020 result in a global economic crash, despite early predictions of widespread disaster.) The citizens of the world's democracies are being taught, both by political entrepreneurs and by their own inflated sense of expectation, that the ordinary pressures, worries, and temptations of life in an open society are serial catastrophes for which the only remedy is the abandonment of their own freedoms.

The diminishing of threats and the elevation of expectations, coupled with the dullness of daily life in a society gorged on more forms of leisure that it can comprehend, is both the triumph of liberal democracy and a danger to it. Eric Hoffer, who wrote his classic work *The True Believer* in 1951, warned:

There is perhaps no more reliable indicator of a society's ripeness for a mass movement than the prevalence of unrelieved boredom. In almost all the descriptions of the periods preceding the rise of mass movements there is reference to vast ennui; and in their earliest stages mass movements are more likely to find sympathizers among the bored than among the exploited and suppressed. To a deliberate fomenter of mass upheavals, the report that people are bored stiff should be at least as encouraging as that they are suffering from intolerable economic or political abuses.[4]

The conservative writer George Will put it more simply in 2020, noting that affluent societies are often gripped by a "hunger for apocalypse," a wish for a great struggle that could give drama and deeper meaning, a frisson of risk, to the otherwise dull rhythm of life in a country that meets almost all of the needs of its population at almost all times, and entertains them continuously while doing so.[5] Democracy, at its best, is boring, and when a society becomes attached to the idea that boredom is a burden that government should alleviate, the attraction of politics beyond the edge of reason becomes a matter of entertainment rather than of justice or even of necessity.

The real question is not whether the world is in better shape than it was decades ago. It is. Rather, the issue is whether the achievements of the past half century have had the unintended consequence of undermining many of the qualities essential to the survival of a democracy.

If it seems somewhat astonishing to trace the decline of modern democracy to peace, affluence, and technological progress, step back in time for a moment and consider the transition from the old world of the post-1945 Cold War order to the world in which we live today. Before we can think about the views of ordinary citizens, the failures of governing elites, or the challenges facing both of them, we need to think more dispassionately about life in the twenty-first century and why it looks the way it does.

PEACE—AT A PRICE

Let's start with peace. To say the world is more peaceful in 2020 than in 1970 or 1980 is a fact. It also *feels* somehow false. It feels, at some basic emotional level, like a contradiction in a world full of unpredictable threats that can strike Americans closer to home, especially after 9/11, when terrorists killed more people in a day than the Empire of Japan managed to kill in a major action against an entire U.S. military installation on the opening day of a war. Patriotic young men and women showed up at recruiting stations in 2001 and volunteered to fight overseas, just as they did in 1941. To this day, men and women from the United States, NATO, and other democratic nations are scattered about the globe and fighting battles against determined enemies who hate them. Peace? Nonsense.

And yet, as the saying goes, there is no point in arguing over things we can look up. Leave aside for a moment the fact that we no longer live under the constant threat of nuclear Armageddon. (The nuclear weapons are still there, but in much reduced numbers, and without the constant possibility of imminent hostilities.) There are fewer bloody struggles around the world, and they are taking fewer lives. This does not mean that the hundreds of thousands of lives lost in places like Syria, where the death toll after nearly a decade of war is now well over a half million, are not each a tragedy. But to believe that the world is more riven by conflict today than in the past is to engage in a loss of collective memory of places such as Biafra and Bangladesh, where two conflicts between 1967 and 1971 killed millions, or of Rwanda in 1994, where well over three-quarters of a million people were butchered in just over one hundred *days*.

Americans and Europeans could respond that such places are far away and such incidents are long ago, and that their own daily experience is one of threats and violence. A generation with no memory of the time before 9/11 is convinced that America is endlessly "at war." To lament that the American military is constantly deployed to violent areas, where they must engage in actual combat, is literally true, and it is fair criticism to ask why. To believe that such engagements only began after 9/11, however, or that they are more destructive now, betrays yet another failure of memory or a willful disregard of history. (In a similar vein, many Americans also refuse to believe that violent crime at home is down even from just a few decades ago. Violent crime rates have been on a steady decline since the 1990s, but the idea that the United States is in the grip of a crime wave is yet another persistent myth in the twenty-first century.)[6]

Consider how differently Americans regard their current engagements from the searing national effort their parents and grandparents poured into Vietnam. I began high school in 1975, only two years after the national draft had ended. The kids in my hometown, even at my younger age, were more aware of the war than others, perhaps, because our city was home to a major U.S. Air Force base whose B-52s had flown bombing missions directly to Vietnam. Some of my first memories of television are of the evening news footage of Americans fighting in Southeast Asia. My parents, whose son would soon be of draft age, usually stared at these images silently but with evident anxiety. And yet by the time I arrived at Chicopee Comprehensive High School that autumn, the war was over. It was already someone else's nightmare. But at least I knew it occurred and I could see the toll it took on American society, even as a clueless freshman in no danger of being called to serve anywhere.

By comparison, when my daughter began high school in 2016 in our small Rhode Island town (which is home to a large U.S. Navy installation) in the supposed era of "endless wars," the idea of war as a massive national effort was completely alien to American society. A draft is unthinkable. The wars in Afghanistan and Iraq are more like global policing; by the time my daughter was old enough to pay attention to the news, these engagements had been going on for some fifteen years as prophylactic measures against the general threat of terrorism and had produced only a fraction of the casualties taken in Vietnam. By comparison to what I knew even as a young child in the 1960s, these overseas conflicts were mostly invisible to her and the generations just before her. Vietnam was a war whose large engagements with both guerrillas and the uniformed soldiers of an enemy state were broadcast into American homes. The "endless wars," by the time President Joe Biden announced a 2021 withdrawal from Afghanistan, had dwindled mostly to engagements with irregular forces and gangs of murderers, and barely made the headlines anymore.

For all the talk of "war weariness" among Americans, citizens who are not in the military or who are not part of a military family or community have not had to endure even minor inconveniences due to U.S. military activity and commitments, much less shoulder major burdens such as a draft, a war tax, or resource shortages. Aside from the occasional indignities at the airport, most people would be hard-pressed to describe themselves as living in a country under threat. Little wonder that the soldiers who served overseas in those first years of major operations soon felt forgotten. "America's not at war," went a common complaint among the troops. "The military's at war. America's at the mall."

The martial spirit that overtook the United States and other nations after 9/11 long ago dissipated into frustration with the lack of progress abroad and irritation with overly expansive security measures at home. American military engagements since the fiasco of Iraq twenty years ago—it is almost too much to call them "wars"—have been conducted by a small sliver of the population. For the general public, despite our reluctance to say so, it has been a stable peace. It is, to be sure, peace bought by exhausted volunteers, but it is peace, nonetheless.

This peace has had paradoxical effects. As the Tufts professor and *Washington Post* columnist Dan Drezner wrote in 2019, Americans might complain about foreign entanglements, but by and large they ignore foreign policy. "Public opinion," he notes, "has ceased to act as a real constraint on decision-makers," because the combination of geographic isolation, overwhelming power, and an all-volunteer force have allowed most Americans "to stop caring about vital questions of war and peace. The apathy has only grown since the end of the Cold War, and today, poll after poll reveals that Americans rarely, if ever, base their vote on foreign policy considerations."[7]

In fact, the Global War on Terror only briefly interrupted a tradition of apathy about foreign affairs that long predated 9/11 and Iraq and stretched back into the Cold War itself. When the USSR fell and took with it the daily fear of nuclear annihilation, America stood alone and unchallenged. The democracies after 1991 became safer from an existential threat to their way of life, but they also lost a sense of purpose about why they valued that way of life in the first place. Andrew Bacevich, a relentless and often excessive critic of American decadence, nonetheless put it well in 2020:

> Winning the Cold War brought Americans face-to-face with a predicament comparable to that confronting the lucky fellow who wins the Mega Millions lottery: hidden within an apparent windfall is the potential for monumental disaster. Putting that windfall to good use while avoiding the pitfalls inherent in suddenly acquired riches calls for prudence and self-awareness—not easily demonstrated when the big house, luxury car, and vacation condo you've always wanted are yours for the asking.[8]

The end of the Cold War, of course, did not mean a new Lexus waiting for all of us in the driveway. Bacevich, however, has a point that within a few years of the Soviet collapse, any notion of a common struggle against a mortal threat seemed almost silly, and most of us moved on almost immediately rather than thinking seriously about the long struggle from which we'd just emerged.

With the Soviet Union gone and no serious challenge from an alternative to liberal democracy, multiple U.S. and Western leaders tried to recast the fight against al-Qaeda and ISIS as something like the former East-West struggle, and a rudderless nation, alone at the apex of power, briefly found new purpose in a war against mass-murdering terrorists. I was tempted by this same parallelism: I wrote a book shortly after 2001 in which I argued that the United States might well be in a long-term battle, an ideological struggle similar to the Cold War with forces that were, in every sense, anti-Western. As it turns out, Western strategists (including me) overestimated their opponents, who were relatively easy to defeat on the battlefield but difficult to eradicate in detail. Eventually, the U.S. and its allies abandoned the notion that they were in an epochal struggle against a new horde of barbarians, and the "war on terror" devolved from major battles in Afghanistan into a series of street brawls in various parts of the world against loosely organized forces whose military skills were often directed mostly to the rape and murder of unarmed civilians.

The final act of the 9/11 era was the self-inflicted wound of the Iraq War in 2003. This was a discretionary crusade, popular with an American public and a U.S. national security establishment that had wanted to settle scores with Saddam Hussein for over a decade. And yet, even after the George W. Bush administration bungled the postwar occupation of Iraq, Bush was returned to office with over 50 percent of the vote; congressional Republicans took their punishment in 2006, only to return to a majority four years later. If the public was enraged about all of this military adventurism, they seemed unwilling to make it a priority at the ballot box. (Donald Trump, for his part, bombed Syria twice and courted war with Iran. His supporters later lauded him for having started no new wars overseas, which was true as well of Obama, evidence yet again that exasperation with military deployments, among the general public, is mostly a matter of partisan point-scoring.)[9]

By 2016, "endless wars" were talking points among the far right and far left, but the petering out of the campaigns against terrorists and the failure of either Russia or China to emerge in the interim as a powerful anti-Western nemesis removed any sense of urgency from the American public about war and peace. The heroic Cold War narratives about fighting radical Islam were replaced by the reality of young U.S. and NATO soldiers, volunteers all, grinding out their days in the desert trying to find terrorists like the cowardly Jihadi John, a failed hip-hop artist from London who went to the Middle East to gain his fame by beheading helpless aid workers on YouTube. To this day, the civilians back home, for their part, are annoyed not by the ubiquitousness of conflict but by things like airport screenings and other minor practices of a new security theater that now seems only like a series of random indignities untethered from any substantive threat.

The Cold War compromised democratic societies, and especially the Americans, in ways their citizens still do not like to think about, including the institutionalization of expansive statist policies built around national security. But the Global War on Terror made us all into something worse. This time, with no viable challenge to American democracy on the horizon, the fighting was outsourced to volunteers without a draft, without anything like a national mobilization or any other requirement for shared sacrifice. And Americans were, as a nation, fine with that—at least to judge from their electoral choices every two to four years.

IT DOESN'T FEEL LIKE AFFLUENCE

Most people, on reflection, might concede at least some of the point about a more peaceful world. A more "affluent" world is a tougher sell; in his 2016 speech in Europe, Obama tried to make the case for living in the "most prosperous, most progressive era in human history," but when I have suggested to students and other public audiences over the past decade or so that we now live in an affluent time, I am met with looks of disbelief. (Even younger students who intensely admire Obama will shake their heads at the former president's cluelessness in a classic case of generational disconnection.) Honestly, professor! These are terrible times and have been for ages—*everyone* knows that.

Part of the problem with judging the times in which we live is that it is common for people to think times are bad even if their own situations are happy enough. There are multiple reasons for this, many of them rooted in human psychology.[10] Older people, for example, tend to remember their youth fondly because they're old, and because their minds have filed away the bad times and are now replaying the good times. Also, by our nature, we do not like to jinx the present by saying that things are going well. Moreover, there is the problem of immediate experience. As every economist—and every politician—knows, explaining the low unemployment rate to a woman who is unemployed is both cruel and pointless. For her, the rate is 100 percent, and the fact that someone in another time zone has a job illuminates little and changes nothing.

This is why it seems almost crazy to talk about the impact of "affluence" at this point in history, since so many Americans, along with rioters in places like Paris and Athens, seem to think they are living in an economic hellscape. This, in part, is a lingering response to the Great Recession of 2008, when the global spending party came to a crashing halt, but it is also a response to fears *about* the Great

Recession that remained in the culture after it was over, in the same way that the Great Depression made its mark long after the recovery. The Great Recession has become a touchstone in many of the narratives about why Americans have turned against their own institutions, but, as we will see, it is not an explanation that takes us very far. There is no real coherence in the choices Americans have made since the crash; they remain uninterested in reform, angry at bailouts, and unwilling to embrace even moderate notions of austerity.

Anger at a "broken" democracy persists under economically good conditions because, for millions of people, the modern era doesn't feel like affluence, even when they themselves are well-off. Instead, it feels like China and other competitors are putting workers in the postindustrial democracies on the unemployment line, a case Donald Trump made on the campaign trail to great effect in 2016. It feels like apartments and houses in big cities like New York or San Francisco are out of reach. And indeed they are, even for many well-off professionals. It feels like health care, at least in America, is dangerously expensive—because it is.

This is why compassionate observers will argue that the Americans of the past decade or so, like the others around the world gravitating toward populist and authoritarian alternatives, are just fed up and desperate. These citizens are not political scientists or philosophy professors trying to parse each candidate and assign them a score on some cosmic scale of moral rectitude. They just want a roof over their heads and food on the table. They want to believe that they will not have to work until their dying day and that their children will have a future in a country that once promised them that opportunity.

Under these reasonable concerns, however, are several nearly insoluble problems for the liberal democracies. Perhaps most important is the degree to which people are now fixated on a sense of *relative* deprivation. Even when people believe they are doing reasonably well, they are infuriated when they also believe that they are worse off than others or are doing more poorly than they should be doing. The twenty-first century is an era of massive income inequality, and that's a problem in itself for a variety of reasons. But as a political matter, inequality becomes even more salient when citizens are highly aware of it.[11] Paradoxically, this can sometimes become a source of greater social friction between people closer in status than those further apart. (As Hoffer presciently wrote in 1951: "Our frustration is greater when we have much and want more than when we have nothing and want some."[12]) It is one thing for people to know that others are doing better than they are, which produces uneasy resentment; it's another to know how *much* better off they are, which spurs a hotter sense of raw injustice.

Add to this the influence of the media, and especially of social media, which encourages all of us to examine the idealized lives of others, and thus us to conclude that our own lives are somehow less fulfilling. Once this notion becomes ingrained in voters, it becomes difficult to ever convince them otherwise. Their current situation is always stacked either against the lives of their friends, celebrities, or absolute strangers, or, even worse, against an imagined alternative future.

What's really going on here is an intensifying cycle of expectation and disappointment, of progress and change, of dislocation in one place and prosperity in another. Writers such as E. J. Dionne disagree, noting that "certain views take hold because they comport with both lived experiences and the data. So it is with the belief that the American Dream, as we have come to understand it, is in grave jeopardy."[13] But note here Dionne's important caveat: the American Dream *as we have come to understand it.* Likewise, in an examination of Europe, the Estonian leader Toomas Ilves objects to the framing of the inequality debate, noting how much it "ignores real data":

It takes but a look at the Gini coefficient in these countries—the measure of income inequality—to see this is nonsense. Income inequality across the whole of the EU has been stable, and in some cases declining. Across the board it is much lower than it is in, say, the United States, where it has been high and rising, especially under the current populist administration. And there is no absence of populists in the countries with one of the lowest income differential coefficients, Hungary.[14]

Once people believe that the bad times are terrible and the good times are never good enough, there is little chance of changing their minds. In 1994—a time of American economic growth and prosperity— an employed yet angry Ohio steelworker named Rick Crum told a *New York Times* reporter that politicians were all "leeches;" when pressed about his anger, he said: "If inflation is so low, how come cereal is $4.75 a box?" (Mr. Crum made an exception for one politician: his own member of Congress. "I get a lot of mail from her," he said. "She seems to be trying.")[15]

Another thorny problem is that these notional harms are almost impossible to remedy, because they are open-ended. This is related to the problem of "hedonic adaptation," the human tendency to regard one's current state of comfort as the baseline. A 2019 survey of American spending and saving habits commissioned by the Charles Schwab investment firm, for example, found that Americans, particularly younger people, feel a "pressure to spend as a result of social media envy and the desire to not be left out of friends' experiences," and they believe it takes an average $2.3 *million* in personal net worth to be considered "wealthy"—or, put another way, more than twenty times the actual median net worth of U.S. households. (Millionaires, in case you were curious, feel that "rich" begins at $7.5 million.)[16] In 2020, the *New Republic* writer Bruce Bartlett— a former official in George H. W. Bush's Treasury Department—fumed against people making six figure incomes and yet still wanting $1,200 checks in COVID relief from the U.S. government. Bartlett noted that these "whiners who earn $200,000 and complain they're broke" do not lack wealth; rather, because they are spending to the very edge of their income, they lack *liquidity*, "and therefore essentially live hand-to-mouth."[17]

For the rest of us, hedonic adaptation is a simpler matter. If you've had a queen-size bed for a while, anything else feels small. If you eat sirloin long enough, everything else tastes like leather. The memory of a time of more austere living fades away; whatever the current state of life is like is the new baseline and anything below it is intolerable. Citizens caught in this hamster wheel of ever-rising expectations will, sooner or later, exhaust every type of government.

The economist Donald Boudreaux took on the issue of living standards in a 2020 debate about whether "middle class stagnation" in the new century was a myth, or at least whether it is the crisis Americans believe it to be. Perhaps I am victim of my own confirmation bias, but I was struck by a passage that resonated with the similarity to my own life and generation:

> I'm a time traveler from the 1970s. Born in 1958 into a working-class American family, I lived through the 1970s. And while it took me several decades to arrive in the year 2020, now that I'm finally here I can report that my recollections of the 1970s remain vivid. Here's the bottom line: Ordinary Americans today have a material standard of living that is vastly higher than was the standard of living of ordinary Americans forty or fifty years ago.
>
> Examples of this improvement are legion. Smartphones, personal computers, the Internet, overnight package delivery, GPS navigation, streaming music, hi-definition television, on-line

debates. . . . We Boudreaux would have danced with delight had
we in the 1970s been given access to any one of these wonders.[18]

This feeling of amazement would have applied as well to the Nichols
family, waiting in the late 1960s for a verdict from the television
repairman—and I wonder if those even exist anymore—on the
health of our only set. (As it turned out, our loyal living room companion just needed a small and inexpensive part that cost less than
the visit itself.) The experience, however, is the same: I am living at a
standard I could not imagine as a working-class child a half century
ago, or even as a struggling graduate student thirty-five years ago, and
not because I am well-off, but because much of what surrounds me in
my daily life simply did not exist in the 1970s and the 1980s.

Boudreaux's fellow economist Branko Milanović reacted, as
many critics of the current era might, with incredulity at what he
deemed to be Boudreaux's insinuation that Americans should be
happy with gadgets instead of growth. Boudreaux, he complains,
"compares income of today's middle-class Americans with income of
the middle-class Americans 40 years ago using the goods that were
inexistent 40 years ago," a "peculiar metric" that produces the desired
conclusion that since nobody had a smartphone in 1980, the existence of any smartphones at all shows that the growth rate of income
is therefore infinitely high.

I am a political scientist, and the last thing I want to do is get
caught in a brawl between economists. But it is telling that Milanović
objects that "in no country or time (especially if the world income
is growing), have people judged their situation by comparing their
income with that of their grandparents." That is demonstrably false;
in our current era, all many of us *do* is compare our income and our
living situation to that of our parents and grandparents. While it is
invidious, and even cruel, to tell people to be glad that they are not
having their teeth pulled and their spleens removed by medieval

barber-surgeons, it is fair to take the critics of the globalized world to task for comparisons made *within living memory*. I do not remember a time before television, but smartphones actually exist and were introduced within my adult lifetime. This technology has changed my productivity and my standard of living in a way that I cannot measure purely by income.

When judging the track record of liberal democracy, these changes in living standards cannot be dismissed as mere anecdotes. They matter in a real and concrete way. As the economist Michael Strain wrote in 2020, "the argument—and even the implication—that quality of life hasn't improved for typical households and individuals in decades . . . borders on the absurd." Strain objects to a tendency among populists of arguing by "highlighting pockets of (actual, serious) problems and confusing them for the common experience of typical people in the United States today." As Strain notes with some frustration, this populist insistence on treating ordinary citizens as victims who are somehow bereft of human agency not only "miscalibrates" their expectations, but does so in order to sell them a "message of economic and social despair" even in the midst of rising living standards and social progress.[19] This is the cycle in which populists and political opportunists raise expectations, and then use the inevitable failure to meet those inflated expectations as the justification for illiberal solutions.

At the risk of engaging in dueling statistics, it is important to understand the difference between the false nostalgia for the past and the reality of the present. Is college, for example, now more expensive? Yes. The cost of attaining a degree has risen to absurd levels, for reasons that range from stingy state legislators to administrative bloat to the endless supply of loan money. But the cheaper schooling of an earlier age wasn't distributed very widely. In 1980 (when I was still in college), only 14 percent of women had a college degree. By 2018—again, within a single adult lifetime—that number jumped to

55 percent. (Men in the same period went from 21 percent to 35 percent.) In 1983, as the U.S. was coming out of a brutal recession, the
median net worth of an American family was $52,000; by 2016 it
was $97,300.[20] The jump was far higher for richer people—but this
unequal increase still means that all families were better off. We could
do this for pages, about any number of indicators from heart attack
survival rates to vehicle fatalities to the number of years of a human
life taken up by work.

In the end, Barack Obama was right: if you could choose a time
to be born, it would be now. That doesn't mean we can't do better,
but to dismiss the progress of the past fifty years achieved by free
societies—and the experts who serve them—is a foolish basis for the
rejection of democracy.

Critics could argue that exceptions also matter, and that a society
in which most people do well while some do very poorly is not a just
society, and that to ignore such suffering is as dishonest a method of
argument as that employed by the decline-obsessed populists. There
is, without doubt, a fair amount of bad faith in arguments about
whether people are better off today. One side glibly waves away the
problem of averages, adding the few incomes of the super-rich to the
mix to make the world overall seem like an equitable place, and they
ignore the sense of injustice created by the emergence of a class that
will soon include *trillionaires*, something that once was impossible
because there literally was not enough money in the world to create
such a class. I am an upper-middle-class professional who begrudges
no one their success, and yet I find that I, too, reflexively recoil at
the notion of someone who has to count that many zeroes in their
net worth. (Or, more realistically, who has to pay someone to count
those zeroes for them.)

The other side, however, romanticizes life in a previous century
based purely on economic data. They carefully, and in my view dis-
honestly, ignore the reality that almost no one would really prefer to

live in the world of fifty years ago. It is an argument based on selective memory, presenting certain realities—cheaper college tuition and single-earner families among them—completely out of the context of the times in which they occurred. The world of a half century ago, one within the living memory of millions of adults around the world, was one of oxygen tents, unsafe cars, smoking at work, and, just in case we were having a carefree day, the constant threat of complete global annihilation. It was a time when women stayed in the house whether they wanted to or not, when a married male's income could support a family—and had to—because those men had no competition at home or abroad.

The issue of justice is crucial and one we'll take up when thinking about solutions later in the book. But the question of living standards matters because it is in itself an important measure of the performance of a system of government. The old Soviet Union had a lot of income equality, achieved by keeping people at low standards of living. For most people, it was an unjust but relatively equalized system. Those who will argue that "the system is broken" have internalized only some of the economic facts of the past century while conveniently ignoring all the other realities that went along with that world. If you were a working, non-draft-age, white male, whose memories of childhood were formed in the Great Depression, you might think quite fondly of the 1950s, even right up to the 1980s. If you were a person of color, a woman, gay or lesbian, a draftee, mentally or physically disabled, or a member of any number of marginalized communities, perhaps not so much.

This raises another set of challenges to democracy that come from the paradoxical impact of affluence. The question of economic justice would have far greater resonance if the attacks on democracy were coming from the very poorest in every society. They're not. Instead, populist and authoritarian alternatives are often driven by resentments among and between the upper and middle classes. The most disadvantaged members of society, if we are honest enough to say it, do not have enough of a voice to destabilize a government or a political system. They aren't even likely to vote; as a 2019 study of nonvoters found, they are people "who are generally below the poverty line, with a lot of job turnover and family disruption, whose lives are busy living paycheck to paycheck."[21]

European observers, perhaps because they are more comfortable talking about class issues, have zeroed in on what *Financial Times* writer Martin Wolf calls "plutopopulism"—the bankrolling of antiestablishment celebrity candidates by people who are very much part of the new establishment, at least if measured by sheer wealth. Likewise, the British writer Simon Kuper noted in 2020 that the "comfortably off populist voter is the main force behind Trump, Brexit and Italy's Lega," a fact cagily ignored by opportunistic politicians who instead claim to be acting on behalf of stereotypes like "the impoverished former factory worker," even if there are few such people left to represent.[22] Or as the British think-tank analyst Charles Kenny, a forceful advocate of globalization, put it: "The voters who were won over by [Trump's] antiglobalist message were not legitimate victims of globalization," meaning that they were not, in the main, people who had actually suffered the job losses or deprivations they claimed were behind their vote.[23]

Sadly, faux populists hoodwinking ordinary citizens is not new. The American icon Will Rogers was famous for his down-home observations about the rich and powerful, and many of his sayings about politicians remain part of American folk humor today. ("With Congress, every time they make a joke it's a law, and every time they make a law it's a joke.") But Rogers knew exactly what he was doing. His son, Will Rogers Jr., once admitted as much to the Hollywood screenwriter Budd Schulberg. "My father was so full of shit, because he pretends he's just one of the people, just one of the guys," Rogers told Schulberg after a few too many drinks. "But in our house the only people that ever came as guests were the richest people in town, the bankers and the power-brokers of L.A. And those were his friends and that's where his heart is and he (was) really a goddamned reactionary." The elder Rogers died in a plane crash, and his son was running for Congress. "Jesus, Will," Schulberg replied. "You'd better keep your voice down, because you can't knock Will Rogers."

The younger Rogers was elected to Congress once, and then failed in subsequent political bids. In the 1950s, however, Schulberg used the elder Rogers as the inspiration for the character Larry "Lonesome" Rhodes in the American film masterpiece *A Face in the Crowd*. Rhodes, like Rogers, is a humble and charming character in public. He is discovered crooning songs and dispensing wisdom in a rural Arkansas jail cell by a producer who catapults him to stardom. In reality he is a ruthless grifter and rogue; he becomes a media sensation and is on the verge of an unstoppable political future before he is exposed and destroyed in a fit of guilt by the same producer (now his spurned lover) who made him famous. *A Face in the Crowd* was made in 1957, but—for obvious reasons—it enjoyed a revival of interest after 2016.[24]

Nothing shone a harsher light on the class disparities of modern American populism than the 2021 Capitol attack. The mob that overran the House and Senate was not made up of the poor and dispossessed seeking redress of grievances. They were a bored lumpen-bourgeoisie—middle-class citizens whose incomes allowed them to visit Washington. Many at the riot were wearing expensive military gear, and in some cases they were accompanied by their parents as travel companions. Many of them prattled and postured for their cameras even as they committed any number of crimes, which facilitated their eventual arrests around the country. The attackers included a realtor from Texas who went live on video during the violence to assure her audience that she was, in fact, committed to getting inside the Capitol, "life or death, it doesn't matter," but that upon her return to Texas everyone should know that she is a person who can handle even the toughest real-estate deals. Another rioter asked for supervised release after her arrest so that she could attend a pre-scheduled "work related bonding retreat" in Mexico.[25]

In any case, even if we grant that globalization and technological change have produced more pain than its advocates want to admit, these processes have also produced a world in which a high standard of living is so woven into the lives of the democracies that voters now view affluence as a *given* rather than as an *achievement*. There are, indeed, laid-off factory workers. And there are people (and always will be) who struggle to make ends meet. But American voters of all classes have come to expect continual improvement in their standard of living, from an economy they expect to provide a stream of ever-better and ever-cheaper goods and services. The American Dream cannot produce "rags to riches," but it has, as Strain puts it, delivered reliably on the promise of "rags to comfort."[26] As the *Financial Times* columnist Edward Luce wrote in 2017, we barely notice that the price of items like food and clothing—basic things all human beings need, "the products you find on Walmart's shelves"—are in fact cheaper compared to thirty years ago, in part because we are all too well aware of the painful fact that health insurance and college tuition are hundreds of percent higher.[27]

These increases, and the vanishing jobs and professions of the twentieth century, are part of the restless anxiety of a squeezed middle class. But Luce adds the revealing condition that people in the advanced West feel betrayed because they had counted on a belief that "by the end of their lives our children would be three to four times better off than we are."[28] Most children, however, are in fact already living better (again, by almost any measure of general well-being) than their parents did *at the same age*—an important proviso—and so the formula of doing "far better" can only end in political disaster. If every generation thinks the next will be three to four times better off than itself, then the near future will look like the movie *WALL-E*, with obese, immobilized citizens reclining on their couches in space-faring luxury liners while robots feed them bon-bons and change the channels of their television screens.

For a democratic government, relative deprivation and hedonic adaptation combine to create a no-win scenario. When times are good, they are not good enough and the political institutions and their elites have failed. When times are bad, they're bad, and the failure of the elites and the system they inhabit are obvious.

Peace and affluence are not anomalies in the American experience, and they need not be, in themselves, drivers of democratic discontent. Unfortunately, late twentieth-century Americans convinced themselves that the boom that followed World War II should never have ended (as though somehow other nations would never recover from the war); they likewise came to believe that their security at home was unrelated to the dispersal of U.S. troops all over the world. Political and economic changes, some hurtful and others beneficial, were inevitable with the rise of a global economy and the decline of the Soviet threat. The impact of these transformations on citizens of democracies and dictatorships alike, however, was supercharged by startling technological advances that changed daily life in ways, once again, that we now take for granted, from electronics to computing power to the explosion of bandwidth. These technological leaps were more than just enablers for entertainment and gadgetry: they have contributed both to our progressively better standard of living and to our democratic decline.

TECHNOLOGICAL PROGRESS AND SOCIAL DECLINE

Gordon Moore, who cofounded the computer chip maker Intel, predicted as far back as 1965 that computing power would get much faster and much cheaper at the same time, but "Moore's law" didn't really heat up until the 1990s. These rapid advances in computing, combined with improvements in technologies such as satellite communications and advances in miniaturization, gave ordinary citizens access to information, entertainment, and labor-saving benefits at speeds and capacities that would have been rare even at the most advanced scientific or military organizations only decades earlier. It is within living memory that engineers routinely used slide rules and people who may now FaceTime a friend almost anywhere on the planet had to wait hours even to make a transatlantic telephone call from the United States to Europe. (For younger readers, a "slide rule" was a calculating device made of movable pieces of wood or plastic, and the "telephone wait" back in the old days was the time it took for a U.S. operator to find an open line on one of the busy telephone cables underneath the ocean.)

Technology has also been the enabler of drastically higher standards of living in a much shorter time than ever before, and this has not only accelerated hedonic adaptation but has also served to drive ever higher expectations about living standards. The entrepreneur Peter Theil, referring to the ubiquity of Twitter, famously snarked in a 2013 presentation at Yale University about disappointment in the future by saying that "we were promised flying cars and all we got was 140 characters." The writer David Frum, however, put this into perspective only seven years later when he retorted (via Twitter, no less) that "I was promised flying cars, and instead all I got was all the world's libraries in my pocket and the ability to videochat 24-hours a day for free with my grandchildren on the other side of the world."

The internet and the subsequent revolution in communications brought us something else, however, that was, like so many innovations, an advance full of promise that turned on us because of our own bad habits. We are now locally and globally connected to each other at a level of involvement that is unhealthy for us on both a social and political level. This is not just a problem of social media, although that is the breeding ground for so much of what plagues modern democracy. It is more than global connection. It is a persistent presence in each other's lives that encourages us never to leave each other alone in the virtual world while avoiding any real human contact in the physical world.

This is deadly to a democracy, which relies as much on reflection as it does on civic interaction. We have become a performative culture, where our politics and even our tastes and preferences are displayed at every moment. The competition for attention and approval has become as fierce as the fight for any other scarce resource, and like any other zero-sum game, it often ends in disaster. Michael Goldhaber, the academic who years ago popularized the notion of an "attention economy"—in which those who can gain attention gain political and cultural strength—described the 2021 attack on the U.S. Capitol as one example of this kind of competition, calling it a predictable result of "thousands of influencers and news outlets that, in an attempt to gain fortune and fame and attention, trotted out increasingly dangerous conspiracy theories on platforms optimized to amplify outrage."[29] And because we now experience our lives as citizens through the mediation both of the internet and media outlets that have nothing but time and bandwidth, we can continue this social and political combat with just a few clicks on a keyboard or the remote to our televisions.

It sounds "undemocratic" to say it, but the democracies were more stable when political news and exposure to political leaders came in smaller packages, such as a daily newspaper, or the twenty-eight minutes of the evening news. When we took in political information in smaller doses, we could (if we were so inclined) take time to think, to reflect, and to discuss. It is a cliché to say now that acceleration of technology has progressed beyond the point where human beings can process the improvements raining down on them at ever shortening intervals, but it is a cliché because it is literally true. By 2015, U.S. consumers were taking in so much data on their various devices that, by one estimate, the average person would need more than fifteen hours a day to see it all.[30] This is bad enough when the average consumer is trying to take in both entertainment and information. Add to this the virtualization of our social and political life and it is a democratic disaster in the making.

And yet all this virtualization helped to blunt the impact of an international crisis when COVID-19 struck. The ability to relocate our workplaces, to stay in touch with each other even in isolation, even to be able to limit the spread of disease by cutting the amount of time it takes to pick up groceries, showed that the interconnected world was a lot more resilient than many of us might have thought. (There was a spate of "the pandemic means the end of globalization" pieces in early 2020, but as the globalized economy proved to be a great advantage in fighting the pandemic, those voices became a bit quieter.) Still, after being trapped in front of our screens for so long during the COVID pandemic, it is possible we will fall out of love with our personal technology. Years of rhapsodizing about how advanced societies could transition education and meetings and social gatherings to the virtual world have been undone by the reality of "Zoom Fatigue" and headaches from staring at other people on screens all day. Children do not learn as effectively sitting in their rooms while their teachers and other students stare at glowing screens. But many of us will, as we have for some thirty years, draw the opposite conclusion, and continue to see the online world as the great equalizer, a giant arena for the political and social equivalent of primal scream therapy.

HAPPINESS IS A HARD MASTER

In the end, the challenge to democracy isn't from continual war, economic scarcity, or the difficulties of daily life, all of which were features more characteristic of the late twentieth century than of the early twenty-first. Democracy is not in danger from new tribulations, but from new achievements: Democracies, it seems, cannot cope with peace, affluence, and progress.

To say this as an observation is not to wish for an economic catastrophe, nor is it a call for the national unity of "blood and iron." (Some of the opponents of people like Trump and other populists actually hoped for an economic downturn before the 2020 election, thinking that it would be a bucket of cold water over the heads of an irrational crowd, but populists are clever enough to use such moments as confirmation that the elites have failed yet again and that their views were right all along.)[31] The unity of war, of course, is temporary, and democracies, like any other regime, bear its burdens at great risk.

Peace is a great gift. Global economic cooperation is, in some form, inevitable. Technological change is irresistible. But if these advances turn us into self-absorbed and petulant children, then we have not gained very much. Democracy is a set of behaviors and beliefs that make institutions work, not a machine that grants wishes. The United States and any other nation that calls itself "democratic" must reinvent a way to protect democratic values and the inherent rights of each of its citizens while solving real problems—and taking advantage of real opportunities—produced by the new century. Blaming "the system," the elites, the economy, immigrants, and anything else has turned out to be a dead end.

In Aldous Huxley's *Brave New World*, a group of "World Controllers" eradicate war and social disorder in the far future by inundating human beings with pleasure, including sex, drugs, and pneumatic massage chairs. The Controllers do not outlaw democracy; they don't have to. They make happiness the highest value, define happiness as sensory pleasure, and provide it at will. As one of the World Controllers says near the book's conclusion, "happiness is a hard master," referring to the giant effort poured into keeping the population sated and docile. But it works.

Brave New World was written in 1932. Seventeen years (and a world war) later, in 1949, George Orwell posited a different end for democracy in his classic dystopian novel *1984*, in which a dictatorial Party wins by grasping the central truth that the wielding of power for its own sake will always triumph over watery ideas about truth or law or morality. Orwell, writing while Hitler was only recently dead and Stalin was very much alive, feared that human beings could be controlled far more effectively through pain and fear than through pleasure. Both Huxley and Orwell, interestingly enough, believed that their new dictators would emerge after a terrible war, but during the Cold War struggle with the Soviet Union, most Westerners feared Orwell's image of a boot stomping on a human face forever more than they did Huxley's warning that the end of democracy would be a drug-assisted suicide rather than a totalitarian murder.

In the mid-1980s, however, a New York University professor named Neil Postman wondered if maybe the Cold War struggle was blinding us to the possibility that Huxley was right after all. And what, Postman wondered, if we were already subjugating ourselves, by our own volition, with no need of World Controllers or the Inner Party of Orwell's Oceania, and willingly embracing a world ordered around entertainment and fueled by material plenty? Postman worried, as the title of his book announced, that we were in the process of "amusing ourselves to death," and he dedicated his book to the notion that maybe Huxley, not Orwell, was right.[32]

Postman was thirty years ahead of his time. But to discover why, we have to start even farther back in history. It is typical almost to the point of ritual to begin every examination with a nod to Alexis de Tocqueville and his reflections on America in the 1840s. It does not help us much today, however, to dwell on the behavior of homesteaders and frontiersmen two hundred years ago. Those who can find answers in Tocqueville are people who already understand the nature of democracy and citizenship. Instead, we must look to a small Italian village in the 1950s. An American scholar who could not understand why his own people could not get along with each other and make their own lives better went looking for answers in places like Utah and Arizona, and finally in Italy. He found a small community where nothing seemed to get done, and where no one gave a hoot about democracy. It was full of good people who loved their families but who somehow did not care about each other.

In the next chapter, we'll visit this lovely village and meet its people. Their story is a cautionary tale from the past that could turn out to be our collective future in our own brave and dystopian new world.

The Nicest People You'll Ever Dislike

When Good Neighbors Are Bad Citizens

The idiot is one who lives only in his own household and is concerned only with his own life and its necessities. The truly free state, then—one that not only respects certain liberties but is genuinely free—is a state in which no one is, in this sense, an idiot: that is, a state in which everyone takes part in one way or another in what is common.

—Hannah Arendt

THE NICEST PEOPLE YOU EVER DISLIKED

Democracy, in its raw form, is about counting votes. Liberal democracy is about much more than that. Choices made at the ballot box reflect the values and beliefs of the people casting those votes, which is why Election Day itself is often less important than what took place on all the other days before it. If citizens approach voting with a purely mercenary sense of self-interest and devoid of any sense of civic responsibility, liberal democracy cannot last long. There might still be elections, but they will be a collection of shams and illiberal plebiscites, and the history of such exercises in other nations shows that this kind of voting does not mean very much. No society can maintain a good democracy—one that respects human rights and puts the needs of the individual over the interests of the state—if it must rely on a population of bad citizens.

What does it mean to think of our neighbors as bad citizens? Even to ask the question feels wrong. "Good citizenship" awards are for children; adults do the best they can while balancing busy lives. To judge the civic behavior of our neighbors feels, well, judgmental. It certainly feels that way to me: I am an ordinary man with manifest personal and political failings, and I have done any number of things, including ballots I have cast, that I regret. (No, I'm not going to list them. I'm glad that the voting booth keeps our secrets.) Who are any of us to turn to the next person and blame them for the decline of our system of government?

Worse, such recriminations tend to result in platitudes that only sound like so much moral hectoring: "Be a conscientious voter. Show up for elections. Think about the future." If any of us were that easily advised to become paragons of civic rectitude, we wouldn't need democratic institutions, including the myriad social and political organizations whose aim is to encourage us to be better people, in the first place. This is the kind of advice that ends up being something like a lesson with a golf pro who keeps telling you to keep your arm straight and your head down—if you could do *that*, you wouldn't be paying a coach. This discomfort is one reason why it comes more naturally to all of us to blame "the system." When we feel like things are going wrong and our institutions seem to be failing us, the last thing anyone wants to hear about is their own part in it all and how they could have served those institutions better.

But there *is* such a thing as being a bad citizen, even among people we might otherwise think of as good neighbors. When we disengage from society and ignore our civic obligations, we are bad citizens.

When we listen only to those with whom we already agree and believe anyone else is wrong as a matter of first principles, we are bad citizens. When we insist on one standard of treatment from the government and the law for ourselves and for people whom we happen to like, and a different standard for others, we are bad citizens. When we continually blame the world around us for our nation's troubles while refusing to consider whether we've had any part in them, we are bad citizens. And when we only do what's best for ourselves, we are not citizens at all, but rather we become mercenaries, loose in the ship of state and plundering the hold, with no interest in our direction and no regard for our eventual survival

Genuine civic spirit is not the same thing as mere sociability. It's easy for most of us to be pleasant and sociable. We wave cheerfully at our neighbors from our driveways or nod politely to each other in our shared elevators and hallways. When we move into the public arena, however, we might find that we are *only* neighbors. Suddenly, we are aware that our disagreements are over more than taxes or potholes. We may find that we do not agree on things that are far more important to us. It might be immigration, or abortion, or minority rights, or civil liberties. It might be over how to defend ourselves against a foreign threat or measures to protect the health of the public. Our political differences, at that moment, become differences over basic values. The people with whom we thought we had so much in common turn out to be the nicest people we've ever disliked.

The temptation at such moments is to withdraw into ourselves and to take part in the political process purely as a matter of self-interest or even self-defense. We seek our own good and then retreat to our sanctum with our families. But as Hannah Arendt long ago reminded us, the Greek root of the word "idiot" comes from the word "idion," meaning things pertaining only to oneself as opposed to the common good. Even in the city-states of ancient Greece, those who cared only about themselves and were unwilling to contribute to the efforts of the community were judged to be bad citizens, insofar as one could think of them as "citizens" at all. The city was more than a collection of households, it was a living thing in itself, one that had to be tended by the public or lost. To be unable or unwilling to understand this was, literally, to be an idiot.

Readers who love their families (and who might not care very much about their neighbors) could well stop here and say: What's wrong with that? After all, who puts the welfare of strangers over their own family? What would it even look like *not* to act this way? We don't have to imagine what a society plagued by daily mistrust and the absence of a commitment to liberal democratic values might look like. There are plenty of examples around the world, from Russia to Colombia to Nigeria. There are any number of permutations in which societies are run by informal arrangements, corruption, kinship, tribal loyalty, or other arrangements that fill the vacuum left by the absence of shared norms, the rule of law, and civic commitment.

But one example in particular provides a warning for the citizens of the democracies, including the United States. It is a small Italian village nestled in the hills just above the ankle of Italy's "boot," and in the 1950s it was full of warm and charming people who were wonderful company. But they did not care very much about democracy and could not for the life of them make their town work, economically or politically. They cared very deeply about their own children, but almost not at all about those of other people. They were more willing to rent a mule for farm work than to hire their fellow townspeople for the same price.

Their experience was long ago and far away, and yet life in their village should sound familiar—and worrying—to Americans, as well as to the citizens of the other liberal democracies.

"NO ONE INTERESTS HIMSELF IN THE GENERAL WELFARE"

In the late 1940s, a young man named Edward Banfield switched careers after a stint in government. Initially an optimist about the role of government and planning, his work with the Farm Security Administration during Franklin Roosevelt's New Deal gave him second thoughts, and he headed for the University of Chicago, where he wrote a dissertation about farmers in a U.S. government program in Casa Grande, Arizona. More specifically, he wrote about how the inability of the farmers to cooperate with each other undermined the project. He then did a similar examination of farmers in Gunlock, Utah, but he still was puzzled not only by the question of why people who had every reason to work together refused to do so, but also why this problem seemed mostly impervious to government intervention.[1]

Banfield decided to look abroad for more answers. In 1956, he and his family headed for Italy and settled for several months in the village of Chiaromonte—a place, as he described it, of such "extreme poverty and backwardness" that Banfield chose to protect the town's identity with a pseudonym: Montegrano.

Banfield arrived in "Montegrano" only a decade after the end of World War II, thirteen years after Benito Mussolini had been hung by his heels and three years after Italy's last king, Umberto, was told far more gently that his services were no longer needed. Montegrano was part of a republic, a nation stitched together from Italy's fractious regions, and hardly a perfect democracy. But Italy was also a founding member of NATO and one of the first members of the European Economic Community, the forerunner of the European Union. It was a country in which the citizens had the right to express their views freely—as if anyone could prevent Italians from doing otherwise—along with the other basic guarantees of a democratic nation. There was even an active and sizable Communist party, although during this early period of the Cold War, the Communists were kept from power by various coalitions led by the Christian Democrats—along with some secret infusions of cash to anti-communist politicians from the American intelligence agencies.

Both the United States and Italy in the 1950s were free nations, at least to judge from the constitutional guarantees of civil and human rights, and the noisy and active public spaces in both countries. Despite the formal similarities between two Western democracies, however, Banfield could see immediately that something was amiss in this little corner of Italy. "Democracy" in Italy did not mean what it did in America, a nation at that time full of active civic, religious, and social organizations. All of these associations seemed to be missing in places like Montegrano. Banfield had seen the effects of the lack of trust and cooperation among the farmers of Arizona and Utah, but these problems were even worse in Italy. The townspeople were poor and mistrustful, and they were destined, it seemed, to stay that way.

Things were so bad in Montegrano that when Banfield wrote a book about the village, he titled the work *The Moral Basis of a Backward Society*. (You can see why he was kind enough to change the name of the village.) In effect, Banfield said that development was blocked in "Montegrano" and other backward places not because of the government, or capitalism or socialism or any other "ism," but by the people who lived there. Democracy in such places was just a word; the townspeople were free, of course, but they lacked the fundamental moral qualities that make democracy work and allow citizens to cooperate, to respect each other's rights, and to regard each other as members of a community, rather than to act like brutish children playing a game of musical chairs. Scholars now refer to these horizontal relationships among people as "social capital," the reservoir of trust and goodwill that allows citizens not only to advance together but also to endure the inevitable bad times without turning on each other, and towns like Banfield's "Montegrano" had precious little of it.[2]

When Americans think of a small commune in Italy, they probably think of a town much as Montegrano looked to Banfield at the time, with Mediterranean sunlight shining down on artisans and farmers, and the gentle southern Italian mountains holding lovely white stone homes in a reassuring embrace. The reality was far less appealing, as Banfield wrote:

There are no organized voluntary charities in Montegrano. An order of nuns struggles to maintain an orphanage for little girls in the remains of an ancient monastery, but this is not a local undertaking. The people of Montegrano contribute nothing to the support of it, although the children come from local families.

There is not enough food for the children, but no peasant or landed proprietor has ever given a young pig to the orphanage.

There are two churches in town. . . . The churches do not carry on charitable or welfare activities, and they play no part at all in the secular life of the community.

The doctor, although he has called upon the government to provide a hospital, has not arranged an emergency room or even equipped his own office. The pharmacist, a government-licensed monopolist, gives an absolute minimum of service at extremely high prices.

Most people say that no one in Montegrano is particularly public spirited, and some find the idea of public-spiritedness unintelligible.[3]

The local teacher was even more blunt and despairing when asked about civic involvement. "Many people positively want to prevent others from getting ahead," the young educator told Banfield. "Truly, I have found no one who interests himself in the general welfare. On the contrary, I know there is tremendous envy of either money or intelligence."

Banfield created a term for this kind of civic disengagement, an academic mouthful that we will note in passing and then leave aside: *amoral familism.* Basically, it means a society in which people act in their own interest without regard to any moral code other than what they believe is best for them and their families. Civic involvement in such a society is a waste of time, a snare for suckers. In a place like Montegrano, Banfield observed, values greater than the self and the family are mostly irrelevant, because there is "no connection between abstract political principle," on the one hand, and "concrete behavior in the ordinary relationships" among the townspeople, on the other. It is a society in which people think that what's good for the family is the only real rule of politics, and ideas like "democracy" or "socialism" or "communism" are mostly just so much noise.

Montegrano was in southern Italy, and it is no accident that the most extreme version of this kind of thinking is at the root of the Italian Mafia mentality, in which the clan is more important than anything else. To see an excellent depiction of "amoral familism," think of the final scene of the 1974 movie *The Godfather Part II*, written by Mario Puzo and Francis Ford Coppola, both Italian Americans from immigrant families. Set in 1941, the youngest son of the Corleone crime family, Michael, is talking to his older brother Sonny about the attack on Pearl Harbor. Sonny—who is no coward and often exhibits great physical bravery—nonetheless thinks the men now crowding the military recruitment stations are "saps." Michael, born and raised in the United States, asks Sonny why he thinks this way. "They're saps because they risk their lives for strangers," Sonny answers.

When Michael says they're risking their lives for their country, Sonny says: "Your country ain't your blood. You remember that." When Michael reveals he has dropped out of Dartmouth and enlisted in the Marines, Sonny is so enraged that he attacks him.

In Montegrano and villages like it, Banfield found that civic life reflected a basic rule expressed in one form or another by all of the villagers: "Maximize the material, short-run advantage of the nuclear family; assume that all others will do likewise." These Italians lived by a purely transactional code, according to which every man used "his ballot to secure the greatest material gain in the short run." Nothing else was remotely as important. "Although he may have decided views as to his long-run interest, his class interest, or the public interest," Banfield wrote, "these will not affect his vote if the family's short-run, material advantage is in any way involved."

It is difficult to govern a town like Montegrano, insofar as it can be "governed" at all. There are elected offices, but no one trusts anyone else to hold them. This is just as well, since being a local official was hardly an honor and certainly not a vehicle for improving the life of the town. Mostly, democratic politics produced misery for everyone involved.

> In Montegrano and nearby towns an official is hardly elected before the voters turn violently against him. As soon as he gets into office, his supporters say—often with much justice—he becomes arrogant, self-serving, and corrupt. At the next election, or sooner if possible, they will see that he gets what is coming to him. In Montegrano there is no better way to lose friends than to be elected to office.

This is not an environment that encourages talented or virtuous people to engage in public service, even if there were people who understood such positions to be a matter of public service in the first place.

The voters projected their own self-centeredness onto their elected officials, because the townspeople knew what they would do with political power, and they assumed that everyone else would do the same. The goal in every election was not to return political leaders to office for the public good, but to squeeze out whatever benefits could be gotten in the immediate circumstances.

If this sounds suspiciously like the modern United States or some of the wobblier democracies in Europe, it should. In his time, however, Banfield saw far fewer similarities with the United States. Instead, he contrasted Montegrano with St. George, a community he saw while living in Utah where civic interaction was the order of the day, from the Red Cross to the local farm bureau. Banfield was being a bit too clever here, since St. George was a Mormon community and was, for religious and cultural reasons, likely to exhibit more civic engagement than most places even by the standards of the United States in the 1950s. The contrast was nonetheless striking, and most of the associations and their goings-on in St. George would be familiar to anyone today who grew up in almost any American community of the mid- to late 20th century, including fraternal organizations, trade associations, school committees, and the Chamber of Commerce.

Montegrano, by comparison, had none of these. Even the church and its services in this nominally Catholic town were mostly ignored, except for a small group of village women and some of the men who "remain standing near the door as if to signify that they are not unduly devout." There were local newspapers; the major dailies from Rome and elsewhere in the region were delivered by bus to the commune, but there was nothing in them of local affairs, and they were thus read by few villagers. And as for civic engagement, Banfield found about twenty-five "upper class men" in a town of over three thousand who "maintain a clubroom where members play cards and chat. Theirs is the only association."

Again, this sounds terrible and yet familiar. The collapse of trust in institutions and politics is a well-known story in the United States.[4] The American public, whose generally low participation in elections is itself a departure from most other democracies, not only has ceased to trust government institutions, but many Americans have come to believe that these institutions and the elites who inhabit them are actively hostile to ordinary citizens.[5] America's many civic and fraternal associations, the intermediate institutions that provide the social foundations for democratic government, are declining in numbers and activity. Levels of trust in everything and everybody but the military (which should be a warning sign in a democracy) have fallen to historic lows. To run for office in America in the 2020s is to invite the same kind of instant disrepute it garnered in Italy in the 1950s.

Americans always have plenty of excuses for their cynicism. It's too hard to vote; the rich just get richer; nothing matters anyway. The Italians had all of the same excuses, as did observers who objected to Banfield's account and who applied what they saw as obvious answers of their own to the village's political and economic dysfunction. *Of course* poor people loathed the authorities; those are the elites who kept them poor. *Of course* the village distrusted the Catholic Church; those clerics and bureaucrats concentrated land and wealth and power in their own hands for centuries. And *of course* the commune wanted nothing to do with politics; those Fascist pretenders joined an insane war and devastated their country within recent memory.

Banfield thought of those explanations, too, and found that they did not explain very much. Perhaps the villagers were selfish and disengaged because they were poor. That's a popular excuse, but, as it turned out, not one that held much water. When it came to attending church services in this small Catholic town, for example, Banfield wryly noted that the typical villager "uses his poverty as an excuse for not doing what he would not do anyway: he does not go to mass on Sunday, he explains sadly, because he must be off to his field at dawn. But his field is a tiny patch of wheat on which, except for three weeks a year, he can do almost nothing." More to the point, that same villager does nothing else for the town, even for the orphanage whose walls were falling down around the ears of the little girls housed there. "None of the many half-employed stone masons has ever given a day's work to its repair," Banfield observed, despite the fact that "there is hardly a man in Montegrano who could not contribute a third of his time to some community project without a loss of income."

Banfield plowed through several other explanations, including ignorance, class hatred, and the attachment of peasants only to their own plot of land. None of them seemed to capture the problem. The best Banfield could do was to note that many of the villagers themselves had been orphans or desperately poor children—not that this increased their empathy toward others in the same situation—and so they feared the kind of poverty and premature deaths that would relegate their own children to a life of similar misery. Rather than cooperate and endure any longer-term risk to their families, Banfield surmised, the villagers took what they could get in the near term and let the future be someone else's problem.

In the end, Banfield found no solution. His remedies, as sensible as they were, amounted to little more than recommendations that encouraged people to be better citizens. "The individual must define self or family interest less narrowly than material, short-run advantage," he wrote. "He need not cease to be family minded or even selfish, but—some of the time, at least—he must pursue a 'larger' self-interest." And who will do this? Well, Banfield hoped (for that is all he could do) that "a few persons, at least, have the moral capacity to act as leaders. These need not act altruistically either; they may lead because they are paid to do so. But whether they give leadership or sell it, they must be able to act responsibly in organizational roles and to create and inspire morale in organization."

And if all that can be done, somehow, then the citizens must be sure not to throw it all away: "Voters and others must not destroy organizations gratuitously or out of spite or envy." Banfield, even after his disillusionment with the New Deal, still had the instincts of a social planner, and he wanted to be able to translate his findings into some kind of policy. All the more desolating, then, that he admits at the end that planners who want to defeat these cultural land mines would have to identify the "key elements" that created them in the first place, "something which may be impossible."

Banfield died in 1999. His book, for a time, became an academic classic and for years was part of the education of future social scientists, back when such books were readable both by scholars and the general public. Eventually Banfield ran afoul of the prevailing views of the academy in his day, which returned to a faith in government solutions and rejected his emphasis on culture and human agency when trying to explain persistent poverty.[6] He is also somewhat less read these days because his case study has been overtaken by newer and better works not only on Italy, but on democracy in general. A landmark study in 1993 by the Harvard professor Robert Putnam, for example, found—as Banfield might have expected—that when Italy attempted to impose similar institutional reforms in the north and south of the country in the 1970s, the same set of arrangements performed differently depending on where they were, an outcome explained primarily by social context and history rather than by institutional design.[7]

Comparisons between Italy in the 1950s and America in the 2020s are naturally limited, especially when Banfield loaded the dice by comparing impoverished villagers who had just survived a war to relatively prosperous Mormons in Utah. There are fundamental economic and political differences that matter as much now as they did then, including the important differences in voter behavior when faced with the Italian proportional representation system and the

American system of separated powers and fixed terms. And an agrarian society in an underdeveloped region of a defeated nation is not a good comparison to a thriving town in an emerging superpower.

But even within Italy itself, the flaw at the heart of the villages like Montegrano has bedeviled Italian politics over the many years since Banfield lived among its residents. Italian democracy has survived and Italy has become a major political and economic power, and yet the attitude of the self-centered villager is still a part of the political culture. As the Italian scholar Maurizio Viroli notes, Italy is still a free country, if "free" means that "neither other individuals nor the state can prevent us from doing as we choose." But Viroli calls this the "liberty of servants," rather than the liberty of citizens. It is the liberty of human beings who are subjects in a new kind of democracy that is really just the "court of a *signore* surrounded by a plethora of courtiers, who are in turn admired and envied by a multitude of individuals with servile souls."[8]

The *signore* to whom Viroli refers was Silvio Berlusconi, a media mogul and gleeful sybarite who led Italy for nearly a decade. Berlusconi was like one of Banfield's villagers—if those villagers were plutocratically rich and given control of an entire country. He entered politics to protect himself and his interests, he methodically enriched himself and his friends, and he had no real attachment to any governing concept other than what was best for Silvio Berlusconi. Like all demagogues, his antics and promises finally exhausted the public, and he resigned in 2011. Viroli, for his part, rejects the idea that Berlusconi and the regime he produced was some kind of accident. When he reflected in 2010 on how his country had come to such an unfortunate state, Viroli did not hesitate to speak of what he describes as "Italy's longtime moral weakness," and despite the "examples of greatness that have honored our past and our present," he did not spare the voters from their own responsibility:

By moral weakness I mean the quality that so many political writers have explicated, that is to say a lack of self-esteem that in some cases masks itself with arrogance, and which makes men willing to become dependent on other men. If I believe that I am not worth much, why should I not serve the powerful, if I profit considerably thereby?[9]

"To put it concisely," Viroli adds, "if we are subjected to the arbitrary and enormous power of a man, we may well be free to do more or less what we want, but we are still servants."

WE'RE ALL VILLAGERS NOW

But maybe this was all just a story about Italy. Maybe this kind of selfishness and delusion, as Viroli wrote, is just a recessive gene in Italy's political DNA, reasserting itself every few generations as a reminder of some sort of flaw or original sin that dates from the first time Romulus and Remus set their eyes on the Seven Hills. Maybe Americans and others can reassure themselves that this is "just how Italians are." Unfortunately, the story of Montegrano matters today because the democracies—and even the United States, which once seemed so much healthier than Italy—are looking more and more like that long-ago village. The story of Montegrano is a cautionary tale precisely because it could be the American future.

Consider, for example, how many Americans think that the major defect in the U.S. political system is a combination of both their own incompetence as voters and the moral failings of the group of politicians for whom *they themselves have voted.* A national study done some twenty years ago by two University of Nebraska professors found that nearly half the respondents from national focus groups "believed that the country would be better off if politicians and not the American people decided political issues."

> We were taken aback by the extent to which focus group partici-
> pants believe that the American people generally do not have the
> time, motivation, orientation, knowledge, and even intelligence
> it takes to get up to speed on the political issues of the day, *unless*
> *those issues might be of vital interest to the person.* . . . And it was an
> extremely rare voice that said the American people were willing
> to shoulder the responsibility of deciding tough political issues.
> (emphasis added)[10]

And yet among that same group, anywhere from a quarter to some 40 percent of Americans believe that "obvious, commonsense solutions to the country's problems are out there for the plucking," and that the main reason these obvious solutions are not enacted is that "politicians are corrupt, or self-interested, or addicted to unnecessary partisan feuding."[11]

No Italian peasant could have set up this no-win situation more elegantly. The voters hold out hopes that somehow better decisions could be made by "leaders who will step forward, cast aside cowardly politicians and venal special interests, and implement long-overdue solutions," but why these citizens never manage to find such unicorns is left unexamined. Worse, as the writer Jonathan Rauch noted later, it is deeply worrisome to realize that for the voters in this study, "whether the process is democratic is not particularly important."[12]

Generations of Americans were raised with Norman Rockwell's 1943 painting of a man speaking his mind at a New Hampshire town meeting, one of the representations of FDR's "Four Freedoms" Rockwell produced during World War II. They will bristle at reimagining this sturdy and civic man, whose face Rockwell lovingly depicted as having weathered a lot of tough New England winters, as just another lazy Mediterranean farmer lolling about in a half-tended grain field, complaining about others. Americans are doers, volunteers, self-made and motivated. Americans don't begrudge success, we emulate it. We believe in merit and talent and we encourage everyone to be their best. We are not Italian villagers, scheming and nursing grudges against each other.

And yet it is important to remember that Rockwell's image of the common man having his say, politely and with the obvious attention of his fellow citizens, was both an idealized reality and an aspiration. Even as a romantic memory, it is a portrait from a bygone era. For decades, television-addled voters in the United States have been looking for celebrity gladiators, not governors. Here, for example, is a California voter speaking to the *New York Times* in 2016:

> Victor Vizcarra, 48, of Los Angeles, said he would much prefer Mr. Trump to Mrs. Clinton. Though he said he disagreed with some of Mr. Trump's policies, he added that he had watched "The Apprentice" and expected that a Trump presidency would be more exciting than a "boring" Clinton administration.

> "A dark side of me wants to see what happens if Trump is in," said Mr. Vizcarra, who works in information technology. "There is going to be some kind of change, and even if it's like a Nazi-type change, people are so drama-filled. They want to see stuff like that happen. It's like reality TV. *You don't want to just see everybody be happy with each other. You want to see someone fighting somebody.*" (emphasis added)[13]

It was generous of the reporter to note that the subject disagreed with "some" of Trump's policies, as if that mattered; what was more important was that Trump was a television star and Clinton was dull.

Most voters, especially in the United States, would resent the implication that their beliefs are flexible or that their political leanings are not based on some sort of principle. As party identification has grown more rigid over the years, they would reject the idea that they are capable of careening about between political ideologies, embracing socialism one moment and royalism the next, like the villagers of Montegrano. And yet political scientists for decades have noted the political incoherence of the American voter. As far back as the early 1960s, the political scientist Phillip Converse showed that most voters do not have particularly stable ideological views.[14] The voters lack the information—or the interest—to develop a coherent view of politics beyond a general party identification, and this reality plays itself out regularly in U.S. elections.

In the 2016 presidential election, for example, there were stark differences between the major party nominees. More consistent but nonetheless jaundiced and bitter voters could look at Hillary Clinton and Donald Trump—historically, two of the most unpopular people ever to face off against each other for the presidency—and see nothing but two New York-based plutocrats, aging Baby Boomers who hated each other but traveled for decades in the same circles. (A famous picture of the Clintons at one of Trump's weddings encapsulated the cozy similarities between people who claimed to be representing different groups.) If Clinton was the avatar of the Establishment, Trump was merely a different wing of the same oligarchy, another narcissist trying to buy himself an office.

Many of these voters were attracted to the campaign of Senator Bernie Sanders of Vermont. An oddball figure in U.S. politics for decades, Sanders was an unlikely presidential prospect—a tough-talking old man with a Brooklyn honk despite years of representing a rural New England state, and a self-proclaimed socialist in a country where "socialism" is mostly an epithet. Sanders presented himself as the real deal, a man who could turn the system on its head, and his campaign briefly caught fire when he won some important Democratic Party primary contests in 2016 and gave Clinton a run for her money.

And then millions of supposed Sanders voters went ahead and voted for Trump anyway. This was a not a handful of disaffected campus socialists. A significant number of Democratic primary voters—more than one in ten, as it turned out—crossed over and gave their vote to a man who, in theory, stood for everything they hated: nativism, hyper-capitalism, sexism, authoritarianism. They ended up contributing to the margin of victory in the states Trump needed to pick the lock to an Electoral College win that both Democrats and Republicans until that moment had thought was out of reach.

This outcome is only puzzling if we believe the voters have consistent—and civic—views. Insofar as policy does matter, the voters often create policy dilemmas that politicians cannot resolve other than by short-circuiting such debates and running on personality and fame. For years, the standard trope among observers of American politics has been that voters are consistent and moderate while politicians are opportunistic and extreme. Politicians might well *be* opportunists, but Americans are neither consistent nor moderate. Voters love to describe themselves as moderate and independent, but they are, to use President Joe Biden's catchphrase, full of malarkey. As the scholar David Broockman and his colleagues showed in work from the early 2010s, voters are not all that moderate. Rather, "surveys mistake people with *diverse* political opinions for people with *moderate* political opinions." (emphasis added)[15]

Put another way, voters who have strong views on a few issues look like "moderates" if their views are averaged together. Such people—who might, say, want both universal health care because it is in their interest but also favor discrimination against gays and lesbians because of their personal or religious beliefs—are actually difficult to categorize and are often more extreme on any one issue than the politicians who represent them. These voters want their hot-button issues served, even if these issues are almost impossible to accommodate within a coherent worldview. As the political analyst Lee Drutman noted in 2019, "if you're a campaign trying to appeal to independents, moderates or undecided voters — or a concerned citizen trying to make sense of these groups in the context of an election — policy and ideology aren't good frames of reference. There just isn't much in terms of policy or ideology that unites these groups."[16]

This becomes all the more disheartening when the politics of narrow self-interest are blended into a general cynicism and an emotional suspicion of politics. As Rauch argued at the time of the 2016 election:

> Like Trump, Sanders appealed to the antipolitical idea that the mere act of voting for him would prompt a "revolution" that would somehow clear up such knotty problems as health-care coverage, financial reform, and money in politics. Like Trump, he was a self-sufficient outsider without customary political debts or party loyalty. Like Trump, he neither acknowledged nor cared—because his supporters neither acknowledged nor cared—that his plans for governing were delusional.[17]

For voters in an advanced postindustrial democracy, this might seem like just another harsh rebuke from yet another intellectual. For the villagers of Montegrano, however, this would hardly be a rebuke; rather, they would see it as merely a description of the natural order of things. To the transactional and self-interested mindset, politicians are largely indistinguishable other than on the basis on their personalities, and the platforms they espouse are usually irrelevant. All that matters is getting the candidate to do things you want—or to prevent them from doing things *other* people might want.

Consider two voters from Iowa, the emblematic American heartland state, in the run-up to the state 2020 Democratic caucus. A caucus is a far more personal involvement in choosing a nominee than merely casting a vote in a primary; caucus-goers must engage in bargaining with other party members to gain support for their candidates. One might expect greater levels of general consistency in such an environment, but one would be wrong to be so hopeful. The *Los Angeles Times* reporter Matt Pearce, for example, spoke to a woman who caucused for Sanders in 2016 and then voted for Trump.[18] In 2020, she initially settled on Pete Buttigieg, the mayor of South Bend, Indiana, as her choice. If Buttigieg didn't win the nomination, however, she would move from the young, progressive, gay, once-married Buttigieg back to the elderly, right-wing, serially adulterous, thrice-married bigot Trump—a kaleidoscopic change in preferences that only makes sense as a search for a tailored set of narrow promises that would meet her personal satisfaction, rather than the selection of a candidate who must govern across a range of issues.

Another Iowan told the media that she had voted both for Barack Obama and for Donald Trump, "just to shake up Washington, to be honest." (This is sometimes called the "OOT" voter, the person who voted Obama-Obama-Trump in 2008, 2012, and 2016, respectively.) Had Trump not been available in 2016, she said, she might have gone for—of course—Bernie Sanders. "We've just been in a rut so long," she sighed.[19] This voter had for years run her own beauty salon in a county in Iowa that in 2016 had a 2.5 percent unemployment rate, had almost no immigrants (the county is 98 percent white), and boasted a crime rate far below the U.S. average. And yet, like many voters over the years, her perception was that American politics had become too static and needed some sort of disruption to make it more receptive to people like her. If that meant going from Barack Obama to a candidate who had originated the viciously racist "birther" campaign against Obama, so be it.

Move east across the United States, and the story is the same. The reporter Tim Alberta visited Pennsylvania in 2020, listening in to a debate on a porch in Scranton. A voter named Ann said that even as a Democrat, she couldn't vote for Biden because he was, she thought, senile. "The porch," according to Alberta, "erupted in groans and laughter and shouting," but Ann pressed on. "He is! He is!" she said, raising her voice. "I'm sorry, but he is. And Trump, that asshole, forget about it. He should have never been president in the first place. So, I can't vote for either one of them." One of the other people on the porch tried to break the tension by adding another possibility. "What about the one guy—what's his name, the rapper. Canyon West?" A teenager in the house informed the adults that the rapper is named *Kanye* West, adding that West was too late to qualify for the ballot in most states.[20]

Alberta also visited with two brothers in Pennsylvania who made the Iowans and the porch debaters seem almost coherent by comparison:

Neither of the McHale brothers voted in 2016. They are fed up with politics and politicians. Bill, a registered Democrat, "wasn't a fan of Hillary," and Bob, a conservative-leaning independent, "couldn't stomach" supporting Trump. Four years later, their positions haven't changed much. "I'm not real happy with my party these days," said Bill, a custodian with the Scranton Public Schools. "They're too far to the left for me at this point. The older I get, the more to the right I find myself." He stops suddenly. "Trust me, I'm no Trumper. I think the Republicans are insane. But I don't like the guy Democrats are putting up, either . . . I could have voted for Buttigieg; I liked him. Maybe even Bernie."

Jonathan Last, a conservative anti-Trump columnist, wrote of this discussion with understandable exasperation: "Read that again: Bill is a 'conservative-leaning independent' who is worried that the Democrats are 'too far to the left' which is why he does not support Joe Biden, but would have supported Pete Buttigieg or possibly Bernie Sanders."[21] If there is some sort of programmatic coherence here, any candidate would be hard-pressed to find it, especially among voters for whom words like "right" and "left" seem devoid of any meaning beyond proxies for "like" and "dislike."

I have known many such voters personally, including "OOT voters," and felt the same exasperation. One of my closest friends from high school, for example, came of political age when I did. Like me, 1980 was his first national election. Over the years, he cast two votes for Ronald Reagan, one for George H. W. Bush, two for Bill Clinton, two for George W. Bush, two for Barack Obama, and then turned to Donald Trump. When I asked him in 2016 how this lifetime of voting made any sense, he said that he tended to prefer Republicans because he believed that they were generally better for the economy. Why, then, did he vote for the last two Democratic presidents? Because, he said, *those* Republicans, at the time, were just out to protect the rich. But what about Donald Trump, whose entire goal in life is being rich? My friend shook his head and gave up trying to explain it. "Nothing's been good since Reagan," he said, a statement we both knew was not true and might well have been more a reflection of the gloom of middle age than of any political preference.

I do not know how he voted in 2020.

There are plenty of people like my friend, and at first blush that might even seem reassuring. People *should* change their minds if they think they're being offered a better candidate or a better deal. But at some point, such voting goes beyond people merely changing their minds. To vote both for Barack Obama and for Donald Trump is beyond "flexibility." Better candidates and better deals require an electorate capable of comprehending the contenders and what they offer, but such reflection becomes impossible when emotion, cynicism, and self-interest congeal into tribal loyalty and "negative partisanship"—the idea that all parties are bad, but that yours is far worse than mine and so I therefore must vote against yours.[22] This is the worst of all political worlds, in which the voters believe they are being true to a set of political ideas but are really acting out of contradictory emotions and conflicting rationalizations.

It is not news that American voters often do not understand the ideologies they claim to support. As Jonathan Rauch noted in 2019, people are sorting themselves into parties that are themselves mashups of contradictory ideas. "We are not seeing a hardening of coherent ideological difference. We are seeing a hardening of *incoherent* ideological difference" (emphasis in original).[23] Insofar as people are loyal to parties, much of it is the result of traditional attachments or reflexive partisanship. Unaffiliated voters, meanwhile, often go shopping for deals, and then retroactively apply partisan rationalizations to their choices.

Self-interest is the normal engine of normal human day-to-day behavior, and there's nothing wrong with it. Only the saintliest of us do things all day long purely out of the goodness of our hearts; the rest of us have bills to pay. (I wrote this book because I wanted to communicate some ideas to you that I think are important, but I also hope you paid for it.) Politics, in the political scientist Harold Lasswell's classic 1936 formulation, is always about "who gets what, when, and how," but different cultures and societies solve that problem in different ways. And whenever someone gets something in that distribution, someone else will think it is unfair. (Joseph Heller, in his celebrated satire *Catch-22*, described the father of one of the book's characters as "a long-limbed farmer, a God-fearing, freedom-loving, law-abiding rugged individualist who held that federal aid to anyone but farmers was creeping socialism.") When there is nothing else but raw self-interest, however, liberal democracy is impossible—especially if we define our "interest" as including the psychic gratification of defeating enemy tribes and dividing the spoils.

Without some basic belief that the good of the family and the good of society are intertwined and mutually reinforcing, democratic institutions become little more than temporary conveniences, and democratic values become annoyances. And when we need those institutions and values—especially when our rights are threatened—we will find ourselves alone when facing whatever jackal pack has assembled against us. We will have no recourse through the law or the ballot box, and we might end up relying on criminals, buccaneers, or foreign powers to protect us in the ensuing scrum.

In 2020, the onset of a pandemic forced Americans to confront the question of whether ordinary self-interest had curdled into dangerous selfishness. The answer, at least in the United States, was not pretty.

ALONE AGAINST THE STORM

Pandemics, unlike military crises or other shared threats, tend to divide people and make them more isolated rather than bring them together, because they force us to live alone and to rely on ourselves. The menace of contagion requires us not only to shun contact with our neighbors, but to do so for the common good. There is a difference, however, between "social distancing" and social warfare. Every nation in the world was tested when the coronavirus made its way from bats into human beings in 2019. Some, like South Korea and New Zealand, passed with flying colors. Others bumbled their way to disaster.

The United States, one of most advanced nations on earth and a powerhouse in the field of medical technology, failed miserably.

By the time the president of the United States deigned to wear a mask in public, over 150,000 Americans were dead, and dozens of U.S. states remained mired in partisan combat over everything from mask mandates to school closures. The political writer George Packer addressed this with wince-inducing clarity when he described the United States as reacting to the pandemic not like a technologically advanced democracy, but instead "like Pakistan or Belarus—like a country with shoddy infrastructure and a dysfunctional government whose leaders were too corrupt or stupid to head off mass suffering." Packer even went so far as to describe America during the pandemic as "a failed state."[24]

This last charge was not only too extreme, but it let far too many Americans off the hook for their own disgraceful behavior. In a failed state, government no longer exists. From Somalia to the Soviet Union, a failed state is a place where it is difficult to do so much as deliver a package, turn on a light, or pump a gallon of gasoline without relying on some ad hoc and often personally hazardous arrangements. (I was in Moscow a month before the Soviet collapse in 1991, when money meant little and people mostly traded food or cigarettes for basic services. That's what a failing state looks like.) This collapse of institutions did not take place in the United States during the pandemic. Instead, millions of Americans decided to do what they wanted to do, and to let the consequences fall on others.

In addition to the people who believed that masks and closures were dictatorial, there were others who simply didn't care. States rushed to reopen businesses; younger people congregated in bars; casinos filled back up overnight. And when protests broke out over the video of a police officer in Minnesota coldly crushing the life out of an unarmed and handcuffed man by kneeling on his neck, hundreds of sympathetic medical experts—caught between a just cause and the inevitability of protests—relented on their own advice and blessed the same kind of mass gatherings they had warned against only days earlier.[25] They meekly advised the protesters to wear masks, wash their hands, and self-quarantine themselves in cities where those same experts said church choirs should be prohibited from sitting too closely to each other because it was too dangerous.

President Trump, meanwhile, was caught on tape admitting that he knew that the coronavirus was deadly and that he downplayed it anyway.[26] Trump claimed that he didn't want to cause a panic, but he also held crowded political rallies for weeks after being briefed on the massive threat from COVID. He pushed for ending lockdowns, ridiculed his election rival for wearing a mask, and defied local and state ordinances against large public events. Millions of his supporters applauded him and followed his example.

No one did more to cripple the U.S. response than Trump, but as the writer Damon Linker pointed out in the terrible summer of 2020, Trump was only the embodiment of a much larger social problem revealed by the failure to contain the pandemic.

> What is the source of the failure? It has many names—individualism, cultural libertarianism, atomism, selfishness, lack of social trust, suspicion of authority—and it takes a multitude of forms. But whatever we call it, it amounts to a refusal on the part of lots of Americans to think in terms of the social whole—of what's best for the community, of the common or public good. Each of us thinks we know what's best for ourselves. We resent being told what to do.[27]

Once the death toll began to mount, both the president and his supporters doubled down, over and over. To admit error would be too disempowering. And, perhaps most important in an atmosphere of resentful tribalism, it would feel too much like surrendering not only to science but also to the tribe's political enemies.

At a time when the United States needed to come together like a strong and assured democracy, it reverted to the politics of the village. Banfield didn't live to see it, but he would have understood it. In late 2020, the writer Franklin Foer drew on Banfield's work to deliver a blistering criticism of how the Trump administration's nepotism, and in particular the appointment of the president's inexperienced and incompetent son-in-law, Jared Kushner, to oversee the government's COVID-19 response, made a bad situation worse:

> Banfield argued that amoral familism inhibits good decision making; it's the enemy of efficiency and progress. The pandemic has graphically illustrated this. The country has performed woefully compared with the nations it once regarded as peers. It has become the national version of the stunted village that Banfield studied, ruled by a father and his callow princeling, unable to govern in the name of the common good, because they can see no further than the interests of the clan.[28]

The disaster that followed, however, was more than just the result of the petty corruption of the Trump inner circle. Millions of Americans were already adherents of Trump's version of transactional politics long before 2016, but it was dreadful timing that the most nepotistic and dysfunctional administration in modern history was at the helm during an emergency that did not lend itself to simple partisan or tribal solutions.

The de-evolution of American politics into clannish self-interest may have been weighing on Barack Obama's mind when he spoke to the convention of his own party in 2020. Both the former president and his wife, in separate speeches, went after their political rivals, which is to be expected at a political convention. But Obama went farther, calling on Americans to adjust their expectations and to shoulder their share of the burden of sustaining a liberal democracy. He called upon people "to embrace your own responsibility as citizens—to make sure that the basic tenets of our democracy endure."[29]

Although Obama's comments were aimed squarely at Trump, this was a broader indictment about disengagement, a warning that "those in power—those who benefit from keeping things the way they are—are counting on your cynicism." As one journalist put it, "Obama, suddenly a gray-haired father figure to his party . . . seemed frightened."[30] If the former president was frightened, he should have been. So should we all be.

NO MORE EXCUSES

When democracy first arrives in a place like Montegrano, where people are poor and life is arduous, the odds are already stacked against success. Democracy, a system that relies on sustained cooperation, will always have a harder time gaining a foothold against the immediate imperatives of survival. In difficult circumstances, people will do what's best for themselves, with little interest in high-minded abstractions about politics, even if doing so produces the paradoxical outcome that they remain poor. So it was in the Italian village. Banfield, it should be remembered, really wasn't trying to explain democracy, he was trying to explain poverty. The revelations about how the lack of trust and cooperation undermines development came later.

It's one thing, however, for democracy to face trouble getting off the ground in a place like Montegrano, it's another for it to wither once it is already established and has flourished for centuries among a prosperous and educated people. Americans are turning inward not because they are poor or worried that their children will end up in orphanages as wards of the state. Rather, Americans are devolving back toward the mentality of the village not because they are poor but because they are comfortable, materialistic, and self-obsessed.

They are inspired, at least in the public sphere, not by examples of virtue but by celebrity. They are motivated to compete with each other not because they are fighting over scraps but because they are entitled. They insist on their own rights not as a matter of principle but as a means of crowding out the rights of others. America is becoming Montegrano—but with better cars, cheap air conditioning, the internet, and two hundred cable channels.

Maybe Montegrano never had a chance. But what excuses the rest of us?

"Is There No Virtue Among Us?"

Democracy in an Age of Rage and Resentment

The West's souring mood is about the psychology of dashed expectations rather than the decline in material comforts.

—Edward Luce

The most obvious explanation for American political life since the end of the Cold War is that we have become an unserious country populated by an unserious people.

—Jonathan V. Last

Is there no virtue among us? If there be not, we are in a wretched situation.

—James Madison

AN UNVIRTUOUS NATION

It is disturbing enough to realize that our neighbors might be good people but bad citizens. But what happens if the citizens of a democratic nation, whatever their civic habits, are no longer virtuous enough as a people to sustain their own institutions? Good people can, from time to time, be bad citizens. Nations, like families, can persevere through periods of anger and estrangement. Liberal democracy, however, cannot long survive among an unvirtuous people. The collapse of virtue, public and private, leads not only to bad citizenship, but also to the eventual impossibility of producing good citizens at all.

Even more than questions about what makes a good or bad citizen, questions about virtue seem intrusive and judgmental. Democracies, we might think, are not based on virtue, but on everyone behaving moderately well while minding their own business. To ruminate on who is a virtuous person is a matter for ancient philosophers; to investigate the feelings or beliefs of other citizens is the road taken by the eternal social and political busybody. As Louis Brandeis famously wrote in 1928, "the right to be let alone" is "the most comprehensive of the rights and the right most valued by civilized men." Just as liberal democracies long ago rejected literacy tests and poll taxes for the universal franchise, they cannot today institute some sort of moral test at the entrance to the voting booth. In a tolerant, secular democracy, what's in our hearts when we show up to vote is between us and our conscience.

And yet, as much as Americans may prefer to ignore this part of their national history, the Founders of the American republic understood the existential link between virtue and democracy. They knew that to believe in some magical difference between how we live our lives as individuals and how we conduct ourselves as citizens in a community was only a reassuring fantasy. "Public virtue," John Adams wrote in early 1776, "cannot exist in a nation without private virtue, and public virtue is the only foundation of republics." A year earlier, his cousin Sam (in a letter sneering about the well-known adultery of a doctor who turned to the British during the Revolutionary War) wrote, in his characteristically blunt way: "There is seldom an instance of a man guilty of betraying his country, who had not before lost the feeling of moral obligations in his private connections."[1]

More important, the Founders understood that institutional design could not overcome the worst impulses of human nature if human beings themselves decided to give in to those base instincts. "I go on this great republican principle," James Madison said at the Virginia convention to ratify the Constitution in 1788,

> that the people will have virtue and intelligence to select men of virtue and wisdom. Is there no virtue among us? If there be not, we are in a wretched situation. No theoretical checks—no form of government can render us secure. To suppose that any form of government will secure liberty or happiness without any virtue in the people, is a chimerical idea.[2]

The Founders knew that ballot boxes and legislatures and courtrooms—all of which exist today in even the most repressive states—could not sustain a democratic nation without some understanding among the public of duty, tolerance, sacrifice, cooperation, compromise, and the inherent truth of individual rights.

Nor were the American Founders under any illusions about human nature, including their own. It was Madison, after all, who said that "if men were angels," government itself would not be necessary. The Founders, whatever their many virtues, also fired scalding insults at each other, passed intemperate laws, and in general acted like flawed and sometimes terrible human beings. They counted among their number true geniuses and heroes, but their ranks were also rife with egomaniacs and opportunists. More damning, they left the tumor of slavery intact next to the infant heart of their new republic and set the stage for the greatest bloodletting in American history.

If we can forgive the people of the eighteenth century who founded a democracy, we need not be overly demanding about the failings of human nature two hundred years later. Even in the most admirable democracies, there will be cynical and disengaged citizens. Some will always harbor irrational hatreds and low motives. Others will see government only as a means for purely selfish and transactional gains. At every public meeting of some kind in an open and free society, the law of averages, if nothing else, will guarantee that there are going to be truly terrible people in the crowd, including the usual crank who shows up to excoriate everyone else.

But when we're *all* that local crank—when enough of us are continually angry, entitled, and conspiracy-addled—civic life becomes impossible. The public square empties out. Paranoia and fear become the dominant emotions. In such a world, citizens end up retreating to castles surrounded by moats filled with bizarre rationalizations and parapets loaded with boiling hostility, lowering the drawbridge only long enough to engage in necessary trade for supplies.

Most people do not need to be exemplary human beings or deep political thinkers in order to be good citizens. (And, of course, there are many good citizens who pay attention to the news, cast unremarkable votes for mainstream candidates, and diligently pay their taxes while also being execrable people.) But citizens at least have to *believe* in notions of virtue and civic responsibility and act on them with some regularity, even if they cannot consistently practice them. A "virtuous" people cannot be virtuous only once or twice every two to four years and still expect their own republic to function without them the rest of the time.

Liberal democracies are nurtured by infrequent events like voting but even more so by small but important habits of mind that combine self-interest with civic conviction, a commitment to participation and cooperation that is unrelated to any specific ideology or platform. This civic sensibility, reinforced by time and repetition, allows us to overcome our individual flaws and construct a durable edifice of institutions, laws, and norms that protects our rights and freedoms. In the modern democracies, however, that edifice is now being washed away by the citizens themselves, as civic virtue drowns in narcissism, anger, and resentment. Bad citizenship is a passing malady, and it can remedied by any number of means. But an unvirtuous people is a fundamental and potentially fatal threat to a liberal democracy.

THE NARCISSISM PANDEMIC

The most important ingredient in the decline of modern democracy is narcissism, the true pandemic that is at the root of almost all of democracy's problems. Narcissism, the unhealthy preoccupation with the self to the exclusion of all else—and especially to the exclusion of other human beings—tempts us away from thinking about the needs of other people and to see them only as objects in relation to our own happiness. Its traveling companion is entitlement, the selfish and self-absorbed conviction that our own importance merits constant reward. Narcissism undermines virtue of every kind, but it is particularly deadly to the social trust that allows democracy to endure in hard times. By definition, a democracy is a community. By definition, a narcissist is incapable of holding or granting membership in a community.

How we got here is an important question, but no matter which roads we traveled, Americans, along with a fair number of citizens elsewhere in the developed world, have arrived at the dead end of a stunningly narcissistic and entitled society. This didn't all happen overnight, and more than a few alert social critics saw it coming. Among the most influential was Christopher Lasch, who in a 1979 book titled *The Culture of Narcissism* raged against the arrival of the "new narcissist," a hedonist questing for personal fulfillment while fending off the onset of adulthood and its responsibilities. Lasch painted a portrait of the average late-century American as an overgrown child who "extols cooperation and teamwork" while "harboring deeply antisocial impulses," who "praises respect for rules and regulations in the secret belief that they do not apply to himself," whose "cravings have no limits," and whose constant demands for immediate gratification create a "state of restless, perpetually unsatisfied desire."[3]

Lasch, who refused narrow identification with the left or the right, was not the most appealing critic. Some of his warnings turned out to be the product of blind spots, or just plain wrong. (As the writer E. J. Dionne later noted, Lasch believed that the "ideology of white supremacy no longer appears to serve any important social function," a baffling dismissal even in its time.[4]) Lasch's later work seems to be that of an academic so fed up with the attitudes of his colleagues and other cultural elites that he became, by irascible reaction, a populist. By the time he wrote *The Revolt of the Elites*, published shortly after his death in 1996, he was far more forgiving of the masses, and more prone to excoriate the upper classes, even to the point of excusing the same kind of civic indolence among average citizens that he might have deplored just a few decades earlier.

Still, at the end of the 1970s, Lasch could see the damage already done. In a passage that seems to predict the internet and the continual media cycle, he warned that "historical currents have converged in our time to produce not merely in artists but in ordinary men and women an escalating cycle of self-consciousness—a sense of the self as a performer under the constant scrutiny of friends and strangers." In such a culture, plodding achievement, cooperation with others, and deferred gratification are pointless. When citizens are always performing for each other, they expect accolades and instant psychic rewards, even if they have not earned them, and they become angry and resentful if they do not get them.

Some of this, perhaps, was Lasch's response to the cheap exhibitionism, oily decadence, and overall cultural stagnation of the disco era. (And let me add, for the benefit of younger readers, that compared to the rest of the 1970s, disco was one of the *least bad* parts of that decade.) David Frum has described the decade as "strange, feverish years," a time of "unease and despair, punctuated by disaster," while the liberal Columbia University professor Mark Lilla would later recall how difficult it is "to convey to anyone who wasn't alive and politically aware at the time what a dreary place America seemed in the late 1970s, how lacking in direction and confidence."[5] The post–World War II glow among an older generation was gone, and the energy of their children in the mid-1960s had exhausted itself within a decade. Self-examination became the new hobby and self-actualization the new goal.

In later years, America managed to recover as a military and economic great power. American social and civic culture did not. Thirty years after Lasch launched his broadside, the psychologists Jean Twenge and Keith Campbell published *The Narcissism Epidemic*, a scathing study that laid out in detail the degree to which narcissism and entitlement had become woven into American life. Twenge and Campbell traced the evolution of American society from the late 1960s into the twenty-first century in a complicated tale of the synergy between affluence, entertainment, education, and a persistent youth culture marketed toward the natural human fear of aging.

These economic and cultural developments produced an ongoing problem Twenge and Campbell described as "the odd perpetual adolescence of many American adults."

[W]e imagine narcissism in society resting on a four-legged stool. One leg is developmental, including permissive parenting and self-esteem focused education. The second leg is the media culture of shallow celebrity. The third is the Internet: Despite its many benefits, the Web serves as a conduit for individual narcissism. Finally, easy credit makes narcissistic dreams into reality. The narcissistic inflation of the self was the cultural twin of the inflation of credit. They are both bubbles, but the credit bubble popped first.[6]

This is a description of American society that will anger many readers, who may see a "blame the victim" accusation underneath reproaches about parenting and spending habits. But the growth of narcissism in the United States and other developed nations was not some unavoidable accident. From Lasch's warning in the 1970s, to the political scientist Robert Putnam's landmark work in the 1990s about "bowling alone" (the general tendency of Americans to do things individually that they once did in groups), to multiple cross-national studies of college students done over the past few decades, the growth of social isolation and the concurrent rise of narcissism should not have been a surprise.[7] The rise in narcissism means increasing esteem for ourselves while our connections to others are decreasing, a terrible confluence of loving oneself more while loving one's neighbor less.

Perhaps the most obvious example of the effect of narcissism on political life has been that Americans have become vastly more embracing of narcissistic public figures, especially at the national level. Previous traditions of stoicism in politics were always a mixed blessing, a way of hiding the medical and moral frailties of national leaders from Franklin Roosevelt to John F. Kennedy to Richard Nixon. But the idea that every candidate for national office had to be somehow authentic or relatable on a personal level became a disturbing trend in American politics in the wake of the Cold War. The writer Joan Didion captured this new sensibility in 1992 when she noticed that candidate Bill Clinton spoke about difficulties in his childhood regularly "and rather distressingly, in connection with questions raised about his adulthood."

> He frequently referred to "my pain," and also to "my passion" or "my obsession," as in "it would be part of my obsession as president." He often spoke, at low points in his primary campaign, of those who remained less than enthusiastic about allowing him to realize his passion or obsession as "folks who don't know me,"

and about his need to "get the people outside Arkansas to know me like people here do."[8]

This was the Clinton campaign's attempt, as Didion wrote, to create a "dramatically more interesting character than candidate, a personality so tightly organized around its own fractures that its most profound mode often appeared to be self-pity." Until the 1990s, this was not a quality voters normally found attractive in their prospective commander in chief.

But Bill Clinton was merely a warning of things to come. There is no way to talk about the increase in narcissism in American public life without talking about the rise of Donald Trump and the cult of personality that formed around him during his time in office and continued to surround him even in defeat. Trump has been widely described by medical professionals, colleagues who knew him, and his own niece—herself a clinical psychologist—as a narcissist.[9] But even in a crowded field of narcissistic celebrities, Trump stood out in 2016 not just for his self-love but also for the slashing hostility he deployed against anyone who threatened his ego. Those who had watched Trump for decades as a tabloid celebrity knew that his public persona was based on outlandish and overblown claims, shameless lying, and merciless attacks on anyone, including his own family, who got in his way. The surprise was the degree to which millions of Americans embraced this kind of behavior and rewarded it.

Political candidates are always, to some extent, celebrities, especially since television became an indispensable part of political campaigns. The days when a William McKinley could run for president by sitting on his porch are long gone, not only in the United States, but in every nation that has electricity. But there was also a time, not so long ago, when it was unthinkable that someone as dysfunctional as Donald Trump could survive in modern American politics. Even the most self-centered American politicians were expected to rationalize their electoral bid as a call to public service. Glamorous candidates who came from privilege or previous fame, such as JFK or Ronald Reagan, had to demonstrate a common touch, often by mastering the art of the self-deprecating quip. Trump challenged this tradition by extolling himself in flat, self-aggrandizing terms that would have washed previous candidates from American public life: "I alone can fix it." "I am the elite." "They're jealous of me."

Whatever Trump's personal shortcomings, what was most disturbing from the perspective of democratic stability was how many Americans seemed to identify with him. Ordinary voters sat through hours of Trump's alternating litanies of narcissistic grievance and self-adulation and then said of a man who, by his wealth and lifestyle is unlike almost any other American, "He's like one of us."[10] As the scholar Eliot Cohen wrote, the most disturbing possibility is not that these voters were hoodwinked, but that they were *right*, and that they were, in fact, much like Trump. "American culture," he wrote in early 2016, is "nastier, more nihilistic, and far less inhibited than ever before. It breeds alternating bouts of cynicism and hysteria, and now it has given us Trump." This, Cohen, argued, was a symptom of cultural and moral rot, and whatever Trump's personal pathologies, his rise was "only one among many signs that something has gone profoundly amiss in our popular culture."[11]

Not everyone who voted for Trump was a narcissist and not everyone who voted against him was Mother Teresa, and American liberals have their own brand of narcissistic dysfunction and celebrity worship. The adulation of former president Barack Obama, for example, at times became indistinguishable from a personality cult, such as when *Newsweek* ran a cover story referring to Obama's second term as "The Second Coming." This might have been easy to dismiss as a poor editorial choice, except that four years earlier, *Newsweek*'s editor, Evan Thomas, greeted Obama's first election by saying on MSNBC,

"I mean in a way, Obama's standing above the country, above the world, he's sort of God."[12]

Another less serious but unsettling example was the self-help guru Marianne Williamson ending up onstage during the Democratic Party's 2020 primary debates, a spectacle possible only because Williamson, a wildly popular author before her presidential run, managed to clear the initial low polling bar for inclusion. Williamson made it through two rounds of debates, and her campaign outlasted some of the party veterans, despite her participation devolving into airy pronouncements about "harnessing love for political purposes." In the end, Democrats nominated an establishment figure in Joe Biden, but even to see Williamson on the stage was a tableau from a new American political landscape.

If narcissism were confined to small pockets of self-absorbed citizens or limited to a particular demographic or socioeconomic background, the threat to democracy would be more easily contained by the numerical realities of voting. Narcissism, however, is spreading in the United States and abroad. Twenge and Campbell—in language now even more uncomfortable after the arrival of the coronavirus—wondered whether the epidemic of narcissism in the United States could become a global pandemic.

We already know that both individual Americans and our shared culture are becoming more narcissistic over time. Thus a host is in place. And narcissism has a means of transmission through the media and the Internet. The narcissistic behavior that brings attention to one person can, through the magic of the Internet, be spread instantly around the globe. Other cultures are increasingly becoming infected with narcissism, becoming hosts for the fast-moving virus of egotism, materialism, celebrity worship, entitlement, and self-centeredness. As epidemiologists can tell you, a virus that spreads from many people and many points can quickly overtake an entire population.

Using a disease model and comparing the outbreak of narcissism to the increase in obesity from poor eating habits, the authors warned that "it is much easier to spread narcissism than fast-food restaurants."[13] Much like junk food, narcissism is destroying our communal health.

YOUR HATE HAS MADE YOU POWERFUL

Anger is bad for you. We know this from medical science. While it sometimes provides a release of tension, long periods of anger damage your heart, marinate you in stress hormones, raise your blood pressure, and harm your relationships. But anger also feels good—sometimes, really good. Rage is liberating, empowering. This is a part of our makeup as human beings and central to our myths of good and evil. "Let the hate flow through you," the evil Emperor Palpatine of the *Star Wars* saga cackles as he tries to turn the young Luke Skywalker to the Dark Side. "Your hate has made you powerful."

Hate is power, but it is also poison to liberal democracies. And yet liberal democratic societies are immersed in it, hijacked by a diffuse and nihilistic rage that seems to exist for its own sake. A 2019 poll found that two-thirds of Americans are "angry about the way things are going in the country," over 60 percent are angrier over current events than they were five years before, and 58 percent say that their friends and family are angrier too. At 74 percent, Democrats were the angriest of all—an understandable reaction from a party mostly out of power until the congressional elections of 2018. But over half of Republicans reported feeling angry as well, with majorities of both Democrats and Republicans feeling "like a stranger in my own country."[14]

This is not a phenomenon unique to the United States. In 2019, the Gallup organization found that over a fifth of respondents across 142 countries said they felt angry, a slight increase from 2017 and a new record since the first such survey was conducted in 2006.[15] Armenia and Iraq were at the head of the pack with the angriest populations, while Chad and Mozambique led in perceptions of worry and stress. Still, the Americans made a strong showing. "Even as their economy roared," Gallup pollsters noted in 2018,

> more Americans were stressed, angry and worried last year than they have been at most points during the past decade. Asked about their feelings the previous day, the majority of Americans (55%) in 2018 said they had experienced stress during a lot of the day, nearly half (45%) said they felt worried a lot and more than one in five (22%) said they felt anger a lot.[16]

Even if we consider that Americans were about as angry as everyone else in the world, this is a remarkable finding in itself, considering that people in most other countries in the world have more reasons to be angry than most Americans. But Americans were also 6 percent more likely than people in other nations to express worry, and a whopping 20 percent more likely to report stress, a number that puts the United States on the same level as Greece, Iran, and Uganda— and three points of ahead of Venezuela, a country that is both a political and economic disaster.

Cross-cultural comparisons of emotion are always tricky, but there is almost a ridiculousness to this level of stress and anger in the wealthiest and most powerful country in the world. These emotions are especially challenging for a democratic government when citizens report that they are miserable while at the same time explaining that they are also quite happy, a finding that complicates locating actual solutions to these general anxieties. In early 2020, for example, Gallup found that "nine in 10 Americans are satisfied with the way things are going in their personal life, a new high in Gallup's four-decade trend," and topping the previous high of 88 percent recorded in 2003, five years before the Great Recession.[17] Two-thirds, in fact, are *very* satisfied with their lives. Of course, being rich helps; the very happiest Americans are those who make over $100,000 a year. But even among the *least*-affluent respondents—those who make under $40,000 a year—80 percent are satisfied with their lives, and over half are very satisfied. Wealthy, married Republicans report being the happiest of all, while "lower-income Americans, Democrats and those who are unmarried report more tepid satisfaction," but the bottom line, according to Gallup, is that the "vast majority of Americans in all major demographic and political subgroups are content with the way their lives are going."

How can people be happy and furious at the same time? One explanation is that the people who are happy and the people who are furious are not the same people. But polling—and voting behavior—suggests that this is not true. Social anger and personal satisfaction seem to coexist side by side in multiple groups of voters, who report great happiness while voting for some of the angriest populist candidates.

A better explanation is that human beings are bad at assessing risk, at judging the state of the economy, or at estimating their own welfare relative to others, and always have been. Citizens tend to judge the state of the world by who they think is running it at any given moment. At the 2016 Republican convention, for example, the journalist Michael Grunwald noted that the "delegates all seem to agree the Obama economy is a ghastly mess. Except for the economy wherever they happen to live."[18] This could have been written about almost any American political gathering over the past half century; as a 2010

Pew study noted, Democrats and Republicans reversed positions on the state of the economy after the Great Recession—that is, after Democratic candidate Barack Obama's election—with Republicans far more pessimistic and Democrats far more upbeat, even though Democrats had lower incomes, less wealth, and suffered more job losses during the recession.[19] Likewise, American citizens over the years regularly report being satisfied with the quality of life in their communities while thinking the *country* is on the wrong track.

At this point you may be congratulating me for discovering something called "ordinary human emotions." And yet there is something wrong when an affluent democracy like the United States has a constant high voltage of anger running through its political veins regardless of actual local or national conditions. Indeed, "anger" might not be a big enough word to capture the sourness of American civic life. In 2019, the scholar Arthur Brooks worried that Americans had blown past mere "incivility" or "intolerance" only to arrive at "something far worse: contempt, which is a noxious brew of anger and disgust. And not just contempt for other people's ideas, but also for other people."[20] Many of us are no longer angry about any particular condition of our lives, or about any particular policy with which we disagree. We are now a more foul-tempered version of Banfield's villagers, immersed not only in amoral and transactional politics, but gripped as well by the contemptuous dismissal of everyone who is not part of our family or trusted circle.

I am not immune to this feeling. A few years ago, I gave a lecture on the problem of expertise and democracy at a prestigious university in a beautiful but geographically remote region, and at dinner with the faculty afterward, we began to talk about the politics of America's rural areas and small towns. Despite the fact that I personally came from a relatively small city and working-class roots, I was fed up, I said, with the recalcitrance of a minority of Americans whose electoral behavior seemed utterly hostile to everything from

civil rights to basic science. Some of the academics at the table nodded along, but one of the professors who did not share my views eyed
me for a moment and said, "Your contempt for the voters is palpable."

I was taken aback. I noted that his contempt for urban and more
liberal voters was just as evident—because it was—and after more
discussion about what we deplored among which groups of voters,
we moved on. But my colleague was right. I not only felt disconnected from voters with whom I disagreed, but I had given up on
them and viewed them, if not with contempt, with disdain. (For his
part, my colleague was convinced that his deeply hostile view of liberal voters was rooted in moral righteousness about issues like abortion and free speech and therefore completely reasonable.) I had to
think seriously about my own failings because his comment struck a
chord that I could not deny. I still think about it.

There are always reasons in a democracy to be dissatisfied, angry,
or even enraged. Sometimes, we are fed up when local authorities
are squandering tax payments while uncollected garbage sits on the
streets. More severe problems, from the mismanagement of the economy to the bungling of a military conflict, can and should produce a
tidal wave at the ballot box. And some wounds—such as the delayed
promises of equality to women and minorities—will call justifiably
enraged citizens into the streets to demand actions from recalcitrant
authorities who have been in power too comfortably and too long.

But anger should not be the default condition of a democratic
electorate. In our current political era, especially since the end of
the Cold War and the subsequent rise of a powerful and wealthy
America, drama and anger have become the normal state of affairs,
and these emotions have supplanted deliberation and compromise. They leave no room for reasoned debate about policy, which
is complicated and boring. As Lilla has put it: "Romantics chafe at
this undramatic conception of politics. They prefer to think of it as a
zero-sum confrontation—the People against Power, or Civilization

against the Mob. And it's not hard to see why. What could be more stirring . . . ? And what could be more dreary than the history of parties and public administration and treaties?"[21]

Instead, citizens now elevate political differences to existential struggles, because to do so makes for a more interesting and all-consuming confrontation between good and evil. In 2016, for example, future Trump appointee Michael Anton dubbed the coming presidential contest the "Flight 93 Election." He argued that the voters, like the passengers of that doomed plane on 9/11, must rush the cockpit and risk the possible damage of Donald Trump in order to stop the certain death represented by Hillary Clinton.[22] This was not only an inept metaphor, but one that ought to be deeply offensive to any sensible person after 9/11. In something of a *mea culpa* four years later, the conservative evangelical writer Erick Erickson admitted to his own capture by such a mentality: "I really was one of those people who believed every election was an existential crisis and we were on the verge of destruction. I cannot bring myself to lie to you. I used to really believe the nation would collapse if Obama or Clinton or Biden got elected."[23]

It should not have been a surprise, however, that this odious sophistry found a home in the American political lexicon. For years, each election has been cast by partisans as "the most important election in our lifetime," the last charge out of the trenches, after which there would be nothing left and no second chances.[24] The distance from a "Flight 93 election" to "other citizens are literal monsters" is not nearly as far as we might hope. As the conservative writer David French said in 2020, "conspiracy theories are nothing new in American life."

Behind it all is a simple conviction, an unstated premise that lends credibility to any claim, however outlandish: "they" are so evil and so loathsome that they'd happily unleash an epidemic on the world or crush the livelihoods of millions merely to obtain a political advantage. These are not the convictions of a healthy society. These are the convictions of people consumed by rage and fear.[25]

Right-wing populists of the early twenty-first century have raised apocalyptic rhetoric to an art form. (To his credit, French is not one of them; he has been attacked by his former comrades on the right with shocking personal smears for his writings.) But it has become something of a tradition over several decades for Americans of all persuasions to talk in this way not just about elections, but about almost everything.

These apocalyptic narratives are dramatic nonsense. They undermine the sober reflection and deliberation that sustain democracies. The especially vexing irony here is that citizens seek out this turbocharged drama in politics not because things are bad, but precisely because life is generally good and there is usually not that much at stake in any one election. When we face ennui and relative comfort, we make up for the emptiness by replacing ordinary politics with the emotions we would normally bring to bear in wartime. We cease to be citizens so that we may imagine ourselves as crusaders. As Eric Hoffer wrote: "Faith in a holy cause is to a considerable extent a substitute for the lost faith in ourselves. . . . Take away our holy duties and you leave our lives puny and meaningless."[26] When politics becomes a crusade, citizens are no longer merely going about the mundane business of choosing representatives, they are donning suits of shining armor that make them, if only for a day, the most important human beings who have ever lived.

The addiction to political drama is especially tempting because it combines with narcissism to provide people with rationalizations that make life's humiliating pains and tribulations seem like part of a grand adventure. Losing a job, for example, is traumatic. (Yes, I've experienced it, and I have suffered the depression that comes with it.) Losing a job because "the system is broken" transforms a personal tragedy into a national cause. To be mugged in the street is terrifying (and I've experienced that, too), but to be mugged because "society is breaking down" elevates the experience from a police report to a war.

Even something as prosaic as being on the wrong side of an election—and who hasn't experienced that?—is unpleasant and disappointing, but to lose an election because "everything is rigged against people like me" turns an electoral loss into a cause for revolution in the name of the oppressed. (Sometimes it's more than disappointing. When I was a teenager, my mother ran for re-election to a local office in our small city. I was her campaign's deputized observer at the vote count, and I had to go home and deliver the news to the candidate—my own mother—that she'd lost.) Why should any of us accept any of these indignities as part of the many vicissitudes of life in a large, open society, when we can instead cast ourselves as warriors securing the gates against the barbarians?

In politics, anger can propel otherwise untalented politicians and meaningless campaigns to victory. It is an emotion, however, that tends to be short-lived. It burns brightly and then burns out. The more durable and lasting fuel for illiberal politics is resentment, the reflexive expression of envy and ego that drives human beings to view political life not as a requirement for cooperation, but as an opportunity for revenge.

THE POWER OF RESENTMENT

Resentment in politics is the externalization of envy. If there is one thing authoritarian governments do especially well, it is the way in which they mobilize resentment as a weapon. Democracy, on principle, is based on the public's acceptance of regular cycles in which winners and losers exchange places, sometimes unexpectedly. Authoritarians, by contrast, promise stability and equality. They offer placidity by promising, without favor or exception, to make losers of everyone outside of the ruling group. By reducing all citizens to the same miserable condition, they build a constituency among those who are willing to endure oppression as long as the people they hate have to endure it as well. Resentment is about leveling rather than leadership, about vengeance rather than virtue.

Resentment, like narcissism, undermines the civic virtues of tolerance, cooperation, and equal justice, because it fuels demands for rewards and punishments based on jealousy and unhappiness rather than reason or impartial justice. It is more than just irritation at the success of others; it is an anti-democratic desire to see those others torn down in the name of "equality." There is a more evocative word, *ressentiment* (imported from French by the philosopher Friedrich Nietzsche), that captures this vague but powerful envy of others. Mere "envy" or "resentment" isn't enough to express the lasting toxicity of *ressentiment*. As the writer Joseph Epstein has explained, ordinary resentment is a "quick, stabbing thing, set off by an act of ingratitude or injustice, but that can, fairly quickly, melt away."

> But *ressentiment* is of greater endurance, has a way of insinuating itself into personality, becoming a permanent part of one's character. *Ressentiment*, then, is a state of mind, one that leaves those it possesses with a general feeling of grudgingness toward life. . . . So much so that those suffering *ressentiment* come almost to enjoy the occasions for criticism that their outlook allows them.[27]

If you're an academic (like me), Epstein has a particularly uncomfortable example of how people in a perfectly comfortable profession like mine can be happy and yet still itch with *ressentiment* about others whose talents seem more valued than our own. "Why does some ignorant lawyer have enough money to buy a villa in Tuscany when one knows so much more about the art of the Italian Renaissance? What kind of society permits this state of things to exist? A seriously unjust one, that's what kind."[28]

Ouch.

This sort of thinking—and as an academic, I admit to nothing here—is why the philosopher Ian Buchanan describes *ressentiment* as a "vengeful, petty-minded state of being that does not so much want what others have (although that is partly it) as want others to not have what they have."[29] (Epstein himself seemed to suffer from the same affliction in 2020 when he unburdened himself at length about the new First Lady, Jill Biden, using the title "doctor" because she has a doctorate in education.)[30] Or, in the words of the German philosopher Max Scheler, it is existential envy "directed against the other person's very nature," and thus unresolvable: "I can forgive everything, but not that you are—that you are what you are—that I am not what you are—indeed that I am not you."[31] Citizens engulfed by *ressentiment* seek to bring others down to what they think is their own underappreciated station and to identify scapegoats to bear the blame for their own sense of inadequacy, and to answer for the oppression, real or imagined, they feel has befallen them.

Note that both the right and left in the United States think the other suffers from *ressentiment* and is out to inflict its revenge. "Our society is shot through with Nietzschean *ressentiment*," the conservative writer Jonah Goldberg said in 2015, while Alan Wolfe, an avowed liberal, declared in 2018 that *ressentiment* is just another way of describing the "populism of the right." Sadly, they both have a point.[32]

There is a very old joke about this kind of social resentment in the context of a peasant culture. I have heard versions of this joke in both Greece and Russia, but it can be found almost anywhere: God summons people of various nationalities, including a peasant, and offers to grant their greatest wish. Other nationalities wish for greatness for their nations, but the peasant asks nothing more than for God to kill his better-off neighbor's plow horse. (A variation of this joke has a genie offering the peasant anything he wants, but whatever it is, his neighbor will get twice as much, so the peasant says, "Poke out one of my eyes.")

In the 1988 American film *Mississippi Burning*, the screenwriter Chris Gerolmo used a much darker version of this parable in his fictionalized account of the actual murders of three civil rights workers in 1963. Two FBI agents, one an idealist from Robert Kennedy's new Justice Department and the other an older man who had served as a sheriff in the Deep South before joining the Bureau, are discussing why there is so much hatred in the rural South. The older agent tells a story from his childhood about how his father secretly killed the mule of a prospering African American neighbor, eventually driving him to leave town, because his white father could not bear being inferior to a Black man. "Is that an excuse?" the young agent asks, appalled. "No," the older man says. "It's not an excuse. It's just a story about my daddy."

Gerolmo's script was meant to represent a particular kind of hatred and racial animus in the Jim Crow era in the American South. But his depiction of *ressentiment*, of hating the idea that others whom we despise might do better than ourselves, could apply to any number of cultures and times. Sadly, however, the racial version is still alive and well in the United States. In 2019, the psychiatrist Jonathan Metzl conducted research among poor and middle-class white voters in an attempt to figure out why they were supporting "political positions that directly harmed their own health and well-being or the health and well-being of their own families."[33] What he found was that cultural and racial resentments among these voters were stronger even than a sense of self-preservation. Metzl wrote of his discussions, for example, with a 41-year-old Tennessean named Trevor who was dying of liver disease brought on by "years of hard partying" and hepatitis C. "Ain't no way I would ever support Obamacare or sign up for it," Trevor told Metzl. "I would rather die." Trevor was adamant that his tax dollars—despite the fact that he was broke, unemployed, and unlikely to be paying any taxes at all—would go to "Mexicans and welfare queens."[34]

Metzl called this phenomenon "dying of whiteness," a blend of racism and an attachment to myths about independence and masculinity. These beliefs are exploited by cynical populists, who feed simmering resentment among people who are neither independent nor particularly privileged because of their race. But the appeal is about more than race. It is the idea that others, whether racial minorities, immigrants, or the far-away city dwellers, are doing better, somehow at the expense of the "real" Americans who pay the bills but get none of the benefits. This is equality achieved by destroying the playing field rather than leveling it. If Trevor can't have a new liver without risking accidentally giving care to someone who does not look like Trevor, so be it: no one gets one.

These attitudes are not limited to the rural poor. A 2011 study of "Tea Party" populist conservatives of the early twenty-first century, for example, found that these voters—spread throughout the United States, older, white, mostly male, and middle-class—shared Trevor's destructive beliefs but stopped short of being willing to sacrifice themselves to make the point. Indeed, these more affluent citizens showed "considerable acceptance, even warmth, toward longstanding federal social programs like Social Security and Medicare" to which they felt "legitimately entitled." Rather, their opposition to programs like the Affordable Care Act was concentrated on "resentment of perceived federal government 'handouts' to 'undeserving' groups, the definition of which seems heavily influenced by racial and ethnic stereotypes."[35]

A more prosaic example of this kind of resentment in modern America is the voter in Florida who was furloughed from her public sector job during a 2019 budget impasse between the White House and Congress. Initially a supporter of President Trump, she turned on her candidate in helpless anger. "I voted for him, and he's the one who's doing this," she said. "I thought he was going to do good things. *He's not hurting the people he needs to be hurting*" (emphasis added).[36] By 2021, this call to "hurt the right people" was a literal call for violence. As the assault on the U.S. Capitol was being repelled by police, a crying, hysterical protester said in bewilderment: "They're shooting at us. They're supposed to shoot [Black Lives Matter protesters], but they're shooting the patriots." A man nearby said: "Don't worry, honey. We showed them today. We showed them what we're all about."[37]

Democracy is always replete with calls to tax the rich and disempower the powerful—almost by default, because there are so few of them and so many of everyone else. But the more generic idea that candidates have an obligation to hurt others, to punish one's enemies, is different. Populist voters in the modern democracies have no interest in wonky policy debates and are happy to see leaders like Trump, or Berlusconi in Italy, or Rodrigo Duterte in the Philippines, or Jair Bolsonaro in Brazil, promise to hurt the right people—in some cases, actually to shoot them—whoever they are.

This urge to punish others can overwhelm simple calculations about self-interest. In a famous work titled *What's the Matter with Kansas?*, the leftist writer Thomas Frank asked nearly twenty years ago why so many poorer Americans, especially in the rural heartland, were willing to ally themselves with political movements on the right rather than with those on the left that were more likely to help them. Conservative writers, of course, have asked the same question about staggeringly high levels of minority commitment to the Democratic Party, but the answer there is at least partly obvious: minority voters know they're getting a better deal from one party than the other, both in the larger protection of their rights and in the prosaic question of resources directed to their communities. Frank, by contrast, was trying to explain why people in dying towns insisted on praising the very people intent on supporting economic policies that were "grinding those small towns back into the red-state dust."[38]

Interestingly, despite Frank's politics as a man of the left, some of his observations match those of conservative critics of "culture rot." Frank was struck by a moment, for example, at the homecoming parade at Emporia State University in the late 1990s. "A fraternity boy in an enormous black cowboy hat," Frank recalls, "shouted out to his best gal" as he passed by on a float:

He: Where's my sweatshirt?
She (lifting sweatshirt to flash him): It's right here, bitch.[39]

College kids do stupid things. But, as Frank notes, "you probably haven't heard much about this aspect of the heartland" because Mardi Gras–like behavior in a small town in Kansas is the "kind of blight [that] can't be easily blamed on the usual suspects like government or counterculture or high-hat urban policy." He points the finger directly at a capitalist system that treats towns in Kansas as collateral damage in the search for profit.

The economic explanation, however, only goes so far (and, in fairness to Frank, he has a lot more to say on the relationship between capitalism and culture). This kind of behavior helps drive political resentment when the parents, or more likely the grandparents, of the students at Emporia State realize that their heirs have become part of some new culture they detest. They resent what they see as cultural decay, but they would rather not think about the source of that decay, especially if it means looking inward. Their beloved granddaughter isn't exposing herself on the street because something went wrong at home or in their community; it's a large, nebulous thing called *the culture* that was created by someone else, and is therefore, by definition, someone else's fault.

The unfocused rage at *the culture*, at *the elites*, or at some other culprit is not just a distraction; it provides a wellspring of political energy that savvy operators exploit by affixing it to hot button moral issues. An anti-abortion activist in Kansas, for example, admitted as much bluntly to Frank: "You can't stir the general public up to get out to work for a candidate on taxes or the economy. People today are busy. But you can get people who are concerned about the moral decline in our nation. Upset enough to where you can motivate them on the abortion issue, those type of things."[40]

"People are busy"—but not too busy to invest in pure fury about "those type of things," issues that are morally important but that are more of a symptom rather than a cause of their world collapsing around them. Frank captures the seething *ressentiment* about culture among older, well-off Kansans of the early twenty-first century in a passage written long before the 2016 and 2020 U.S. elections that is worth quoting here at length.

The angry men that I knew personally were not aggrieved blue-collar folks, by any means. They were all fairly successful people, self-made men who had done quite well in their fields of accounting or construction or sales—the sort of folks who are supposed to regard American life with a certain satisfaction, not infinite bitterness. And yet something had gone so wrong for them in the [1960s]—and had stayed so steadfastly wrong ever since—that life had permanently lost its luster. It's not that they had any real material beef with the world. These guys were comfortable and prosperous. But the culture—the everyday environment they lived in—rankled them the way pollen affects someone with hay fever. Their favorite magazines, movie heroes, and politicians would never let them forget it, either, parading before them an ever-swelling cavalcade of grievances: tales of foul-mouthed kids, crime in the streets, foolish professors, and sitcom provocations, each one sending them deeper and deeper into the fever swamps of bitterness.[41]

This is the same sense that European observers have noted among the middle-class populists of Poland, the UK, Italy, and elsewhere. American conservatives, for their part, would likely agree that whatever galls them began sometime in the 1960s, but it's been a long time since those days, and college girls in Emporia born sometime in the 1980s (a time their grandfathers probably liked well enough) did not end up acting trashily in public because of hippies or rioters in the 1960s. Something else went wrong—something inside the culture itself of their own homes and families—and they know it.

Liberals who might feel satisfaction at the idea of *ressentiment* driving right-wing populism should pause for a moment to consider their own contributions to the same problem. As Edward Luce has pointed out, the West's urban liberal establishment pays "lip service" to progressive ideas that mask their own resentful separation from other citizens. The global middle class might hate the new generations of enlightened city dwellers, but a lot of those urbanites hate the middle class right back, even if they are more muted and polite about it. For all the talk of multicultural egalitarianism, the well-off are perfectly comfortable with the reality of a new urban oligarchy. "We really couldn't ask for a nicer elite," Luce notes drily, but "the effects of how they spend their money are hardly progressive."[42]

Nor should liberals forget how much of left-wing populism is motivated by a similar culture of irresolvable grievance. Lilla, for one, argues that modern liberalism apes the selfish and resentful individualism of the right, but does so under the cover of rigid and obsessive divisions on race, ethnicity, and gender. This "narcissism with attitude," Lilla said in one of many comments that likely infuriated his fellow liberals, is essentially "Reaganism for lefties."[43] Worse, in the perverse world of tribal extremism, neither side has much of an interest in winning. Escalating demands for power come from losses, not triumphs, and so the strategy is to stay in the fight, deny the reality of incremental victories, and maintain the permanent and valued status of "victim."

The grievances of the left are different from the *ressentiment* of the populist right, however, because American culture—indeed, global popular culture, at least in the developed world—is primarily a liberal culture. Liberals cannot plausibly claim to be losers in the "culture wars" any more than conservatives can claim that they have lost the struggle to define capitalism, a contest they won at least forty years ago. Liberal grievances nonetheless produce claims that are hard for democracies to cope with, because in the teleology of the left, equality is as unreachable a goal as rolling back the clock on the culture is for the disaffected right.

The United States and other established democracies long believed they had succeeded in harnessing the power of envy, replacing victimhood with citizenship, and restraining the dragons of resentment. This optimism was buoyed by the ability of dynamic market economies to paper over these emotional dangers with high growth and material plenty. But voters afflicted with *ressentiment* view life, and not just the race for material wealth, as a rigged competition. Like the villagers of Banfield's "Montegrano," Americans view education with suspicion and envy because esteem and self-respect, too, are now a zero-sum game. Anyone who does better than anyone else, in any way, is clearly using brains or connections or some other magical device to get ahead, to secure more benefits, and to look down on others.

In a democracy, and especially one with free markets aimed at ever-growing consumer consumption, people get what they want, and, as it turns out, getting what they want makes them miserable. This produces both powerlessness and guilt. There is nothing the business leaders of Kansas can do to make their granddaughters put on their sweatshirts in public and stop talking like reality-show Mafia wives; they can only feel humiliation that it has happened and wince at the suspicion that they themselves might have had something to do with it. And while they cannot vote to elevate themselves and better their own culture, they can vote to impose solutions on others that will make everyone else as miserable as they are. In a corroded, unvirtuous society, that might be good enough.

NOSTALGIA: THEY'RE TEARING DOWN TIM RILEY'S BAR

Finally, it is important here to say a word about nostalgia, the powerful emotion that alternately taunts and comforts us with memories—true or false—of a better life in the past. It is an emotion, strangely, that can produce warm feelings even about terrible times once such days are far enough in the past and can be revisited with a sense of safety. And sometimes it produces a yearning for times that never were, providing a new narrative not only about how much better the past was, but also about who is to blame for the ruinous condition of the present. This latter kind of memory, to use the Russian writer Svetlana Boym's term, is "restorative" nostalgia; Americans (and, as Anne Applebaum notes, a fair number of Britons and other Europeans) have been in its grip for years.[44]

Nostalgia is common among both people and societies, especially after traumatic changes. American popular culture in the 1970s—that is, in the wake of the upheaval of the 1960s—included beloved 1950s period comedies like *M*A*S*H*, in which the Korean War was used as a gentle and comic allegory about Vietnam, and

Happy Days, in which the fifties were recreated as a gauzy memory of a happy and prosperous Middle America. The 1950s craze eventually subsided, and television went on to handle the 1960s a bit more gingerly. *Tour of Duty*, a series about a U.S. Army platoon in Vietnam, appeared in 1987 in the wake of the Best Picture Oscar win for Oliver Stone's *Platoon*. A year later, *The Wonder Years* premiered; set in the late 1960s, it was more about childhood sweethearts than about the 1960s. A decade later the seventies got an idealized, *Happy Days*–style treatment in *That 70s Show*. A highly successful look at adults in the 1960s, a glamorized depiction of martini-guzzling Manhattan ad agency executives titled *Mad Men*, would not appear until the early twenty-first century.

Rage, however, occasionally peeks out of these previous periods of nostalgia, an important reminder that the choleric nostalgia of the current era is neither new nor unique. In 1970, for example, the television icon Rod Serling penned an Emmy-nominated episode of his gothic horror anthology, *Night Gallery*, that was out of character for a show that was usually about ghouls and vampires. In "They're Tearing Down Tim Riley's Bar," aired in 1971, a widowed, alcoholic plastics company executive named Randy Lane is on the verge of being forced out of his position after twenty-five years. Randy then learns that Tim Riley's, the long-closed bar where he celebrated his homecoming from World War II, where he danced with his wife and sang with his father, is about to go under the wrecking ball to make way for a bank. Randy descends into delusion, summoning the ghosts of the dead as he tries to return to the world of 1945.

Serling, a World War II combat veteran himself, was a writer consumed with nostalgia, and "Tim Riley's Bar" was one of his most personal scripts. It echoed some of his earlier work in which harried, middle-aged men somehow magically visit a simpler and happier time.[45] But Randy Lane's rage against the modern world in 1970, as the bar crumbles around him and the ghosts fade away, sounds almost exactly like the angry populist venting, especially of men, in the 2000s.

> I rate something better than I got! . . . Hey, I've put in my time. Understand? I've paid my dues. I shouldn't have to get hustled to death in the daytime and die of loneliness every night. That's not the dream! That's not what it's all about!

> I can't survive out there! Pop? Tim? They stacked the deck that way! They fix it so you get elbowed off the earth! You just don't understand what's going on out there now! The whole bloody world is coming apart at the seams!

At the close of the episode, as the wrecking ball closes in, Randy is saved at the last minute by his secretary and finally acknowledged by his company. This was a standard television happy ending, but lead actor William Windom and others recall that Serling wrote an earlier version in which Randy, alone and defeated, stands outside of the demolished bar in a soaking rain.[46]

Perhaps not coincidentally, 1971 was also the year in which the landmark series *All in the Family* made its debut on network television. The centerpiece of most episodes was the intergenerational conflict between Archie Bunker, the middle-aged, right-wing patriarch of an outer-borough New York family, and his hopelessly liberal son-in-law. The theme to *All in the Family* was written by the Broadway composers Charles Strouse and Lee Adams—both born in the 1920s—and while it was jaunty and hummable, it evoked the nostalgia of millions of real people just like the fictional Queens factory worker. Each week, the show opened with Archie and his wife Edith at the piano, singing Strouse and Adams's melancholy hymn to a world only thirty or forty years in the past. Misty eyed and holding a cigar as he sang, Archie invoked Glenn Miller, Herbert Hoover, a world where "men were men," and his family's old LaSalle automobile, which "ran great."

The LaSalle was introduced in the Roaring Twenties and went out of production thirty years before the premiere of *All in the Family*. But viewers understood why Archie was grieving in a world that was now full of Japanese Datsuns and Toyotas and German Volkswagen Beetles, a countercultural symbol that Americans of the time associated with young people. Edith, played by veteran actress Jean Stapleton, would bang away at the keys, smiling and content, but Carroll O'Connor, who played Archie, would look away in a reverie, lost in a time when men like him still mattered. At the close, the couple would lean against each other and smile.

It was all very heartwarming, if you didn't think too much about the heartbroken lyrics underneath the catchy tune. And indeed, the second verse was so dark it wasn't even used in the show. A lament about "freaks," who belonged in a circus, long hair and short skits, and how it's all gone wrong, Serling's Randy Lane couldn't have said it better. (The theme to *Happy Days*, by contrast, was a fluffy, perky homage to early 1950s rock written by two other reliable hitmakers, Charles Fox and Norman Gimbel, that broke into the top 10 on American pop charts in 1976.)

All in the Family, unlike the other programs of its time, was a constant argument between the past and the present about who was to blame for everything being terrible. And yet Americans could smile at Archie Bunker's bitter nostalgia because so many American families had an Archie in it that they knew and loved—my own father was pretty close—and, perhaps even more to the point, because no one *really* wanted Herbert Hoover to be president again. The Depression was within living memory, and viewers knew that Glenn Miller died over the skies of Europe during World War II.

Just as Archie was making his way into American living rooms, real life was imitating art, but in a considerably more violent way.

Just six months before *All in the Family* premiered, a riot broke out in New York City between construction workers on one side and college student protesters on the other. Known as "the hardhat riot" (also called "Bloody Friday" in New York), scores of people were injured when hundreds of construction workers building the nearby World Trade Center waded into a crowd of several hundred students and other protesters picketing the Vietnam War in front of the New York Stock Exchange. The New York City Police, hardly fans of the students, were too few to stop the violence even had they been so inclined—which they assuredly were not.

Over the next two weeks, the union workers and other groups held their own rallies, including a gathering of some 150,000 people in front of City Hall in Manhattan. Their grievance at the time—now remembered as a golden age for American workers—was indistinguishable from the same battle cries of their grandchildren a half century later. "Nobody has been speaking to the average worker," one woman who supported the hardhats said after the riot. "Nobody cares what we want or how we feel."[47] It mattered little to such aggrieved voters that Richard Nixon, the choice and champion of the "Silent Majority," had already been president for almost two years and would be returned to office in 1972 in an electoral landslide.

Americans (and a fair number of Europeans) today once again sound as anguished as Archie Bunker or Randy Lane, or as angry as the hardhats of lower Manhattan. This is because they, too, are once again obsessed with irrational nostalgia. As the scholars Edoardo Campanella and Marta Dassù wrote in 2019, this attachment to restorative, delusional nostalgia is now spreading throughout the developed world.

> The world is marching backwards into the future. More and more countries are becoming trapped in a past that no longer exists— and probably never really existed at all. Millions of people, particularly in advanced economies, believe that life was better fifty

years ago: job opportunities abounded, local communities were intact, and the pace of technological change was under control. The age of nostalgia has begun. It is an age of false myths, unparalleled political miscalculations, and rising tensions between nations—a time of regression and pessimism.[48]

Some of this is the product of an aging population, but the idealization of the past is also, they point out, now mobilized by "jingoistic leaders" as "an emotional weapon in the political debate." The young, meanwhile, howl against the injustices of the past while wishing they could go back and live in it—or, at least, in the parts they think they'd like.

Nostalgia is an insidious challenge for almost any form of government, or at least for those that have not perfected time travel. Authoritarian systems handle such emotions by squashing expressions of dissatisfaction while also pandering to the public with triumphal stories of the past and identification of the betrayers and scapegoats who must be punished for any misery in the present. Democratic regimes have no such alternatives. They can only defend the state of the present, admit its shortcomings, and promise to do better. If the demand from the public, however, is to return to an imagined past in 1970 or 1980 or 1990, any government, no matter how responsive, will find itself on a treadmill that will produce exhaustion and eventual collapse.

A serious people know the difference between righteous anger and resentful rage, between material deprivation and unmet wants, and between reality and nostalgia. But when an entire population slides after years of peace and plenty into narcissism and resentment and entertains itself with comforting lies about the past in order to avoid the responsibilities of the present, the political environment sinks into a corrosive slurry that eats away at the foundations of democracy. Most dangerous of all, in such conditions even a great people will be unable to handle the trials that inevitably befall every nation, including (as we now see) a pandemic. Such challenges require sacrifice, stoicism, and civic commitment; instead, many Americans want a full apology for a twenty-first century that has somehow not measured up to their expectations. This inability to deal with adversity has crippled the ability of many of the democracies, the United States among them, to respond to real problems.

We turn to those issues in the next chapter.

System Failure?

Human Suffering and the Case against Liberal Democracy

Populists identify real concerns—but their answers amount to a fraud and a scam. The failures of a basically good system do not justify overthrowing it and replacing it with something evil.

—David Frum

DYING TOO HARD IN A DEMOCRACY

"You'll want to read this," my wife said, handing me the *Sunday Boston Globe*.

The cover story that week in late September of 2020 was about a woman who died at sixty-two in a nursing home. She had suffered from a number of conditions until her most serious affliction, colon cancer, soon metastasized and took her life. She passed away in a facility because her husband was also in poor health and could not take care of her at home. I was only weeks away from my sixtieth birthday, and I found it a bit unsettling to read of someone so close to my own age succumbing to a highly preventable disease.

The dateline, however, was the reason my wife had given me the paper. The story was from my hometown in Massachusetts, and the facility mentioned in the account was down the street, literally walking distance, from my childhood home. When I was a boy, it was the place we joked about, far too easily, as the place we'd "put" people when they got old. In later years, the joking ended when my father had to stay there briefly as his health began to fail. My brother then passed through its doors on his way to the final stop in a VA hospital. The couple in the story were strangers, but they were from my town. They struggled for survival in the neighborhood where I grew up. And now, as the *Globe* put it, one of them had suffered the "the kind of death all too typical for people who work hard jobs for modest pay," dying "too young . . . and too hard."[1]

It was the kind of story that shakes your faith about whether you live in a truly good society. How can two people who spent a lifetime in a rich and technologically advanced country, just a mile or so from your childhood home in a region known for being at the cutting edge of medical discoveries, die in the gray twilight of working poverty? If liberal democracy is worth defending, who will be left to defend it when the gap between the wealthy of the coasts and the people in my hometown becomes so great there is nothing left but a handful of elites in glittering skyscrapers and everyone else in the shanty towns spreading out beneath them?

The critics of liberal democracy—and especially those who advocate for its replacement with illiberal alternatives—have seized upon exactly these realities to make their case against the injustices of the modern world. Whatever successes liberal democracy might have enjoyed in the storied past, they would argue, it has since been defeated as a system of government by a slew of economic and military traumas, from the impact of globalization to a series of protracted military engagements. Some of us now live in the best of times, while the rest live—and die—in the worst of times.

These critics might concede that rich and poor alike live in an era of marvels and miracles, but those achievements do not matter as much as who benefits from them. What difference does it make to millions of people trapped in a stagnant hell of underemployment and drugs if there is a generic treatment for psoriasis, or that the new Windows operating system has a cool image viewing app? How can anyone fail to see, as the author Max Brooks said in late 2020, that "globalization has ripped half the heart out of America and automation is about to rip out the other half?"[2]

In this telling, liberal democracy is no longer a tolerant, secular, rights-based system of government—if it ever was. Instead, it is an economic and cultural free-fire zone in which atomized, unconnected human beings are easy prey for elites who are better educated, better organized, and better connected than the helpless masses scattered across the globalized landscape. Worse, these global elites are not truly "liberal" or even tolerant; in order to sustain a planetary version of the *Hunger Games*, they stamp out wrong-think on any number of issues, from abortion to climate change, to prevent ordinary citizens from challenging the rules of the new economic killing fields. Like Stalin breaking the back of the peasant communities during the Soviet Union's forced collectivization of agriculture, the globalists are out to destroy the remnants of traditional society to create the New Global Worker.

It's a tale, as it has often been in the past, of the lotus-eating elites destroying the honest and authentic life of the hard-working commoners.[3] It's a hell of a story, and it is rooted in the reality of actual human suffering. But as a criticism of liberal democracy, it is not new and it is not true.

It is difficult to grapple with any of these criticisms of liberal democracy without sounding either patronizing or heartless. From invocations of Christ's reminder that the poor will always be among us to repetitions of Anatole France's ironic observation about how the law, "in its majestic equality, forbids the rich as well as the poor to sleep under bridges, to beg in the streets, and to steal bread," every defense of democracy against the inevitability of suffering sounds either like a bland acceptance of the status quo or a blithe dismissal of human pain as the necessary collateral damage required by freedom and capitalism.

But these are false choices. A truly humane system leaves open the possibility of collective action, of decisions for change, of accountability from those we appoint as the stewards of what the U.S. Constitution calls "the general welfare." These mechanisms, wedded to the liberal idea that every human being has inherent value and—if I might steal a phrase—unalienable rights, are the heart of modern democracy. To recognize honestly and with compassion that these systems, their arrangements, and the people who run them can produce awful outcomes is not an admission that liberal democracy is hopeless; rather, it is the societal self-examination that is among the greatest duties of a citizen and a sign of virtue itself in a democratic society.

The reality of suffering is the cudgel used by populists and illiberal elements of both the right and the left to attack the foundations of modern democracy. Liberalism thrives in the center, between the extremes, where negotiation and compromise and trust must rule the day in order to produce consensus and solutions. But the center—a place that discourages performative anger and drama, and instead is filled with the boring necessity of deliberation and trust—is difficult ground to defend when the pain of other human beings is mobilized in the battle for power.

THE UNLUCKY HORSESHOE

One of the most striking features of the rise of illiberalism in modern democracies is the "horseshoe" effect, in which the complaints of the right and left become more alike as they become more extreme, the way the two ends of a horseshoe meet in a near-circle. This happens especially during democratic breakdowns (such as in Germany in the 1920s) as people abandon the political center for the extremes of right and left. Follow each end of the horseshoe far enough and you'll end up in the dead ends of fascism on one side and communism on the other, with the left identifying class enemies of The Workers and the right nominating ethnic and foreign traitors to The People.

Populist extremism is a comforting morality tale of heroes and villains, usually imbued with an element of social revenge. Consider this bombastic blast from a seasoned American commentator and former political operative, describing his admiration for an American politician who led a populist backlash against the elites: "He was cheered because for four years he was daily kicking the living hell out of people most Americans concluded ought to have the living hell kicked out of them."

> If [he] was so horrific, why, after years of charges and counter-charges, hearings and headlines, of incessant warfare with the American political establishment, Republican and Democrat, did he enjoy such public support? . . . To the Americans who sustained [him] for four years, he was saying that the governing American Establishment, our political elite, was no longer fit to determine the destiny of the United States.

A ringing endorsement, you might think, of Donald Trump and his anti-elite tirades. And the speech was, indeed, by a supporter of the defeated forty-fifth president.

But the passage is not about Trump. It is from a book written over thirty years ago by Pat Buchanan about one of his heroes even further back in history, the late Senator Joseph McCarthy, one of the most appalling and destructive opportunists in American history.[4] A former aide to Richard Nixon, Buchanan never hid his admiration for McCarthy and other authoritarians, from Augusto Pinochet to

Francisco Franco. (As his conservative colleague, the late Charles Krauthammer, once said of Buchanan, "The man is a menace, but no mystery.")[5] What is more revealing is that Buchanan's twentieth-century populist rants—even about Tailgunner Joe—could now, like so many others, be transported into the twenty-first century without anyone noticing.

No single political movement has a copyright on this kind of populist-driven pessimism. From the left, for example, Thomas Frank (the chronicler of late twentieth-century Kansas decline) described the new economic landscape created in the wake of globalization and technological change as "part of a beautiful Davos fairy tale in which high achievement and virtue became almost indistinguishable," and he pointed to deindustrialization, the 2008 financial crisis, the opioid epidemic, and "everything related to the 2016 election" as "elite failures."[6] (He later described the doomed presidential campaign of the democratic socialist and U.S. senator Bernie Sanders as a glimpse of "modern-day populism.")[7]

Victor Davis Hanson, meanwhile, is one of the many commentators on the American right who has welded economic and social themes to reactionary nativism. In an emotionally charged yawp of cultural resentment titled "The Origins of Our Second Civil War," he described the division between the new urban globalists and the sturdy burghers of Real America this way in 2018:

> Ideologies and apologies accumulated to justify the new divide. In a reversal of cause and effect, losers, crazies, clingers, American "East Germans," and deplorables themselves were blamed for driving industries out of their neighborhoods (as if the characters out of *Duck Dynasty* or *Ax Men* turned off potential employers). Or, more charitably to the elites, the muscular classes were too racist, xenophobic, or dense to get with the globalist agenda, and deserved the ostracism and isolation they suffered from the

new "world is flat" community. London and New York shared far
more cultural affinities than did New York and Salt Lake City.[8]

I do not know who has argued that industries left the American
heartland because of reality television, and Hanson does not name
them. But Hanson was once a respected professor of classics, and he
certainly knows that New York and London have *always* been more
alike than New York and Salt Lake City. The more insidious point,
of course, is that Hanson creates a story in which these new elites
intentionally and punitively took jobs away from less progressive
citizens. Like others at both ends of the horseshoe, he argues that
there is hostile agency behind economic and social change, and that
reversing those changes means defeating the system that keeps those
malevolent agents in power.

Rightist critiques often point an accusing finger at "individualism"
and "liberalism," and I sometimes find myself nodding in agreement
with such charges. I am the product of a more community-oriented
time, a churchgoing believer who is so old-fashioned about community involvement that I joined the Elks, just as my parents did in the
1960s. I, too, lament that the nature of work and leisure means that
Americans today are more isolated, less civic, and, as I have argued
here, more narcissistic than they once were. I sometimes am wistful
at what has been lost now that modern living requires less cooperation and less interaction, especially with fewer of us having to share a
common workplace. I wonder if it was a better time before modernity
offered us more solitary entertainments and luxuries, from games to
sporting events to movies, that we might have once enjoyed in groups.

But the critics of modern democracy go even farther, charg-
ing that liberalism itself, with its emphasis on individuals seeking their own happiness, over-empowers individual decisions on
everything from spending to sex. They argue that liberalism as
an ideology intrinsically produces outcomes that are destructive

to human communities. In 2019, for example, a group of conservative intellectuals in the Catholic journal *First Things* issued a broadside against the "fetishizing" of personal autonomy. Claiming that Americans take more pride in their identity as workers than as consumers—an assertion that would have been arguable even forty years ago—the writers invoked the archaic terminology of the 1960s to decry the new "jet-setters" who call themselves "citizens of the world" and who can "go anywhere, work anywhere." Donald Trump's election in 2016, they proclaimed, showed "the potential of a political movement that heeds the cries of the working class as much as the demands of capital."[9]

This leaden prose could have been penned by the editor of a Soviet newspaper in the mid-twentieth century, but it is a crystalline example of a "horseshoe" moment, in which the rhetoric of the far left and the far right become almost indistinguishable. As is often the case, such complaints are framed as unprecedented reactions to the failure of democratic elites to meet qualitatively new challenges. Whatever the deals we all made in the past, such critics argue, those compacts have been rendered null and void by the elites breaking that bargain in ways that have never happened until "now"—whenever "now" might be.

The critics of liberal democracy might retort that if their arguments all sound the same after a half century, it's because they've always been right, and that "left and right" matter less than "the people and the elites."[10] The same charge made over and over, however, regardless of circumstances and shifting through various rationales over time, is a sign of social and cultural dysfunction. If the political judgment is that we are always in dire peril, and the political solution is always to attack the system itself, even if under the false flag of bringing the "elites" to heel, then the underlying project is about power, not democracy. The political scientist Jack Snyder put it well in 2019:

Scholars debate whether populist nationalism in the United States and Europe arises mainly from economic or cultural grievances, but the most persuasive explanation is that nationalist political entrepreneurs have combined both grievances into a narrative about perfidious elites who coddle undeserving outgroups—immigrants and minorities—while treating the nation's true people with contempt. In this view, elites use bureaucratic and legal red tape to shield themselves from accountability and enforce politically correct speech norms to silence their critics.[11]

"This story," Snyder notes, "doesn't fit the facts." Snyder admits that liberal elites need to be held to greater accountability in a world in the midst of rapid change, but he rightly sees the game of illiberalism for what it is: the manipulation of grievances and perceived threats for political gain.

To say that the critics of liberal democracy are drawing our attention to real problems is not an answer. As the conservative writer David Frum once observed in calling for a more sensible and honest debate about immigration, demagogues "don't rise by talking about irrelevant issues. Demagogues rise by talking about issues that matter to people, and that more conventional leaders appear unwilling or unable to address."[12] But this is not enough, as Frum notes, to justify a conclusion that the system has failed—especially if the goal is merely to displace the current government and take its place. Even more well-meaning critiques that somehow always reach the same drastic conclusion are untrustworthy. After all, even hypochondriacs experience actual illnesses, but that does not mean they are reliable narrators of their own health, and treating them as if their complaints are real can do more harm than good.

Real problems inflict real pain that is expressed in all of the ways human beings can exhibit their suffering: depression, substance abuse, crime, family disintegration, suicide, or other forms of early and preventable death. In a narcissistic age, however, almost any negative outcome, whether truly a disaster or only an inconvenience, is recast as an intolerable failure not of any one government, but of the idea of government itself. And when everything is a catastrophe, we lose the ability to create workable solutions because the diagnosis is always to replace the system with something else—often, something morally and practically worse.

GLOBALIZATION AND DEMOCRACY: "IT'S *NOT* THE ECONOMY, STUPID"

No villain in the modern era takes more of the blame for the destruction of the golden past and the ushering in of the miserable present than globalization and its reliable henchman, deindustrialization. Or, to be more accurate, the enemy is "globalism," the idea that globalization—a process that began as goods and people and capital began to move more rapidly and freely in the mid-1960s—is somehow a good thing in itself rather than a process to be managed and restrained.[13] (Other critics use the more overarching concept of "neoliberalism," but we need not wade into a terminological debate here.)[14] From unemployed conservative workers in the American "Rust Belt" to left-wing rioters in the world's major cities, activists and protesters blame their alienation from liberal democracy on globalization and the elites who disproportionately profit from it.

Resentment about globalization is also a good example of how the two ends of the horseshoe often meet in shared anger. The first salvos against globalization emanated primarily from the political left in the 1990s, but the charges of economic Darwinism were soon adopted as the fight songs of the populist right. The first major protests against adopting "globalization" as a conscious policy choice took place in

Seattle in 1999, and the protesters, as the *Bloomberg* columnist Noah Smith later recalled, were

> a hodgepodge of groups—unions worried about competition from cheap foreign labor, environmentalists worried about the outsourcing of polluting activities, consumer protection groups worried about unsafe imports, labor rights groups worried about bad working conditions in other countries, and leftists of various stripes simply venting their anger at capitalism.[15]

Soon, citizens across the board in the United States and Europe agreed that the world economy had come crashing down around them, which provided an opening for the illiberal exploitation of real economic distress. By 2012, just a few years after the global financial crisis and the Great Recession of 2008, 40 percent of Americans cited the economy as their top concern, and populists of both right and left plowed ahead with charges that democracy was no longer up to the task of providing a stable life for its own citizens.[16]

The political window of resentment over trade and globalization, however, did not remain open for long. Five years later, in 2017, that same number dropped to 10 percent. As the Brookings Institution scholar Shadi Hamid observed, this forced populists to move their arguments from economics to cultural grievances. "If there were a tagline for today's populist moment," he wrote in 2018, borrowing a line from Bill Clinton's 1992 internal campaign memos, "it would probably be something like 'It's not the economy, stupid.'"[17] On a global scale, Francis Fukuyama has noted the paradox that globalization seems to have "triggered" populism, but if the "fundamental cause were merely economic, one would have expected to see left-wing populism everywhere; instead, since the 2008 financial crisis, parties on the left have been in decline" while right-wing parties opposed to immigration and focused on national identity have been on the rise, which suggests that cultural anger, rather than economic anxieties, is driving the new populism.[18]

This is not to say that fears of economic change are baseless. How much of the changes that arrived in the late twentieth century were the result of heartless elite malfeasance, however, is an argument that began after the so-called "China shock," in which Beijing's autocrats and their millions of cheap workers were invited into the World Trade Organization. The scholars David Autor, David Dorn, and Gordon Hanson made the case for the "China shock" in an influential 2013 article in the *American Economic Review*, in which they argued that cheap imports from China caused higher unemployment, lowered labor force participation, and reduced wages in local labor markets where there were industries vulnerable to such competition.[19] (There was also a moral case to be made at the time. When I worked in the U.S. Senate, I advised my Republican boss in 1990 to oppose liberalized trade relations with China in the wake of the 1989 Tiananmen Square massacre, which only shows how naïve I was about how quickly America had committed itself to expanded economic ties with China.)

Other experts, however, contend that the "China shock" might not have been such a shock after all, that much of the change in the U.S. and global economies predated changed trade relations with China, and that the shock revealed weaknesses not in "globalization" but in U.S. domestic policy. In fact, the "China shock" argument seems to get weaker as it recedes further into the past. Writing two decades after the WTO's China decision, the trade analyst Scott Lincicome challenged the idea that the working classes were somehow "permanently scarred" by changes in China's trade status, especially in light of the reality that many of the jobs lost at the end of the twentieth century were due to improvements in productivity rather than to offshoring and were replaced by other jobs, albeit in different vocations or regions.[20] Lincicome points out that even Autor, one of the original authors of the 2013 piece, has since softened some of his claims, including the idea that trade with China and its resulting economic disruptions were the primary driver of young American men's unwillingness to marry. (Even a layperson might wonder about such a claim, given that the age of first marriage in the United States has been steadily rising for fifty years and likely has more to do with sexual mores than Chinese imports).[21]

Moreover, the collapse of the American economy predicted back at the turn of the new century by some of democracy's more dire critics did not happen. The Great Recession was not forever; it wasn't even that long of a recession. In fact, the economic death spiral wasn't even happening while people *thought* it was happening: *Bloomberg's* Smith, among others, noted that new data shows that the 2010s were better for American incomes than the 1990s, suggesting that the American economic situation—even during the "China shock"—was always more stable than its critics asserted, and that "a vast overhaul of the U.S. economy might not be as necessary as more radical reformers believe."[22]

The globalization argument has never been a strong case against liberal democracy, but it has always been a good case for making better policy. In retrospect, it is firm ground to charge that the governing elites of the 1990s and 2000s should have been both more prescient and more candid. These elites in the U.S. and Europe oversold the benefits and downplayed the costs of accelerating the move to a globalized economy; whether they did so out of incompetence or dishonesty, it is always in the best interests of national leaders to say the part about "winners" loudly and then to mumble the part about "losers." Perhaps they and the experts who serve them should have been less optimistic, and without doubt they should have made more provisions and strengthened social safety nets to cushion the blow.

If some of these painful outcomes must be assigned to the elites as failures to anticipate the effects of tectonic economic shifts, however, we must also make room here for the behavior of actual consumers. The ordinary citizens of the American and European economies are conspicuously absent from the trade-driven narratives of democratic failure. There is good reason for this: those ordinary citizens are also voters. Just as no national leader wants to admit the possibility that in a competitive economy some will suffer while others gain, it is political suicide to talk about the choices of the electorate itself. But in a democracy, the people rule, and to forget what the people actually *wanted* is to absolve them—and ourselves—of any responsibility for the policies that now are presented by the critics of liberal democracy as evidence of the terminal incompetence of the governing classes. As the conservative writer Kevin Williamson noted pointedly in the pages of the *Washington Post* in late 2020, the pseudo-nationalism, especially on trade, pushed by Donald Trump and others in the first decades of the twenty-first century was really just "an opportunity for the American people to blame the languishing state of the country on someone—Beijing, 'elites,' anyone—other than themselves."[23]

It is difficult, for example, to confront the challenge of cheap overseas manufacturing without noting how much Americans truly love cheap overseas manufacturing. To stand in a "big box" appliance store on the great shopping splurge after Thanksgiving is to be reminded that Americans buy products made in China and other nations with low labor costs (and products made of cheap components from overseas, as well) at astonishingly low prices and in huge quantities. This is why the average American home has between two and three televisions in it, before counting the multiple screens of computers or phones. This is how even Americans of limited means can amuse themselves with hundreds of millions of game consoles. This is why air conditioners—once an expensive luxury—are now common items sold in local hardware stores for less than the cost of a reasonable family dinner at a restaurant. This is why people who once could go to work all day without hearing from friends and family now

cannot stand idle in a grocery checkout line without texting or playing games. (I am one of those people.)

And if the elites have learned little from the experiences of the past
twenty years, consumers seem to have learned even less. Americans,
for their part, have gone right back to their self-destructive habits of
spending and consumer debt. Defaults on car loans, to take but one
example, began climbing just a decade after the Great Recession, not
because of unemployment, but because Americans keep upgrad-
ing their cars. The *Wall Street Journal* profiled one such case in 2019
while noting the worrisome growth in seven-year car loans, a risky
idea that debuted in the mid-1980s and is now a regular feature of the
car market.[24]

> Mr. Jones, now 22 years old, walked out with a gray Accord
> sedan with heated leather seats. He also took home a 72-month
> car loan that cost him and his then-girlfriend more than $500 a
> month. When they split last year and the monthly payment fell
> solely to him, it suddenly took up more than a quarter of his take-
> home pay. He paid $27,000 for the car, less than the sticker price,
> but took out a $36,000 loan with an interest rate of 1.9% to cover
> the purchase price *and unpaid debt on two vehicles he bought as a*
> *teenager.* It was particularly burdensome when combined with
> his other debt, including credit cards, he said. (emphasis added)

Young Mr. Jones, although perhaps unwise in the ways both of
romance and finance, is not an anomaly. A third of new-car buyers in
2019 who traded in their cars rolled debt from old vehicles into their
new loans, up from a quarter before the financial crisis, many of them
to put themselves into nicer and more expensive cars they could not
otherwise afford.[25]

The problem in all this for supporters of liberal democracy is that
complexity doesn't sell, and it doesn't move votes nearly as well as

rage and resentment. "Global changes create difficult challenges" isn't much of a slogan for popular mobilization. "Think about the connection between your high living standard and the costs it might carry for other parts of your economy" is a clear loser. And "maybe you shouldn't be buying three televisions just because they're cheap" is box-office poison. Meanwhile, partisans of the nativist right or the revolutionary left diligently trace every moment of pain to a guilty party who can be defeated on the field of political battle: capitalists, the Chinese, bankers, Silicon Valley, bureaucratic mandarins. (Combine all of these and you can even get capitalist Chinese bankers in league with tech geniuses who are protected by government bureaucrats, which is a superfecta of modern villainy.) It does no good, as a political matter, to respond to such attacks by noting that the real enemy of the blue-collar working man or woman is technology, or that most of the losses in the manufacturing sector over the past few decades were due to improvements in efficiency rather than to cheap foreign labor.[26]

More important, moving the focus away from larger technological trends and consumer choice and onto identifiable enemies allows citizens themselves to dodge important questions. What costs should we be willing to bear to ameliorate the effects of globalization? Should we have more expensive cars but also more automobile industry jobs? (Probably not, especially as the increased cost of transportation would fall hardest on the working poor.) Should nations protect favored industries against competition, perhaps even embarking on trade wars? (We've tried that; it hasn't worked very well.) Should we institute price controls? (We tried that, too, in the early 1970s. That didn't end well, either.) Should we pay more for common items— or for luxuries we have translated from "wants" into "needs"? (No one *needs* three televisions or an advanced smartphone.) Or maybe we should attack what populists of the left and right see as the root of all evil, corporatism, and demand that corporations—and their shareholders—take less profit and keep the prices of their products lower. (The answer likely depends on whether you're looking for a job or looking at your 401k.)

Regardless of the answers, the bottom line, if we may excuse that phrase in this context, is that the economic impact of relentless consumerism is a price democratic societies chose to pay long ago. Such consumerism is often unhealthy and destructive. But for good or ill, consumerism is a *choice*, not a force of nature. And yet millions of people have allowed themselves to become convinced that they had no part in the creation of the modern world. Awash in easy calories and cheap distractions, these citizens in the advanced postindustrial democracies nonetheless believe that they are living in misery.

A WORD ABOUT RACE

The twenty-first century obsession with economic grievances and "the failure of democracy" carries a distinct racial character in the United States. If unequal distribution of income is a characteristic of modern American life, the unequal distribution of empathy has an even deeper pedigree.

In the 1970s, postindustrial decline, unemployment, and drugs swept through America's urban areas. Most Americans—and certainly most American conservatives—did not predict the end of liberal democracy. Instead, white Americans fled the cities while those remaining called for more law enforcement. In the end, nothing seemed to work; in 1979, Christopher Lasch began his classic book on narcissism by noting that "American confidence has fallen to a low ebb. Those who recently dreamed of world power despair of governing the city of New York."[27] America's cities became, in the popular imagination and in iconic films from *Death Wish* to *Robocop*, unredeemable, dystopian nightmares. Millions of Americans agreed with

President Gerald Ford's 1975 decision to deny federal aid to a floundering Big Apple (which prompted the famous *New York Daily News* headline, "FORD TO CITY: DROP DEAD"), not least because they saw violent crime, gangs, drugs, and other signs of urban decay as the moral levy for liberal policies and putatively dysfunctional Black and minority cultures.

And yet when the same phenomena decades later overtook the rural and small towns populated by the white working class, it was a "tragedy" and a "crisis" and an "epidemic" that demanded immediate action. When squalor swept the cities from the 1970s into the 1990s, it was karma and Nemesis; when drugs and unemployment and homelessness fell upon white voters in the 2000s, reporters descended on diners from Appalachia to the Great Plains to ask in somber and respectful tones what the local residents wanted from government and what could be done to help. In 2016, Donald Trump, using language that was once reserved only for liberals talking to inner-city voters, promised a rescue of the small towns and their white citizens.[28]

The economic changes of the past half century brought both prosperity and pain. But complaints about the price of globalization are often a kind of placeholder for a basket of other resentments that are more about class—and especially about race—than about the global economy. It is the lament heard not when jobs leave town, but when the local barber shop, killed off by salons at the mall forty years earlier, becomes a storefront church with a sign in Spanish out front. It is the anger in Montana or Iowa about immigrants pouring over a faraway border in Arizona or Texas. It is the disorienting perception of the sudden visibility of minorities in positions of power, including in the White House. The underlying bigotry of these indictments against modern democracy is why the television commentator S. E. Cupp once exclaimed in frustration that the fabled "Forgotten Man" was "forgotten for a reason—and should be."[29]

WITNESSES TO DECLINE

Some of the most sympathetic views of the problem of decline and deindustrialization and its impact on democracy have come from people who have witnessed it firsthand. This has been an important addition to the debate about democracy because these concerns come from people who are not seeking some kind of political advantage, but who instead are expressing genuine empathy for the challenges faced by their fellow citizens.

In a 2020 interview, for example, the political scientist and Russia expert Fiona Hill (the daughter of a British coal miner) made the point that democracies like the United States and the United Kingdom made the same mistake as the old Soviet Union, by relying too much on heavy industry earlier in their histories and then failing to replace those jobs with anything else later. "Liberal democracy," she said, "hasn't been delivering."

> If I go back to my home town, it's still no better than it was when I was growing up in terms of opportunity. The shops are boarded up in the main street. Nothing new is coming in. There's just no kind of sense of optimism. And when I visit my relatives here in the US in Wisconsin and other places, there's a lot of sense of: the rest of the world is kind of moving on and leaving us behind. People see that as being closely associated with liberal democracy.[30]

Hill served on the Trump administration's National Security Council, but she is no admirer of either populism or of how it was practiced by the president for whom she worked. She rightly notes that populism rarely succeeds because it is too often "style and swagger and atmospherics," while "almost by definition" it produces leaders who are unfit to govern.

This point about the anger of the forgotten places appears regularly among worried Western elites, sometimes out of self-preservation, but often out of genuine empathy, especially among those who, like Hill, are products of a class transition and advancement through education and relocation. The American scholar and entrepreneur Ian Bremmer, for example, grew up in poverty in a housing project in Chelsea, Massachusetts. In a classic American success story, he achieved escape velocity, headed to college far from home, and later earned a PhD at Stanford. Today he is a political scientist who leads Eurasia Group, an influential risk analysis firm.

And Bremmer is worried. "Back in Chelsea," he wrote in 2018, "in my old neighborhood, people are angry. They no longer believe that hard work and education are enough. They don't see a path, and they feel they've been lied to. My brother voted for Donald Trump, and if my mother were alive, I bet she would have too." Bremmer worries that uncritical faith in "globalism" as an ideology has made political and economic elites deaf to the complaints of ordinary citizens, noting that the elites have learned to live with public anger as "a chronic condition" because "the current system works so well for us."[31]

Not everyone from a humble background shares this empathy. Kevin Williamson, who navigated a difficult working-class childhood in West Texas, sees the scapegoating of globalization as "a holistic critique of U.S. economic policy that is wholly bunk," and he argued in 2015 that the romanticized "sense of place," with the implied insistence that every town has a right to exist forever, is little more than "the indulgence of absurd sentimentality."

Change will always inconvenience somebody, it is true, and those great jobs sewing underwear in Southern factories for $100 a week no longer exist. Famine no longer exists and several million formerly poor people get to eat, and the terrible tradeoff is what? A fellow who used to work in a sneaker factory has to go hustle real estate or become a restaurant proprietor? Meanwhile, the poor people of Mississippi, still our poorest state, on average have to get by on a mere 118 percent of the median income in France.

Whatever we do, let's liberate ourselves from the superstition that every spoonful of rice going into a Chinese mouth is stolen from an American pantry.[32]

Williamson is also one of the few writers to acknowledge the racial double standard in such arguments. His answer for what he sees as "the dysfunction" of American white working-class communities is for people to move. "You're a four-hour bus ride away from the gas fields of Pennsylvania," he said in 2016 of a depressed town in upstate New York. "Stonehenge didn't work out, either: Good luck."[33]

Few of us are this tough. Personally, I have no appetite for handing the keys to a trailer hitch to a middle-aged man or woman addicted to alcohol or opiates after a decade of unemployment. And yet I find myself more in agreement with Williamson and others like him than with Hill or Bremmer. I, too, was a witness to decline; I grew up in Chicopee, a Massachusetts factory town much like Chelsea, but a few hours to the west in the Connecticut River Valley. And I drew different conclusions from the experience after seeing multiple cycles of decline and recovery before the sudden obsession among political leaders with processes that began, and whose damage was already done, earlier than the twenty-first century.

Indeed, when Bremmer worries that the people back in Chelsea feel "lied to," I cannot help but think of my own youth just ten years earlier and ninety miles to the west in a similar city and wonder: "Lied to" by whom? When? And about what, exactly? Education and hard work—and more than a little luck—were the path to a professional career for working-class kids like me and Bremmer and Fiona Hill. It still is. But when was this fortunate time when people back in our respective hometowns felt that the system was fair, or that times were good, or that the "elites"—back in the 1960s and 1970s, old Protestant white males who were practically selected before birth to attend fine universities—were somehow invested in the success of the lower classes?

While we are all ruled by confirmation bias, I am hard-pressed to recall when the adults around me as a boy in Chicopee were talking about the healthy economy and the promise of opportunity. What I recall, mostly, is anxiety among our neighbors about jobs, even among the dwindling number of union households. Health care was cheaper, but health was more fragile. When my father had a mild heart attack in 1974, he was confined to the hospital for weeks instead of a few days, and his company allowed him to retire as "disabled." Cancer was so terrifying that the word was not spoken aloud or mentioned in obituaries. Elder-care facilities were often Dickensian warehouses for the old.

More to the point, there seems to be a trick of memory in all of this about what the economic condition of the working class actually looked like before the 2000s. In thinking about the way Bremmer and I grew up, I was reminded of the memoirs of the writer Andre Dubus and his recollection of arriving in Haverhill, yet another Massachusetts mill town not far from either of us, in 1972 with his recently divorced mother.

Haverhill had been named "the Queen Slipper City of the World" because the town's Irish and Italian immigrants worked endless shifts in the mills along the Merrimack churning out a lot of the country's shoes. But in the early 1900s Italy started exporting cheaper shoes and one by one the mills closed and ships stopped sailing up the river from the Atlantic. By the time we moved there in the early seventies, it was a town of boarded up buildings, the parking lots overgrown with weeds and strewn with trash. Most of the shops downtown were closed too, their window displays empty and layered with dust and dead flies. It seemed there were barrooms on every block—the Chit Chat Lounge, the Lido, Ray and Arlene's—and they were always full, the doors open in the summertime, the cackle of a woman spilling out of the darkness, the low bass beat of the jukebox, the phlegmy cough of an old man born here when things were good.[34]

Dubus's memories, including the routine scenes of alcohol abuse (a disease that gripped my mother for years) are more evocative to me than I am comfortable admitting. Dubus and I are about the same age, and, like him, I was part of an early 1970s postindustrial life that we would now generalize as a "culture of despair." My father for a time left the family home, my mother nearly died, my boyhood was spent playing in abandoned buildings and coal yards, and my early teenage years could well have ended in jail. The world of forty or fifty years ago is not a better time in my memory; it was an era that seemed, at least to me, crowded mostly with dead ends and very few avenues out.

Later, I had a front-row seat for the effects of industrial decline when a giant employer left our town and put thousands out of work. The Uniroyal Tire Company, one of the biggest employers in the entire region, began shutting down its operations at the end of the 1970s. The American car industry had been in a slump for a while, and the few customers who were buying cars wanted radial tires, not the older-style bias-ply tires made at "The Uniroyal," an aging and inefficient complex of buildings built in the 1870s in snowy New England. Negotiations between the city, the unions, and the company failed, and by 1980 the factory was set to close.

That summer, my mother—who had finally recovered from her addiction only a few years earlier—was nearing the end of her first and only term as a local alderman. (Mom had won in an upset against a local ward boss a few years earlier on a promise to enforce zoning laws after she got angry about a drug market openly operating down the street from our house.) She did not enjoy the job and she knew her chances of surviving a rematch were slim, but she had spoken well of the integrity and competence of the mayor, a fine man named Robert Kumor, who was new to politics after serving as a lawyer in the Marine Corps and in private practice. I was already working two jobs that summer, but full of temerity (and more than a little boredom), I went over to City Hall and asked Bob if I could get some hands-on, if unpaid, experience. Like many overworked and understaffed public officials, the new mayor was happy for the help, and he took me on with the condition that I couldn't reveal executive business to my mother over on the legislative side of the city government, a promise Mom and I both respected.

Among my other duties, I was assigned to a small task force dealing with the Uniroyal closing. Aside from accompanying the mayor to meetings with the company (an experience I found both fascinating and harrowing), I also kept hours in a small office where men—almost all of them were men—could come and get forms and explanations of how to file for unemployment benefits. I was at first quite proud of myself for wrangling an internship whose only pay was experience and free coffee, but now I found my cheeks flushing with discomfort every day. These workers were old enough to be my father and grandfathers. One by one, they came to my little cubbyhole in City Hall to tell me that they didn't want forms; they wanted a job. They would ask me why all this happened. At nineteen years old, I had no idea what to say. As I recall, I tried to be encouraging. I smiled nervously a lot.

I left to go back to college. The tire jobs never came back. There were various plans for the abandoned Uniroyal property, but today it is still a ghost, waiting either to collapse or be demolished. Later, I worked on the Commerce and Labor Committee in the Massachusetts State House, where I learned how similar stories played out in the other cities and towns of the Commonwealth, like Bremmer's Chelsea and Dubus's Haverhill, as New England continued its shift away from manufacturing and toward the high-tech and medical industries that were turning Boston from a rambling collection of college campuses and dangerous neighborhoods into a technology boom town. (Again, I was fortunate in finding an honest and hard-working boss; the committee chairman, Ken Lemanski, is to this day still a friend and mentor.)

Today, my hometown is doing considerably better. The population loss that began in 1970 was halted some thirty years ago, and there are new businesses where there were once abandoned lots. But the empty hulk of The Uniroyal is even now a reminder that the "forgotten towns" were forgotten a lot earlier than the dawn of the twenty-first century. And yet this reality never seems to matter in political debates. Whether economic times are good or bad, this lament for the old days of factories and mills—jobs that were long gone before some voters were old enough to cast a ballot or even born yet—never changes.

To be sure, any prediction that my city or any other like it would come back from the purgatory of the 1970s would have seemed a reckless bet. But the anti-globalization (or more accurately, the anti-*globalism*) narrative is that stories of recovery are never indicative of positive change. They are just stories. Times are always bad. Nothing gets better. And the past fifty years have not been a temporary economic Purgatory but a permanent Hell, if only the elites would be brave enough to peer through the gloom and see it all for what it is. This is an obsession with decline, and it is one of the myths surrounding postindustrial democracy that will not die.

It remains an article of faith at both ends of the horseshoe that globalization wrecked the economies of the developed democracies and created a literally unprecedented panorama of misery. Millions of us believe this not only because our expectations are high, but because our memories are short.

THE SONG REMAINS THE SAME

It is difficult to capture in economic statistics or population data the strange déjà vu that permeates the debate about globalization, decline, and democracy. So instead I am going to take another unscholarly detour here through popular culture. If the hollowed-out towns, the empty farms, and the deserted streets of the dying cities in the twenty-first century are evidence of an exhausted democracy, then to judge from the signals in the culture, democracy has been on the ropes for nearly forty years.

Like any other American kid born in the late twentieth century, I grew up on rock and roll, and primarily on popular music. My tastes weren't all that sophisticated; I never developed an appreciation for the blues, for example, which is why, at least according to my friends who are professional musicians, I never developed a taste for Led Zeppelin. I wasn't really alienated or angry enough to love punk. Mostly, I was a middle of the road, pop-oriented teen, too young for Buffalo Springfield and later too old for Nirvana.

And yet my abbreviated generation, wedged in between the Boomers and Gen X some forty years ago, had two signature forms of popular music. One was about nuclear war, a genre that peaked in the last years of the Cold War and immersed us in words and images about the end of the world, even on the then-new innovation called "MTV." But the other staple of political rock, a constant even in the age of glitter and lip gloss, was the end of the American Dream. For those of us who came of political age in the years that spanned the presidencies of Jimmy Carter and Ronald Reagan, it sometimes seemed that the only question was which would happen first: utter global destruction or complete economic collapse.

Nuclear anxieties now almost seem quaint and are mostly forgotten. The theme of decline, however, survives, in odes to unrelenting economic pessimism and social decay, to alienation and betrayal about the future. It is the same soundtrack, almost note for note, recapitulated in louder arpeggios of grievance that seem to repeat in every decade. This is worth considering, because if we are to take seriously the idea that liberal democracy has failed in *this* generation, then we must at least recognize that for a half century, *every* generation of liberal democratic citizens has apparently felt the same way. If each era is a time of decline and collapse and then later becomes the Good Old Days, this might say more about irrational nostalgia than about real living conditions.

The people who see the twenty-first century as the end of an American Dream that was within reach only a few decades earlier are, without even realizing it, singing the songs of their mothers and fathers, and maybe even of their grandparents. "The city's dying and no one knows why," Randy Newman sang about Baltimore—in 1977. In 1982 Billy Joel lamented the end of "Allentown" (a song actually written about nearby Bethlehem in the late 1970s), where during a supposed golden age of cheap education and plentiful opportunity "the graduations hang on the wall, but they never really helped us at all" while the "union people crawled away."[35] And John Cougar Mellencamp warned that there was no escape in America's pastoral counties. "Four hundred empty acres that used to be my farm," he sang in 1985. When the bank forecloses, he tells the bank official: "If you want me to, I'll say a prayer for your soul tonight."

The king of American decline-rock, of course, has always been New Jersey favorite son Bruce Springsteen, whose songs about his youth are mostly images of a bleak life among the mills and refineries of his home state. Throughout the late seventies, men in Springsteen's songs walked through the gates of the local factory with "death in their eyes," and then went home and took it out on their families. There's always a "Darkness on the Edge of Town," in every town. His 1984 hit "My Hometown" was a dirge of loss and nostalgia, in which he described "Main Street's whitewashed windows and vacant stores," and how "they're closing down the textile mill across the railroad tracks" while a foreman warns that "these jobs are going, boys." The song was recorded during the recession of 1983, but it topped the record charts in late 1985, just as the U.S. unemployment rate hit a five-year low.

In the British variant, bands like the Kinks grieved for the lost glory of the United Kingdom long before the advent of the European Union. "All the stories have been told of kings and days of old," band member Dave Davies wrote in "Living on a Thin Line" in 1983 (when he was at the ripe old age of thirty-six), "but there's no England now. What are we going to leave for the young?" A year later, Mick Jones of the legendary band the Clash formed a new group called Big Audio Dynamite, and they did "a dance to the tune of economic decline," a groove where the U.S., the UK, and "even the Soviets are swinging away," while the rest of us ask "why did it happen, and who is to blame?" On a more personal level, Paul Weller's 1982 hit for The Jam, "A Town Called Malice," was about his childhood in the 1970s, when "to either cut down on the beer or the kids' new gear" was "a big decision." These men are all senior citizens now, but Springsteen has kept the faith in subsequent works, including a 2012 song called "Death to My Hometown," where he called on his listeners to "send the robber barons straight to hell" for killing the city he told us was already dead some thirty years earlier.

It wasn't always this way, of course. American declinism, in both politics and culture, was a reaction to the end of the unique position the United States occupied in the world economy after World War II. With no real competitors, only America could serve as the

manufacturing base for a wrecked world economy. Once the economies of Europe and Asia were back on their feet—with large infusions of American help, no less—they would grow quickly and start
to muscle their way back into the growing postwar prosperity. Until
the rest of the world recovered, this American preeminence was a
completely unnatural situation, and no future era or subsequent
democratic government could ever measure up to the boom in jobs
and opportunities between 1945 and 1970.

This, in part, is why the pop culture of the 1950s and 1960s is
largely devoid of economic anxieties. (Another reason is that middle-
aged producers and music executives were not fans of socially conscious music until it became profitable.) The hits of this earlier time
of postwar optimism are mostly fluff, often centered on boy-meets-
girl stories. California in this era was the promised land, of course,
but cities were exciting, too: Petula Clark went traipsing through
the lights of "Downtown" to cheer herself up in 1965. But as the
end of the 1960s closed in, the problem was not unemployment
or decline but sterility and decadence.[36] Affluence was ubiquitous.
The songwriters Gerry Goffin and Carole King, inspired by a trip to
suburban New Jersey, gave the Monkees a 1967 hit with "Pleasant
Valley Sunday," a town where there's "a TV in every room," and every
weekend there's "charcoal burning everywhere" in "status symbol
land." Ray Stevens (whose career would later detour into novelty hits
like "The Streak") scored an unlikely top-40 hit in 1968 with a song
called "Mr. Businessman," a blistering attack on a neurotic, adulterous executive with "air-conditioned sinuses" who paid no attention
to his children and was headed straight to an unloved, Scrooge-like
ending in a cold grave.

The darker themes in the pop culture of the sixties, seventies, and
eighties are remembered now with sepia-toned nostalgia, but mostly
by people who could not possibly remember any of it at all. Younger
Americans hear tales from aging relatives of affordable homes and

safe streets in Los Angeles, or of guaranteed union jobs waiting in Youngstown or Gary, but these are now like legends passed down through the generations. In 2020 the political scientist David Cohen at the University of Akron described people in the Ohio Valley as vulnerable to the populism of a candidate like Trump because they saw themselves on "the losing ends of jobs for 50 years," but it is fair to ask how many people other than the elderly actually have such a long horizon of memory.[37] Nor do many Americans want to think very much about what it would actually mean to go back and live in those Kodachrome moments in their minds. As Williamson rightly pointed out in 2019, "you can have a 1957 standard of living, if you really want it, quite cheap," but would anyone really choose to pay the price it would demand from them in living standards—or in social progress, especially for women and minorities?[38]

I might not care very much for Led Zeppelin, but if I may borrow the title of their 1976 concert film, they were right about one thing: the song remains the same. Since the end of the artificial post–World War II manufacturing boom, our shared popular culture has been reliving, over and over, the cycle of blaming governments and scheming elites for selling out the virtuous workers who once made America great. Tell today's citizens of the democracies that their parents and grandparents had many of their same anxieties (and a few, from nuclear war to common medical problems, that have been ameliorated), and the answer is always the same: *Yes, but this time it's different. And someone is to blame.*

That someone, of course, is never the voters.

THE CRISIS OF ACCOUNTABILITY

What we should have learned from the experience of the last thirty years is not that democracy has failed, but that voters and their elected representatives have joined forces in a game of rising expectations, immediate gratification, and very little accountability from anyone at any level. Even critics who might be inclined to agree with this as a general point, however, tend to object (as I have found when discussing these ideas in public forums in the United States) that there is only so much one can ask of citizens who have survived the Great Recession, who face the startling increases in the cost of housing, health care, and education, or who are surrounded by indefensible levels of income inequality.

Every one of these is a problem, but none of them are signs of an essential flaw in liberal democracy. Each of them, in fact, is rooted in the dilemmas of expectation and accountability.

The best example is the Great Recession, of which several good accounts have already been written. There is no arguing that banks, lenders, appraisers, regulators, and insurers turned the housing market into a giant money machine that sooner or later was going to implode, as all pyramid schemes and scams eventually must do. There is no mystery about what happened in the early twenty-first century; as the scholar Jennifer Taub points out, among the many myths of the mortgage crisis is that the collapse came out of nowhere and that nothing could have been done about it, when it was in fact predictable and preventable. Taub and others sum it up as "poor risk management" by institutions that could make money without suffering the consequences of their institutional gambling addiction.[39]

But underneath it all was a popular political goal: universal homeownership. The only way to attain universal home ownership, of course, is if more people buy houses, whether they can afford them or not. As Gretchen Morgenson and Joshua Rosner wrote in 2012, giving the people what they wanted—and letting everyone else get rich off doing so—created a public-private partnership that turned into a bipartisan "runaway train."

Prevailing interest rates [by 2003] were at 1 percent, regulators and Congress were on board for looser lending standards, and a raft of innovative mortgage loans was floating all kinds of new borrowers. Known as "affordability products," these mortgages vastly expanded homeownership, letting borrowers "own" a home but still pay a fraction of what they would have normally. In the early years of the loan, that is.[40]

Bill Clinton thought it was a good idea. George W. Bush thought it was a good idea. Americans who wanted to own homes (and in some cases, more than one home) thought it was a good idea. And when it came time to punish the people who gambled, as the title of Taub's book put it, with "other people's houses," the public decided to keep most of the same leaders they blamed for letting them get into trouble in the first place.

This point about accountability should not be brushed away as merely the power of incumbency or some insurmountable political inertia. Americans, like other democratic citizens, regularly refuse to replace their own leaders after the serial "failures" of democracy. Barack Obama was elected in 2008 at least in part as a sign of the blowback against elite corruption and government malfeasance. "Occupy Wall Street" took to the streets in 2011 to demand that justice be levied on the corporate miscreants who helped crash the economy. The democratic socialist Bernie Sanders surged in the 2016 Democratic Party primaries on a wave of populist anger and promises. The Tea Party movement, which claimed to stand for fiscal sanity and against irresponsible bailouts for the banks, celebrated the arrival of Donald Trump and unified Republican Party government in the 2016 general election.

All of this outrage, however, did not change very much. Obama might not have had much choice, but after his victory he bailed out the banks and was re-elected handily.[41] The Occupy campouts were dissipated mostly by cold weather (and the impatience of New York City officials and residents). Sanders was defeated by Hillary Clinton and his next campaign sputtered out four years later in a loss to an even more obvious stalwart of the political establishment, Joe Biden. The Tea Party, as a political movement, was mostly a spent force by the time Trump was elected, and even its own leaders admitted that Trump—who promised to "drain the swamp" but ended up as the Creature from the Black Lagoon, a big-spending statist whose abuses of power for himself and his cronies was the very embodiment of swamp culture—was the worst thing that could happen to them.[42] In 2020 the process came full circle, and Trump was defeated by Barack Obama's vice president, Biden.

If the past twenty years have been a welling of populist rage, it is a movement that doesn't seem to have much of an interest in results. At the time of the 2020 election, almost every U.S. political leader of both parties, other than Trump himself, had been in office since the days back in the late twentieth century when democracy and the "establishment" were ostensibly teetering on the brink of collapse. In Kentucky, Senate Majority Leader Mitch McConnell (born in 1942, first elected in 1984) won his seventh term; when the Democrats took control of the Senate after special elections in January 2021, he handed the gavel to Chuck Schumer of New York (born in 1950, first elected to Congress in 1980). The Speaker of the House was Nancy Pelosi, who at the time was eighty years old and had been in Congress since 1987. Kevin McCarthy, the House minority leader, was the relative newcomer, with only fourteen years in Washington. For a nation that was fed up and ready to throw the bums out, the bums of both parties have done pretty well at staying right where they are.

As is almost always the case, voters don't really want to fire their own representatives. They just want everyone else to fire theirs.[43]

THE CENTER DOES NOT HOLD

Critics of modern democracy will likely find this litany of electoral longevity maddening. After all, how much can the act of voting mean when money determines the outcome of elections and real power rests in the hands of regulators and administrators and other bureaucrats who are beyond the power of the ballot box? With so much institutional power amassed against the public, telling people to fix their own democracy is yet another heartless reaction to a "broken" system, and the fact that the system keeps propagating itself proves not that people are satisfied, but that democracy is out of reach. Even those who hope for the survival of liberal institutions might glumly quote Yeats and worry that democracy has become a widening gyre of money and power in which "things fall apart" and the center does not hold.

This is too pessimistic. Money helps—a lot—but it is no guarantee of election. Hillary Clinton outspent Donald Trump in 2016 and lost; wealthy business leaders like Michael Bloomberg and Carly Fiorina tried to compete in U.S. presidential primary contests and were crushed. As for the power of the administrative state, the decline of administrative competence in the United States (and in places like the UK, Italy, India, and Brazil) under populist governments in the age of COVID shows that political leaders can easily undermine their own experts and administrators, not least by simply firing them and then refusing to replace them. Power, to paraphrase the Russian revolutionaries of 1917, is always lying in the street, and it is always available to a determined coalition of voters—if they bother to show up.

The gloomier reality we might take from Yeats is how much the "worst are full of passionate intensity" as they try to convince their fellow citizens that the existence of suffering invalidates the liberal democratic ideal. This is an immense and cynical lie. The history of the past century has been a story of increasing liberty and increasing prosperity. Even with the reversals, mistakes, and corruption among the democracies, the autocracies have been the systems that have faced the need to change or perish. They are the regimes that failed to provide for their citizens, whose successes were unsustainable, and whose citizens have repeatedly risen to destroy them.

There are remedies and alternatives, some of them at considerable cost, for many of the troubles that afflict the democracies. But for anything to work at almost any of level of government, citizens first have to accept that they live in a community. They have to begin with an assumption that it is possible to find common ground for solutions, however imperfect they may be. They have to believe that other human beings are sensible and amenable to good will. One might think that the ability to communicate with each other, across the lines of class, gender, race, religion, and even national borders would help this process. In the twenty-first century, social media has provided us all with this opportunity, and we have succeeded in knowing each other better.

Unfortunately, as we'll see in the next chapter, the conclusion we all seem to have drawn is that we don't like each other very much.

Hello, I Hate You

How Hyper-Connection Is Destroying Democracy

No society could survive—and surely no society could be decent—
if everybody in it were able to communicate everything.

—Daniel J. Boorstin

THE GREAT INDIAN FOOD SCANDAL

I don't like Indian food. You may already know this about me. Millions
of people around the world know it too, and the fact that you might
well have heard about it is a problem. In fact, it's a weird story that
serves as a perfect example of how technology is encouraging us to
destroy ourselves.

My trouble began, as every good story of a self-inflicted wound in
the twenty-first century does, with social media. On a quiet Saturday
afternoon in the late fall of 2019, a young man named Jon Becker
asked Twitter's legions to post their most controversial food takes,
and thousands of people responded. There was the usual hatred for
mayonnaise, a few ill-tempered takedowns of lettuce, and even some
swipes at peanut butter and jelly sandwiches. These are hardly controversial: America for decades has had the equivalent of religious
wars over pineapple on pizzas and ketchup on hot dogs.

I, however, decided to go for the gold. I declared that I could not stand the cuisine of over a billion people. And just to be annoying, I added that no one else could possibly like it either. "I think Indian food is terrible," I said, "and we pretend it isn't." (I added this last part as a zinger at my American friends who have repeatedly dragged me out for Indian cuisine, and then insist on telling me how much they enjoy it while they wipe sweat from their eyes and gulp water.) I have never been to India, and so my experience is limited, but I've just never liked whatever passes for Indian cuisine in the United States and Europe, a preference that my friends see as evidence of a parochial and uncultured palate.

The reactions at first were good-natured and funny. "Do you not have tastebuds?" the famous *Top Chef* host Padma Lakshmi asked me. The former U.S. attorney Preet Bharara offered to take me to an Indian restaurant and help me through the menu. Neal Katyal, a prominent legal scholar and Indian American author (and one of my students in his undergraduate days at Dartmouth) simply posted Twitter's iconic riposte: "Unfollow."

Then the responses got a bit darker. I was accused, in various states of unhinged fury, of playing into stereotypes about Indians and furthering a history of oppression. Some proceeded to spin entire narratives of my likely nostalgia for the days of the Raj. (For the record, I was raised not as a son of the Empire, but as an only child. I always assume that no one could like anything I don't like.) A few even suggested that I was supportive of genocide.

On the Monday morning following my weekend tweet, I awoke to an email from an Indian colleague telling me that I was now a news story in India itself.[1] Over the next forty-eight hours, I found myself in the pages and screens of the *Times of India* and other Indian papers, the BBC in Great Britain, the *Washington Post* and Fox News in the United States, and Russia's RT. Both Fox and RT, unsurprisingly, presented me as a heroic white professor refusing to bow to the multicultural mob. I am indeed white, but I wasn't trying to make a point about multiculturalism. Rather, I was making a point that I am often snarky about things I don't happen to like.

When I started getting threatening email messages, however, telling me that I should literally *die* for joking about Indian food, I wondered—and not for the first time—when our hyper-connected global society had become so bizarre and dangerous. This was not the first time I had received death threats and other kinds of harassment, but usually those were spurred by things I'd written about somewhat weightier issues of politics. Now people were sending emails to a relatively obscure, middle-aged professor in Rhode Island and hoping for my swift demise because of a glib take about food on Twitter.

My experience in the Great Indian Food Scandal of 2019 was relatively mild compared to the trials that other people have experienced through the miracle of social media. Our ability to communicate instantly, anonymously, and without reflection has immortalized moments of stupidity (including a few of my own) that in an earlier time would have rightly gone unnoticed. In some cases, the effects have been quite serious, with innocent lives put in danger because of cases of mistaken identity or because of inaccurate—and in some instances, intentionally misleading—information about public safety on issues ranging from shooting incidents to COVID-19 information.

Worse, malicious actors, from states to political hucksters, are now using the internet as their preferred medium for undermining democratic elections throughout the world. The subject of foreign intervention is too big a subject to tackle here; as an expert on Russia, I know that the Russian government and other authoritarian systems gladly exploit social divisions in the democracies.[2] But in the end, the problem rests with the users and consumers, not with enemy regimes poisoning the well. (I wrote extensively about the problem of the internet and its impact on truth and authoritative knowledge in *The Death of Expertise,* and I will not reproduce all of those arguments here.)[3] These attacks play on our divisions and grievances, and they exploit our vanity and ennui. Sometimes they are limited operations against individuals or political parties, but some become destructive wildfires like the QAnon movement, a moral panic based on an insane conspiracy theory about child sacrifice and pedophilia that in 2020 powered at least a few unhinged politicians into the halls of the United States Congress.

The growth of online conspiracy-mongering has had other important real-world consequences as well. On January 6, 2021, the promise of global connection turned into a civic nightmare when thousands of people stormed the U.S. Capitol, invading the House and Senate and injuring well over one hundred police officers in one of the single worst days for injuries to law enforcement personnel since the 9/11 attacks in 2001.[4] The rioters were not disenfranchised or oppressed people in a peaceful assembly. Instead, a detailed analysis by two scholars at the University of Chicago of those arrested for their part in the insurrection found that the January riot was a day-camp outing for middle-aged, middle-class Americans.

> The average age of the arrestees we studied is 40. Two-thirds are 35 or older, and 40 percent are business owners or hold white-collar jobs. Unlike the stereotypical extremist, many of the alleged participants in the Capitol riot have a lot to lose. They work as CEOs, shop owners, doctors, lawyers, IT specialists, and accountants. Strikingly, court documents indicate that only 9 percent are unemployed. Of the earlier far-right-extremist suspects we studied, 61 percent were under 35, 25 percent were unemployed, and almost none worked in white-collar occupations.[5]

In other words, this was a bored "lumpen-bourgeoisie," a narcissistic and mostly affluent middle class of deep pockets and shallow minds who paid lip service to democracy but had no interest in it if the results of democratic elections offended them.[6]

These insurrectionists came to Washington after years of gorging on internet conspiracies and simple-minded memes, and after so much time experiencing political life through a screen, they were weirdly disconnected from the gravity of their actions. They stormed the seat of government while staring at themselves on their phones and frantically posting updates to their Instagram and Facebook accounts—which, of course, made catching them later much easier. One of them told her audience that she was, "life or death," headed into the Capitol, but that on her return to Texas they should keep her in mind as a great realtor who can sell their houses. (She later demanded a pardon from President Trump.) Another, after her arrest, asked the court for release to attend a "work bonding experience" at a resort in Mexico.[7] Almost all of them seemed genuinely stunned that there could be dire consequences from the death and destruction that resulted when their internet-driven, anti-democracy Woodstock turned into a violent, insurrectionist Altamont.

This violence against the American constitutional system was the public expression of a crackpot religion, a cult that could have emerged anywhere but could only grow in the swamp of a hyperconnected country. Its adherents found each other on social media, and they elected the media pundits of cable television as their prophets and high priests. Their oracle, their holy text, was the Twitter feed of the president of the United States, who used the power of instant connection to feed them one outlandish story after another about a stolen election. As lunatics howled and chanted in the Senate gallery and others smeared excrement on the marble halls of the Capitol, the power and promise of engagement seemed less a force for peace and democracy than a bandolier of grenades in the hands of feral children.

Once again, as humanity has managed to do with everything from fire to nuclear energy, we have found a great tool that can advance human civilization. And once again, we are at risk of using it to destroy ourselves. Connectedness, only so recently a marvel and a blessing, is now a curse.

THE VAST AND LONELY SPACES

The sheer size of our interaction with the virtual world, and the speed with which that world has enveloped all of us, has created a vast and yet lonely space, where we are both too connected and too isolated at the same time. We interact with millions of others at our command and our convenience while laundering their presence through the antiseptic interfaces of communications and social media apps. We hardly need each other for very much; if we seek leisure, we can simply ask our phone or computer to provide us a blackjack table or a chess partner, and if humans are not available, machines will step in and make do. If we seek conversation, we can blurt out the first thought in our heads to no one in particular—or to everyone in the world. Even our sex lives have become virtualized to the point where we can relieve our boredom on a bus ride by retreating into pornography while ignoring the discomfort of the people sitting right next to us as we do so.[8]

The ability to send and receive unfathomable amounts of data, from cable television to text messages, has been one of the greatest scientific advances in human history, but like so many such advances in the past, it has come with a price. Liberal democracy requires patience, tolerance, and perspective, but torrents of sensory experiences—it is too much to call it all "information"—assault those virtues. The constant ability to see into the lives of our neighbors, to compare ourselves to strangers, to be in constant contact with the entire planet day and night, is unnatural and pushes the human mind far beyond its capacity for reason and reflection.

The scale of the problem is almost incomprehensible. Hyper-connectivity has invaded our lives in ways we do not even real-ize or fully understand. Even those among us who try to avoid such connection cannot avoid the others in our communities who are plugged in and supercharged. Consider the size and reach of social media: Twitter, as of this writing, has over 325 million users. Facebook has over two and a half *billion* users, and it is now a prod-uct like "cable television" that I don't even have to explain to a mod-ern reader. At this point, Facebook is probably uncontrollable even by its creators; the writer Adrienne LaFrance has called Facebook a "Doomsday Machine" because the social network's destructive algo-rithms now operate almost without human intervention as Facebook seeks to become "the de facto (and only) experience of the internet for people all over the world."[9]

But Twitter and Facebook are just two of the tallest tips of several giant icebergs. In the modern age, anyone with a smartphone or an email account is "connected," and that's a lot of people. In 2012, about a billion people worldwide had smartphones; by 2020 that number had nearly quadrupled, including virtually all Americans.[10] Likewise, over the half the people on the *planet* have email accounts. And we're not just sending messages and keeping our calendars. The company, by some estimates, with the third-largest reach and impact on soci-ety, just behind Facebook and Twitter, but ahead of Microsoft, Apple, and Amazon, is Pornhub, the adult entertainment site that racks up 3.5 billion visits a month.[11]

Again, this level of connectivity is, in the abstract, a remarkable achievement. It is a scientific feat that helps human beings stay in touch with each other, to say nothing of providing access to every-thing from employment opportunities to emergency services. But each smartphone and email account is also a leaky pipe that allows for a lot of political, social, and intellectual sewage. As a Pew Research Center study emphasized in 2016, there is almost no way to use modern technology merely as a tool in isolation from the emotionally supercharged world of cyberspace, especially anything involving social networking.

> In their in-person interactions, Americans can (and often do) attempt to steer clear of those with whom they strongly disagree. But online social media environments present new challenges. In these spaces, users can encounter statements they might consider highly contentious or extremely offensive—even when they make no effort to actively seek out this material. Similarly, political arguments can encroach into users' lives when comment streams on otherwise unrelated topics devolve into flame wars or partisan bickering.

> Navigating these interactions can be particularly fraught in light of the complex mix of close friends, family members, distant acquaintances, professional connections and public figures that make up many users' online networks.[12]

We can try to convince ourselves that we prefer not to engage with the online world, but the online world is constantly engaging with *us*, regardless of whether we want it or like it. The writer Yevgeny Simkin summed it up in one short and terrible, if somewhat overstated, formulation: "All modern social, political, and sociological ills can be traced to social media."[13]

Not everyone is so pessimistic. David Shor, an American data analyst who works on progressive causes, notes that many citizens are not as plugged in to the virtual world as we might think.

> The average voter in a general election is something like 50 years old—in a midterm or primary, it's higher. They don't have a college degree. They watch about six hours of TV a day—that's the

average; there are people who watch more. They generally don't read partisan media. They still largely get their news from mainstream sources. They're watching what's on the *ABC Nightly News*. Maybe they see some stuff on Facebook, but it's really mostly from mainstream sources.[14]

But Shor is underestimating the problem. There's a lot more going on than just "seeing some stuff" on Facebook or other internet locations. More people are online now than at any point in history, and Shor's average voter is marinating in a culture whose priorities are often defined by hyper-connectivity. To hope that all of this remains distant from most ordinary citizens is something like being optimistic about the lower risk of lung disease in a man who has never touched a cigarette while ignoring that he's a coal miner who lives in a house full of chain-smokers.

Connection, for all of its benefits—and despite its power to undermine the rule of authoritarian states—is destroying the culture and habits of a democratic society. It is making us angrier, more narcissistic, more isolated, more selfish, and less serious as citizens. It encourages us to withdraw into ourselves and become the electronic version of Banfield's backward Italian village, a virtual community of surly peasants who no longer even need to leave the house to farm a plot or play cards at the local café.

I am uncomfortable raising this kind of alarm about the sensory glut of available media and the hyper-connection among national and global citizens because I am at heart a technological optimist. I am also part of the problem. Like many people, I have a Facebook account that I use, mostly, to keep up with friends from high school and college. But I also have a very active Twitter account with over a half million followers. I decry the virtualization of our public life while being an active participant in that streaming experience by tweeting, posting, and appearing regularly in podcasts and on television. And yet I want to believe that some good can come of all this, and not just because of my own interests.

Perhaps my optimism is generational. I was among the last cohort of adults in the developed world who grew up in the preconnected, nondigitized world. I had my first email address back in the early 1980s as an office manager in a work-study job when I was in graduate school at Columbia University, an oddity that didn't do very much except allow me to communicate with a small set of office managers at other schools. This impressed my friends not one bit, but with every message I received from some other terminal somewhere, I had the sense that this was a technology that could change the world, and only for the better. But until a more accessible internet blared its arrival through the beeps and honks of a phone modem in the early 1990s, the world still seemed prohibitively large and distant to me.

I do not miss those days. I enjoy the immediacy and comforting familiarity provided by connection now, especially when I travel. But I also admit to a certain amount of nostalgia for a time when there were quiet, isolated spaces in our social lives. I am especially glad that there was no way to create a permanent and public archive of the first thirty or forty years of my life, a revolutionary change I know has already been a source of regret to many younger people. This fortunate timing made me part of a privileged generation that was able to embrace the early benefits and avoid the later drawbacks of connectivity. (A perfect example of this is that I was socialized about relationships by old-fashioned dating back in the 1970s and 1980s, but I met my second wife in middle age via an internet dating site. Truly the best of both worlds.)

This generational vantage point fueled my optimism while allowing me to watch the transition to hyper-connectivity in real time. I was certain, especially in the wake of the fall of the Soviet Union, that connecting the citizens of a globalized world would be a force for peace. I still believe this, and history, so far, seems to bear out this faith. There are few instruments more dangerous to authoritarian regimes than the laptop and the smartphone, with their ability to connect citizens, build gigantic networks, and transmit images and video instantly. In 2021, the repressive apparatus of the Russian state had to cope with thousands of protesters who used the power of instant communications to organize in the streets of major Russian cities after the arrest of opposition leader Alexei Navalny—while also trying to figure out how to stop Russia's teenagers from using TikTok to spread advice about strategies for engaging in civil disobedience. As of this writing, the Russian government is still trying to kill Navalny, an effort that is being followed and documented in real time around the world despite the Kremlin's attempt to isolate him in a prison camp.

Despite all the benefits of a connected world, citizens of the democracies are now poisoning themselves with hyper-connectivity. In much the same way that agricultural mass production and the easy availability of food on every street has made so many of us obese and diabetic, we are gorging on the worst that the internet has to offer— and becoming worse people in the bargain. The scholar Neil Postman warned in 1985 that we were "amusing ourselves to death"; thirty-five years later, not only are we eating ourselves to death, we are also texting ourselves to death, tweeting ourselves to death, and "shitposting" ourselves to death.[15]

HOW CONNECTION DESTROYS DEMOCRACY

The hyper-connected world corrodes democratic culture in several important ways. First, it makes all experiences immediate, instantaneous, and local, which overloads our ability to process information and irrationally heightens our sense of danger. The democracies are becoming nations full of depressed, anxiety-plagued wrecks who believe that they are hip-deep in danger and misery. This helps to make ordinary citizens easy prey for the comforting lies of disinformation, as well as for the reassuring sense of false intimacy created by virtual communities to which many people now feel more loyal than to friends or families.

These problems are bad enough, but the cultural impact of the hyper-connected world is perhaps the greatest danger to democracy. Connection facilitates social interaction, but it also enables an environment of constant awareness of each other and encourages endless comparison. This results in a virtualized, internet-enabled social treadmill that not only feeds envy and resentment but also encourages the kind of performative narcissism that was already overtaking American culture long before the advent of the Information Age. The United States and other democracies are, like all nations, collections of idiosyncratic national and regional cultures. But hyper-connection is speeding up the pace of cultural change, and it creates a sense of competition between subcultures that, in an earlier time, might have only been dimly aware of each other, and better off for it.

Cultural change is inevitable and sometimes invigorating, but it is also terrifying to those who feel themselves on the wrong side of it. One of the main drivers of authoritarian attacks on democracy is the sense among privileged groups that their grip on politics and the national culture is slipping away; the internet is their window on that process, distorted and amplified by clever entrepreneurs who know how to play on feelings of inferiority and fears of threats and injuries, real or imagined.

How people respond to change is always a matter of resilience, but in a democracy it is also a process of compromise and negotiation. And here, the technology of connection is doing its worst work by destroying us as people. It is depriving ordinary citizens of a basic ability to pause, to deliberate, and to reason. The immediacy of the hyper-connected world is facilitating our devolution not just away from being thoughtful citizens but away from maturity and confidence, and away from the seriousness that makes life in a democracy possible. We entered the Information Age as adults; we are leaving it, and heading into the Hyper-connected Age, as children entranced by colorful pictures flashing in front of us while we jab at the "Like" button.

DANGER, WILL ROBINSON!

Readers of a certain age will remember *Lost in Space*, the campy 1960s television show about a spacefaring American family in the distant future that was, well, lost in space. They were accompanied by a giant, neurotic robot who was highly protective of the youngest child of the family. When triggered, the robot—whose name, creatively, was "Robot"—would flail his accordion-like arms and shout "DANGER, WILL ROBINSON! DANGER! DANGER!" The music would swell and viewers knew that something terrible was about to happen.

To be connected all day to the internet and cable news is like being young Will living with Robot. News outlets, social media, and millions of web pages are spinning in circles in front of us and flashing warning lights as we skirt the edge of daily panic. Everything happens in real time: social media users anxiously refresh their news and comment feeds while those watching cable networks are warned of an ALERT or that news is BREAKING or JUST IN. This has become such a problem during moments of crisis that police departments sometimes have had to ask social media users not to broadcast the movement of their officers or other first responders in real time—a problem that raises the question of why anyone would feel the need to do such a thing in the first place.

People do this, of course, because they want to be carried into the thrill of live events. This is part of the narcissistic drama of modern life. In the twenty-first century, not only must we believe that we are surrounded by tragedies, but we must believe that we are personally involved in them. We watch these stories obsessively because to do so feeds our sense that great events and important decisions cannot happen without us. We devour excessive amounts of irrelevant detail in the belief that our wise counsel must be offered without delay in moments of peril, whether about a military conflict in Ukraine or a storm in Canada or an air crash in Thailand. Our hyper-connectedness not only makes possible, but positively demands, that we express our views and emotions about everything, instantly, as if all things are happening to all of us. As the writer Windsor Mann once said to me, the aphorism that "the world is watching" should now be "the world is watching and commenting."

To this end, we not only focus on bad news, but we actively seek it out. Internet consumers can curate their own nightmares by engaging in the habit of "doomscrolling," a neologism that refers to how people obsessively click through linked stories of bad news and turn themselves into nervous wrecks. In the synergy of the internet and cable news, we all experience moments of terror together, even if the stories we are reading or watching are nowhere near us. A truck overturns on an interstate highway, and we are all, at that moment, trapped in the traffic waiting for the rig to explode. Gunfire rings out anywhere, and we are all, at that moment, running for cover. A toxic fire erupts anywhere, and we are all, at that moment, wondering if we should seal our windows.

This obsession with drama and danger produces a constant stream of anxiety that neither statistics nor government policy can remedy. Try to explain to Americans, for example, that their children are safer in public schools now than they were in the 1990s—because they are—and you will be met with incredulous looks, and a fair amount of moral judgment, as if a willingness to accept statistical facts is a sign of callousness.[16] This constant sense of danger feeds on itself and quickly short-circuits the ability to think clearly. More important, as a matter of democratic politics, this constant fearfulness smothers the citizen's ability to determine whether governments are perform- ing well or poorly. If every story on the internet is about crime and unemployment, then the viewer or the consumer—it might no lon- ger be accurate to refer to people grazing the internet as "readers"— will reach the almost inevitable conclusion that their government is a failure and must be replaced.

Editors were once the backstop against this kind of dynamic. They were the arbiters who were charged with curbing the sensation- alism and limiting the falsehoods in the pages of a family newspaper. Today, however, real-time reporting on social media by anyone with a smartphone outpaces a careful presentation of facts and context. Even the layout of a web page, with all stories visible at once and links readily available to less authoritative sources, defeats the ability to signal the relative importance of stories, to prevent voyeurism, and to separate truth from falsity. The term "front page" no longer has mean- ing; I made the mistake a few years ago of referring to an "above the fold" story in a classroom of undergraduates, which then required me to explain that one could once fold a newspaper and thus signify that the upper half of the paper, the part you could see as it was displayed on a newsstand, was the most important part of the first page.

As the scholar Timothy Snyder has put it, this flood of global information without any local background or history "supercharges the mental habits by which we seek emotional stimulation and com- fort, which means losing the distinction between what feels true and what actually is true," and this undermines democracy, because a society that is "post-factual is pre-fascist."[17] We are wired, as human beings, to react to stories of danger and to seek protection. We click on the story, which in turn sends a signal to the content provider that they have captured our eyeballs, and so they send us more of what- ever we just clicked on. We click on those, too, and the provider sends us more. Soon, we are in an anxiety spiral of reading, clicking, finding more horror, clicking, reading again, and on and on, never realizing that the terrifying world we have entered is a chamber of horrors we built for ourselves, to our own precise specifications.

And then, exhausted, we sit back and think: Our form of government cannot keep us safe. Democracy has failed us. We need something stronger.

"THE DEVIL LIVES IN OUR PHONES"

Even if we could somehow stop doomscrolling and recover some sense of proportion about the risks and dangers (and astonishing advantages) of living in the twenty-first century, democracies would still face the problem that our now-established patterns of hyper-connectedness have already changed us all for the worse at an elemental level. More citizens are now isolated, depressed, and anxious than ever before, and a large part of the reason behind all this social dysfunction is that our constant interaction with technology is affecting our ability to engage in normal social activity, which in turn makes us emotionally incapable of functioning as competent citizens in a democracy.

No one knows this better than the people who facilitate our neurotic connectedness, the architects of social media sites themselves. These are people who, it turns out, are deeply apprehensive about letting their own children near the products they have created and sell to the rest of us. A 2018 *New York Times* excursion among the Silicon Valley technology mavens found a "dark consensus" among many of the people who built the social media Doomsday Machines. One Facebook executive said in 2011, after leaving his former company, "It literally is a point now where I think we have created tools that are ripping apart the social fabric of how society works." Another

Facebook worker put it even more starkly: "I am convinced the devil lives in our phones and is wreaking havoc on our children."[18]

This is not alarmism, and one need not believe in the devil to measure the damage done to generations whose lives are now inextricably tied to communications and internet technology. The psychologist Jean Twenge (who follows trends related especially to youth and narcissism) argues that the wave of narcissism and depression that overtook young Americans in the early twenty-first century tracks closely with the introduction of smartphones and the retreat of young people into virtual interactions. She marks 2012 as an important year for American society in particular.

> What happened in 2012 to cause such dramatic shifts in behavior? It was after the Great Recession, which officially lasted from 2007 to 2009 and had a starker effect on Millennials trying to find a place in a sputtering economy. But it was exactly the moment when the proportion of Americans who owned a smartphone surpassed 50 percent.[19]

Looking over this data, Twenge claims that the "results could not be clearer: Teens who spend more time than average on screen activities are more likely to be unhappy, and those who spend more time than average on nonscreen activities are more likely to be happy."

These statistics came into distressing detail when Twenge asked her own students at San Diego State University about their smartphone usage. "Their answers," Twenge wrote, "were a profile in obsession."

> Nearly all slept with their phone, putting it under their pillow, on the mattress, or at the very least within arm's reach of the bed. They checked social media right before they went to sleep, and reached for their phone as soon as they woke up in the morning

(they had to—all of them used it as their alarm clock). Their phone was the last thing they saw before they went to sleep and the first thing they saw when they woke up. If they woke in the middle of the night, they often ended up looking at their phone.

Twenge's students used the language of addiction to describe their relationships with the small glowing boxes that rule their lives. "I know I shouldn't, but I just can't help it," one said about looking at her phone while in bed. Others, according to Twenge, "saw their phone as an extension of their body—or even like a lover," with one saying: "Having my phone closer to me while I'm sleeping is a comfort." Another study, done in the mid-2000s, suggested that mental health risks increase with the number of platforms used, with seven or more—hardly a large number of accounts for many young users— potentially tripling the risk of anxiety and depression.[20]

This might seem a large claim. But if we think of personal technology as something like carrying around a judgmental and argumentative crowd around with us all day, it makes depressing sense. A smartphone with social media apps is like a portable Thunderdome of argument. There are no teachers or editors, no gatekeepers or referees, no one to rule out lies, insults, illogical reasoning, or threats. Instead of reasoned discussion, everything devolves into a duel of pure feelings, with every participant laying out emotionally charged claims as part of an ongoing drama of good versus evil. And it's all available simply by shifting our eyes to a small box in our hands at any moment of the day or night.

The virtual world and its system of structured rewards and treats—the likes, retweets, hearts, smiley faces, upturned thumbs, and clapping hands—become divisive because the way such rewards are earned is practically a training program for narcissism and exhibitionism. It is also politically destructive. Amanda Carpenter, a former aide to Texas senator Ted Cruz who broke with him and the

Republicans over their support of Trump, noted that Cruz adopted the "persona of a Twitter troll" because "owning the [liberals] and generating likes, retweets, and reactions online are the key to success" for a considerable number of modern American politicians.[21] "The demands of leading and governing in the public interest have never meshed well with the demands of winning and keeping office," she rightly observes, but "they have never before been so contradictory" as they are in the age of social media.

Lesser lights who play this game end up in court rather than in the Senate. Ben Smith, the former editor of BuzzFeed, tried to explain how one of his own employees, Tim Gionet, became a white supremacist internet personality—his *nom de guerre electronique* was "Baked Alaska"—who went from a job in a media to a "career arc . . . best described as performative violence."

> If you haven't had the experience of posting something on social media that goes truly viral, you may not understand its profound emotional attraction. You're suddenly the center of a digital universe, getting more attention from more people than you ever have. The rush of affirmation can be giddy, and addictive. And if you have little else to hold on to, you can lose yourself to it.[22]

Gionet finally ended up joining the group that tried to sack the U.S. Capitol on January 6, 2021. "We've got over 10,000 people live, watching, let's go!" he said into his phone. "Hit that follow button—I appreciate you guys." Many of the others who invaded the Capitol that day did the same, leaving a trail of evidence for their later prosecution because they could not stop talking to their phones and posting their own pictures even as they committed an act of violent insurrection.

This is not merely a "kids these days" argument about technology, especially since much of the pollution and divisiveness on social media is driven by older people with Facebook pages and email accounts and nothing but time on their hands. As disheartening as it is to say it, the older generation—that is, people my own age—are mostly a lost cause. No one in late middle age is going to develop a new appreciation for reason and nuance after years of believing that memes are facts. I'm not even sure that's a failing of a particular age group; if social media had connected angry and frightened Americans back during the drama of Watergate in 1973 and 1974, would the "Greatest Generation" have been so great? The United States emerged from Watergate led by a president and vice president no one had elected, and the voters of that time, instead of moving on with their lives, might well have sat in front of their laptops passing around Facebook memes about how Gerald Ford and Nelson Rockefeller plotted with the Soviets to unseat Spiro Agnew and impeach Richard Nixon.

The risk to the young is far more of a concern for the future of democracy. We can hope that the damage is temporary, but the replacement of human activity in close proximity with virtual activity at a distance, whether it is social relationships or political interaction, comes with a clear cost of increasing narcissism, depression, and isolation, all of which have been steadily washing away the emotional resilience of a democratic society.

HOW TO MEET NEW PEOPLE AND HATE THEM

Hyper-connectedness undermines democracy by increasing anger and polarization between ordinary citizens not because it enforces distance, but because it encourages intimacy. People get to know too much about each other, and the more they know each other, the more they find themselves in conflict. We can now get from "hello" to "I hate you" faster and at a greater distance than any generation of humans who have ever lived.

This might sound counterintuitive, especially when, at an international level, increased communication so far seems generally to be a force for better understanding and a contribution to the pursuit of peace. This might be due to the fact that at least some interaction can overcome fear of the unknown. There is a reason, after all, that the three empires continually at war with each other in George Orwell's *1984* forbade communication across their borders: each understood, as do all dictatorships, that their rule depended on the isolation and ignorance of their enslaved populations.

The problem, however, is that at a social level, too much interaction and the familiarity it creates really does breed contempt. Sigmund Freud called it "the narcissism of small differences," and while Freud might have been wrong about a lot of things, he apparently was right that human beings who are otherwise alike will find things to be angry about, no matter how trivial. A Russian and an American have a cultural and political gulf to overcome, and thus may find it a relief to celebrate the human characteristics they have in common. Two people from two different parts of California, however, or from Maine and Mississippi—or from a rich and a poor area in the same city—might be tempted more quickly to argue about things they both feel they have in common but that the other does not respect or understand.

Once people find what makes them more different than alike, they focus on these differences and then transfer them to politics as a way of seeking membership in a tribe. A study early in the twenty-first century found that once people encounter "evidence of dissimilarity," they will process more information about each other as "further evidence of dissimilarity, leading to decreased liking."[23] We then associate with people who feel as we do, and create tribes whose loyalty tests become more precise with each iteration and interaction.

(Social media administrators know this. "Our algorithms exploit the human brain's attraction to divisiveness," an internal Facebook study admitted in 2018.)[24] This tribalism festers into group narcissism that demands, as all narcissism does, constant reassurance—and cable news and social media are happy to provide it in exchange for attention and clicks.

The problem is not so much that there are negative people in the world, but that social media encourages the human tendency to reward fighting as a spectator sport.[25] Crowds, after all, did not go to the Coliseum to watch gladiators work out their differences. Venkatesh Rao calls this not the "internet of things," but the "internet of beefs," and warns that it is everywhere, on all platforms, all the time, and supported by people who should know better.

> Beefing is everywhere on the internet. Bernie [Sanders] and [Elizabeth]Warren beef with each other and with Trump, different schools of economists beef with each other over trade policy, climate hawks beef with climate doves. Here you see Slavoj Žižek and Jordan Peterson taking their beef offline. There you see Ben Shapiro attempt to bait Alexandria Ocasio-Cortez into a live beef for the hundredth time. And over on that side, we find Jesse Singal beefing with trans activists.

> And in one corner by himself, of course, is Nassim Taleb beefing with all comers on all topics.[26]

For anyone who sets foot in the social media arena, there is no escape from these conflicts, and most people are unwilling to take all the measures—as Rao notes, these include "blocks, restricted feeds, secret-group gatekeeping boundaries, and subscribers-only paywalls"—that would allow them to avoid all this negativity. Instead, we all log on, and combat is joined.

Television, too, exacerbates this dynamic and increases the distance between citizens. Over twenty-five years ago, the political scientist Robert Putnam noted that even after controlling for multiple other variables such as "education, income, age, race, place of residence, work status, and gender, TV viewing is strongly and negatively related to social trust and group membership," an effect that is reversed when compared to people who read newspapers. "Within every educational category, heavy readers are avid joiners, whereas heavy viewers are more likely to be loners," which in turn isolates these citizens from the kinds of organizations that sustain democratic institutions.[27] Since the late twentieth century, newspapers have been vanishing at an alarming rate, and news and information are now almost entirely a matter of passive viewing, with predictable results.

The challenge for democracy is that even small differences in lifestyles become magnified over the internet. This helps to convince people that no matter how well they're doing, others are doing better, and therefore that our system of government is broken and unfair. Income inequality is a real problem in American life, but most people do not experience it directly; indeed, beyond a certain level of wealth, the difference in living standards is impossible to measure. It doesn't matter if the person much richer than you are has one yacht or five—she has a yacht and you don't—and further multiples of wealth are almost impossible to grasp in any meaningful way. Constant connectivity, however, allows us to measure, and to resent, differences with people we think are (or should be) our peers, and this leads to deep and abiding envy and resentment that plagues life in the modern democracies.

THE ENVY ENGINE

Hyper-connection enables citizens to parade all of the worst aspects of an affluent culture—especially conspicuous consumerism—in front of each other in a game of perpetual one-upmanship. Americans, permanently connected and constantly performing, now showcase an idealized version of their lives to each other every day, inundating each other with pictures of vacations, cars, and other life achievements and trophies. Instead of building trust, we build enmity, and we do it while feasting on the envy of others. As with all of the sins of the modern era, I am a participant; I have shared my bourgeois tastes in everything from shampoo to watches on social media, and more than once I have posted a picture of myself in some exciting locale in order to share it both with friends and strangers. (Why do I do it? I don't know. Like everyone else, I have an ego and a social instinct. In an earlier era I probably would have been the suburban dad herding my guests indoors from my cookout to bore them all with a slide-show from my last vacation.)

As a thought experiment, imagine if during an earlier time Americans had spent their days taking tours of other people's homes. The results of such house tourism would have been socially disastrous. Those were days when being "rich" meant having air-conditioning, multiple televisions, reel-to-reel recordings, and other luxuries. Most people would have been shocked to see the difference between their evenings sweating in front of a small black and white television and their bosses relaxing in splendid, cool comfort watching their second or third television in bed. When I was growing up in a working-class home, I knew there were people who were far better off than we were, but I rarely found myself in a house or an apartment that was far nicer than my own. I admit that I am glad for it. The rich didn't live in my neighborhood and I had little idea of what their lives were like.

Now, we are in each other's homes all day. Or, more accurately, we are in the homes of our friends and neighbors all day, because the rich, mostly, are smart enough not to post their home improvement projects on Facebook. And even if they did, the living standards afforded by wealth are no longer as immediately obvious as they once were. The rest of us now have air conditioners, too, and two or three big television screens; the homes of the rich are no cooler or drier than ours, nor does their wealth buy them televisions that somehow have extra pixels only for people in the top tax brackets. Wealth now buys better food, better doctors, fatter portfolios, and extravagant personal services, few of which are paraded by the super-wealthy on social media.

And so we focus on smaller differences with those closer to us. Instead of being shocked by the glaring difference in living standards between the upper and middle classes that would have angered us in 1970, the working and middle classes are now busily measuring the differences between *themselves* because those smaller differences are readily accessible on social media. The drama of modern democratic society is being driven not by an unemployed auto worker who wants a private jet, but by the irritation of a middle-class family wondering why another middle-class family—especially if it's a family that looks different from their own or speaks a different language—has granite countertops while they make do with outdated linoleum.

Even if we do not bother with the latest update on our neighbors from Facebook, we can cruise real estate sites like Zillow and Trulia and monitor their home values (and ours). We can take a virtual tour of many of the houses near us any time we feel like it, evaluate the improvements our neighbors are making, and check the taxes they're paying. Many Americans are doing all of these things, to the point— again, like so much of what the internet makes available—where it is almost an addiction, as the *New York Times* reported in 2018:

> A couple of times a week, Nick Spencer checks the value of his four-bedroom house in Haddon Heights, N.J., on Zillow. He has no plans to move, describing the town, located about 10 miles from Philadelphia, as "Americana at its best," and his Cape Cod style home as "a labor of love." Yet there he is, clicking on Zillow

every few days to see what the house he bought for $399,900 in 2006 is now worth.

"It's entertainment," he said. "Like a hobby." The Zestimate has been a Zillow mainstay since the company started in 2006, drawing so many curious visitors that the site crashed within hours of its launch.[28]

As it turns out, these estimates aren't usually very accurate and can vary quickly, but none of that stops people from snooping on their neighbors. "It's conveying a truth that doesn't exist," one realtor told the *Times*. So why do we keep doing it? "Why do you read your horoscope?" the realtor answered.

In other words, modern American society has reached the point where we keep constant tabs on our neighbors and their standard of living as a form of leisure activity. (This has become so prevalent a behavior that it was affirmed as a social trend by the ultimate observer of American culture, the NBC television show *Saturday Night Live*, which ran a parody ad in early 2021 featuring people cruising Zillow and fantasizing about house-buying as a replacement for sex during the pandemic lockdowns.) The "Facebook envy" this produces makes it easier for us to conclude that democracy is broken and that our neighbors are happier than we are not because they are working harder or making better choices (or just experiencing a bit of luck), but because they are somehow shafting us and gaining an unfair advantage in life. Democracies can tolerate a lot of anger between the rich and poor, but when all of the classes between those two extremes—that is, the majority of citizens—turn on each other, civic life becomes far more unstable.

Television encourages this corrosive competitiveness and envy with what is often called the "HGTV effect," named after the "Home and Garden" cable network. This effect is the nagging jealousy and desire to upgrade our houses that comes from watching home-improvement shows. These are not self-help, home-handyman programs that explain how to replace the wax seal in a toilet. They are the chronicles of ordinary couples as they traipse around expensive homes and townhouses while arguing with designers and contractors about how many jets should be in the new whirlpool in the third bathroom. These programs, which make dream homes seem within easy reach, created a twenty-first-century boom in renovations and elevated the expectations of homebuyers.[29]

Back in the 1980s, viewers could watch a show such as *Lifestyles of the Rich and Famous* and take a once-a-week television tour of some actor's mansion while understanding that it was far away and unattainable. Now we can spend all day, every day, watching people like ourselves (artificially funded, of course, by the show's producers) trading in their dowdy homes—that is, the kind most of us live in—for showplaces that in the real world would be far out of their buying power. We know it's all fake, and yet the ordinariness of the people involved lures us to ask: "Why them, but not me?" This is a recipe for bottomless envy. As the scholar Helmut Schoenk once put it, "Overwhelming and astounding inequality, especially when it has an element of the unattainable, arouses far less envy than minimal inequality, which inevitably causes the envious to think: 'I might have been in his place.'"[30]

This preoccupation with other people's lives isn't healthy. As one study found, frequent Facebook users—especially those who use the site to check in on the relative status or happiness of others—end up plagued by feelings of envy and are more prone to depression.[31] This shouldn't be a surprise; if you're using social media to compare your life to others, and the "others" are going out of their way to make sure you think their lives are going flawlessly, you're going to end up feeling shortchanged. It is also unsurprising that a later study found that people who shut off Facebook, even for a month, reported a general improvement in their mood and happiness.[32]

Democracy requires good faith, good wishes for others, and a certain amount of stoicism and detachment about the smaller injustices of life. But resentment and its more durable and more toxic isotope, *ressentiment*, are now driving much of modern democratic politics, and nothing could be a better engine for producing that kind of itching envy, relative deprivation, class hostility, and constant disappointment than social media. The radical slogan in the 1960s was "kill your television," but the internet has turned out to be far more dangerous.

ONE CULTURE TO RULE THEM ALL

In late 2019, an editor at *The Atlantic*, Yoni Applebaum, tried to unravel the mystery of America's plunge into anger and civic disintegration. The drama around the 2020 election and the eventual storming of the U.S. Capitol were a year away, but Applebaum identified an important and more enduring trend than politics.

> What has caused such rancor? The stresses of a globalizing, postindustrial economy. Growing economic inequality. The hyperbolizing force of social media. Geographic sorting. The demagogic provocations of the president himself. As in *Murder on the Orient Express*, every suspect has had a hand in the crime.

> But the biggest driver might be demographic change. The United States is undergoing a transition perhaps no rich and stable democracy has ever experienced: Its historically dominant group is on its way to becoming a political minority—and its minority groups are asserting their co-equal rights and interests.[33]

The transition from the America of the mid-twentieth century to the America of the mid-twenty-first century is a story of great sweep and epic change. Applebaum is careful not to overplay comparisons to the Civil War period (although in a moment of inadvertent prophecy, he notes that "by the late 1850s, the threat of violence was so pervasive that members [of Congress] regularly entered the House armed.") The mobility of large populations means that every major country is going to face demographic challenges in the twenty-first century, but in the United States, the worries among the white, mostly Christian working class about being reduced to a cultural minority are becoming a reality, and to return to the medical metaphor I used earlier in this book, this is the moment when a hypochondriac gets the bad news that he or she really does have a terminal illness, and years of anxiety now seem completely justified.[34]

Social media has aggravated this process of inevitable change in important and dangerous ways. Most directly, it has created awareness of cultural change even in places relatively untouched by such changes. This is why people in conservative hamlets in New Hampshire or West Virginia think they're being overrun by immigrants and drag queens and left-wing Latina congresswomen—because increased immigration, or greater tolerance of sexual subcultures, or the election of New York's Alexandra Ocasio-Cortez is happening *somewhere*, and thus through the magic of the internet, it's happening *everywhere*. There are no pockets of culture, or competing cultures; there is now one culture, mediated through the internet and cable television, and we're all living in it.

Americans, in particular, are expressing this fear of a universalized culture in their voting behavior. Hyper-connection means that voting for one candidate in one district based on local issues is rapidly being overtaken by the sense among voters that all elections are now national elections. Every contest is affected by the behavior of candidates far away whose names, in an earlier time, would have been unknown to most voters. As David Shor wisely warned his fellow Democrats in 2020, the decline of local news and the rise of social media as a source of information means "people are consuming much more national news," and this "accelerates political polarization and decreases ticket splitting," meaning that voters are unwilling to defect from national coalitions in order to support a local candidate of a different party.

> This decline in ticket-splitting means that when people are voting on their local House candidate, they're increasingly doing that on the basis of the news they read about the national Democratic Party. And this creates a hard tradeoff: It's no longer true, in a way that might have been true 20 or 30 years ago, that someone in a safe seat can say whatever they want to energize the base without creating consequences in swing districts.[35]

Shor is obliquely referring to people like Ocasio-Cortez here, a first-term Democratic congresswoman whose use of social media increased her prominence, but also helped make her name a talking point for Republicans all over the country. (Shor points out, however, that this dynamic works in both directions: Republicans likewise lost some winnable seats in 2012 due to astonishingly ignorant and offensive statements made by a few midwestern GOP candidates about abortion in 2012.)[36]

Part of what's going on here has little to do with social media and everything to do with the interaction between connection and liberalism itself. A liberal culture tolerates diversity and offers cultural choices to its citizens, rather than stamping out nonconformity or minority challenges to the dominant ethos. This, in turn, means that people might well be tempted to indulge in those alternatives, even as they recognize that they are undoing the traditions and norms—or even just the cultural tastes and fashions—they claim to value. This leads to a special kind of resentment based in anger at oneself for participating in the culture while hating it at the same time.

This kind of cultural interaction, facilitated by capitalism and spread more rapidly by the ability of cable and the internet to overcome the limits of traditional broadcast radio and television, has been going on for at least thirty years. The *New Republic* magazine, for example, ran a controversial 1991 cover story that confronted the question of who was really behind the growing popularity of urban Black music. As overblown a controversy as it may seem now, the emergence of rap and hip-hop into the U.S. musical mainstream at the end of the 1980s was a culturally and racially charged issue, resulting in warning stickers on albums and complaints from American police departments about songs that glorified violence against cops, among other panicked reactions. The *New Republic* cover took aim at this anxiety—and the hypocrisy behind it—by depicting a blonde, fresh-faced, white, teenaged male in a fashionable rugby shirt wearing headphones. The headline? "The Real Face of Rap."[37]

The story, by critic David Samuels, captured an important reality about how Black music had become not a source of "cross-cultural understanding," but rather "a voyeurism and tolerance of racism in which black [*sic*] and white are both complicit." The larger point, however, was that two musical cultures were now melded into a single culture by the 1990s in an industrial product marketed to a dominant white society that had earlier taken pride in rejecting such music as unworthy additions to the national culture. The early stars of this ostensibly subversive form of culture soon became mainstream entertainment figures in their own right.[38] In later years, hip-hop even glorified rich white men in their lyrics, including regular references to a flashy, vulgar casino boss from Queens named Donald J. Trump, who, as president of the United States, refused to condemn white supremacists and offered encouragement to racist movements.[39]

This is just one example of the ongoing cultural ouroboros that the dominant white demographic in America has found threatening since the 1950s. In the twenty-first century, however, social media and unlimited bandwidth have accelerated these and other cultural conflicts beyond the capacity of the ordinary citizen to absorb them or even to comprehend them. Worse, people are more easily panicked by trends that may in reality only be artifacts of spending too much time in the virtual world at the expense of daily interactions with human beings. With the technology of social media, people can now take anecdotal experiences—or even secondhand accounts, legends, and rumors—and reach out all over the country to find others who will affirm that they, too, have seen these same things and feel the same way.[40] Political identities that were once constructed from life among those we know in places we live are now formed over huge distances among strangers whose bonds are formed mostly over things they loathe in common.

Some observers reject the role of technology in explaining the rise of illiberal populist movements and point instead to other factors, including the increasing social and educational gap between urban and rural populations.[41] But Damon Linker, reviewing these arguments, is correct when he notes that hyper-connection is what makes all of this conflict even possible, because it closes the distance between those populations in ways that were never possible before now.

> The sociological account is correct as far as it goes, but it fails to grasp the politically crucial way that social media networking interacts with the distinctive anger and frustration that prevails in economically struggling, sparsely populated regions of the country. Without that technological piece of the puzzle, it would have been much more difficult to conjure and sustain a

movement of right-wing populism capable of challenging institutions of the political establishment.[42]

The writer Pankaj Mishra makes a similar point, but on a global scale,
when he worries about how "individuals with very different pasts
find themselves herded by capitalism and technology into a common present," a proximity "rendered more claustrophobic by digital
communications, the improved capacity for envious and resentful
comparison, and the commonplace, and therefore compromised,
quest for individual distinction and singularity."[43] Never before have
so many groups who dislike each other, including city dwellers and
rural denizens, been able to know each other's views in such detail
and snipe at each other with such ease.

This urbanized and universalized culture pouring through our
screens, large and small, has helped drive American expectations to
ridiculous levels. A television show like *Friends*, with young people
living in impossibly expensive digs in New York, was understood
in the 1990s to be a fantasy. In 2020, however, a fortyish writer can
complain with dead seriousness in the pages of a prestigious magazine that the middle-class life portrayed in *The Simpsons*—a cartoon
that became a cultural institution—is now unattainable for the average American.[44] And there it is: How can we believe that democracy
has realized its promises for all Americans when none of us can do
even as well as a yellow-tinted animated character supporting a family of five in a four-bedroom house with only a high school diploma
and a job as a nuclear safety inspector?

When the citizens of a dominant culture come to believe that
the end is near for their way of life, they search for scapegoats—
especially if they suspect that they themselves have been the agents
of their own cultural decline. Unwilling to look in a mirror, unable to
confront their own habits and tastes, these citizens choose to believe

that the world they knew has been ripped away from them by stealth and subterfuge. The most insecure and frightened among them will also reach what they think is an obvious conclusion: that democracy, and especially liberal democracy, was the instrument of their culture's destruction, and so to find salvation and assure their own survival, they must therefore reject democracy.

Liberal democracy relies on resilient, civic-minded citizens who think themselves to be members of a tolerant and safe community. Sources and apps that goad us into emphasizing our aggression, encourage us to aggrandize ourselves at the expense of others, and reward us for displaying our most negative thoughts are destroying our ability to function as citizens, even without the slew of emotional problems created when our minds are spinning in a tornado of random sensory input all day.

And yet, at the end, I must admit to my own hypocrisy. I do not know that I have answers for any of this, but if I do, I will probably announce them first on Twitter or Facebook.

For those few answers I might have, let us turn to the last chapter.

Conclusion

Is There a Road Back?

No people will tamely surrender their liberties, nor can any be easily subdued, when knowledge is diffused and virtue is preserved. On the contrary, when people are universally ignorant, and debauched in their manners, they will sink under their own weight without the aid of foreign invaders.

—Samuel Adams, 1775

THE LIMITS OF WILLPOWER

In the last chapter of a book like this one—in which I have scolded my fellow citizens for their various shortcomings—I am supposed to offer solutions to the many problems I've identified.

I have bad news.

Liberal democracy depends on knowledge and virtue, and both of these are now in short supply among the citizens of the developed world. So many of the challenges we now think of as mortal dangers to democracy are, in reality, policy dilemmas we might solve if we were more disciplined in our willingness to learn and more civic in our public life. Around the world, citizens resolutely reject both paths to recovery. Not only do they seek out the streams of disinformation that make them dumber by the minute, but they also then levy demands on government that are contradictory beyond any possible resolution. After decades of international stability and rising living standards, the public wants what it wants, and they want it without any guff from their elected leaders about "costs" or "risks" or "trade-offs." Such a society is not a democracy. It is a troop of ill-tempered toddlers.

This stubborn childishness among modern democratic voters defeats both self-education and compromise. Too often, we assume that better information will improve the character of a democracy, despite the abundant evidence that the most educated and literate generations in American history are now less civic-minded than their under-educated progenitors. The problems of maturity and selfish-ness, however, are far more daunting for modern liberal democracies. In an age of cheap and abundant information, it is relatively easy to be a better-informed citizen. But the commitment to become such a citizen requires changes in even small habits that many people are unwilling to make, including reading a reputable newspaper and turning off the gladiatorial propaganda of social media, video post-ings, and cable shows. If making such changes means feeling less good about ourselves, or even thinking less often about ourselves, many of us will simply refuse to do it.

Democracy, in the end, is an act of will, a continual reaffirmation of faith in a system of government that enshrines and protects our rights and the rights of our fellow citizens. And there are limits to willpower in a world where everything has become easy and threats are notional and far away. Instead of acting like adults who have work to do and problems to solve, we now have the leisure to fight with each other over every imagined slight and every possible gain that might accrue to others at our expense. This is how every problem becomes a catastrophe and every policy debate becomes a fight to the death.

Consider, to take but one example, the problem of medical care in the United States. Health care is a human right, and Americans are justifiably angry about the escalating and often ruinous costs of that care. But these same citizens refuse to deliver clear mandates on what to do about these costs. In the elections of 2020, Americans sent two parties to Washington whose members are in almost exact numerical balance, but whose positions on this issue are fundamentally irreconcilable. In the first new Congress of 2021, American voters created an almost perfectly divided government, giving President Joe Biden and his Democratic Party the thinnest of majorities in the House and a literal 50-50 tie in the Senate. The Democrats hope to expand the 2010 Affordable Care Act (ACA), sometimes called "Obamacare" after it was made law under President Barack Obama. The Republicans, for their part, have gone to court, repeatedly, and to the cheers of their voters, to invalidate the entire ACA.

In one telling of this story, we might simply view this outcome as the messy problem called "democracy." The voters have chosen leaders and sent them to contend with each other over an important issue, just as the U.S. Constitution intended. They are using the instruments of elected government and the impartial courts to find a compromise solution. That's how it's supposed to work, after all— at least in theory. (As the conservative columnist George Will often tells audiences who complain to him about bickering in Congress: "If you don't like gridlock in Washington, your argument is with James Madison, not with me.")

This would be more reassuring if compromise were the objective—or if the public had any real notion of what it wanted. Like "Trevor" in Jonathan Metzl's study of white voters, some Americans will forego health care for themselves if that means denying it as well to anyone who doesn't look like them.[1] Other Americans want health care for everyone, but they do not want to be taxed for it. Yet others are happy to let the uninsured literally *die*, so long as they are not among those uninsured.[2] Some voters want to keep the ACA; others want to repeal Obamacare. And some voters want both to *keep* the ACA *and* to repeal Obamacare because a third of them do not know that the Affordable Care Act and "Obamacare" *are the same thing.*[3]

The state of medical care in the United States, especially in the wake of a pandemic that has killed well over a half-million Americans, is literally a matter of life and death, and yet to this day there is still widespread confusion about the most important reform of heath policy in over fifty years. Public opinion about the ACA, some ten years after its passage, is still divided, with approval hovering around 50 to 55 percent, and disapproval staying consistently near 40 percent. But when the public is asked what would happen if Obamacare were repealed, as political analysts Kyle Dropp and Brendan Nyhan found in 2017, "people were stumped," with some 45 percent of the respondents unaware that this would mean that the ACA would also be repealed.[4] This astonishing public ignorance has fueled extreme levels of partisanship, with people instructing their elected officials to fight unceasingly over something millions of them do not understand as a proxy for the hostility Americans feel toward anyone not in their own party.

There are any number of policies, foreign and domestic, where the aggressive ignorance and selfishness of the public effectively guarantees that the political classes will cut deals among themselves meant to placate the masses on the one hand, and to ensure their own political survival on the other. (Public ignorance about foreign affairs, especially, makes voter incoherence on domestic policy seem almost like a model of probity and judiciousness by comparison.)[5] Without a clear signal from the voters other than the mandate of Banfield's Italian villagers to "do what's good for me and my family and to hell with everyone else," politicians will do exactly as much as they need to do in order to maintain good relations with their donors, protect their own pet projects, and either coopt or overcome the angriest and most active voters.

I promised at the outset of this book that I would avoid too much in the way of moral hectoring, but I am not sure if there is a better alternative when it comes to the problems of selfishness and transactionalism. (I also refuse to let go of such hectoring, because I think social pressure is an invaluable tool for restoring boundaries and guardrails in our daily life.) I am not alone in the temptation to exhort Americans and others to be better citizens; the policy analyst Brink Lindsey, for example, has proposed that the road back from democratic ruin will rely on the adoption of important principles such as "emphasizing doing good over feeling good" and "making peace with the world before trying to change it."[6]

I could not agree more with these rules, and especially with what Lindsey, borrowing from the classic *Star Trek* series, calls the "Prime Directive" of civic life: "Treat all your fellow citizens, regardless of their political views, as your civic and political equals." The historian Alan Wolfe likewise makes an excellent case for a return to a kind of adult seriousness about politics. Wolfe is absolutely right—and it should not be a surprise that I agree with him—about the importance of something he calls "political maturity," an understanding of politics as bigger than the self, a commitment to something that extends beyond the confines of the village. This maturity, he argues, was one of the great achievements of American liberal democracy and was "the antidote not only to Joe McCarthy but to all the demagogues that had appeared throughout American history before him."[7]

But how do we convince citizens to act in such virtuous ways? How does one gain such maturity? Lindsey admits that he is only trying, at this point, to establish benchmarks for what a healthy political culture might look like. Wolfe has no answer other than to say that it can be done by thinking hard enough. "All it really takes for a person to become politically mature," he concludes, "is to want to do so. Making that commitment is the difficult part. Once it has been made, the path to political maturity opens up somewhat naturally."[8] But if we have learned anything in the opening decades of the twenty-first century, it is that people will think hard—or they will convince themselves that they have tried to do so—and still come up with incomprehensible and recklessly anti-democratic conclusions. It is no criticism of Professor Wolfe's admirable advice to note that if the citizens of modern democracies were the kind of people willing to engage in the kind of honest reflection that leads to a commitment to political maturity, we wouldn't be in the mess we're in now.

THE AUTHORITARIAN TEMPTATION

It's not that there aren't solutions to the various problems of democratic life, it's that so many of those solutions rely on inconstant and unpredictable human beings. Maybe, then, liberty really is the problem. Alone in a world full of bewildering options, human beings will prefer the reassurance of the pack and the safety of the herd rather than choose to grapple with the ambiguities and consequences of freedom. This, as Charles Krauthammer called it in 2017, is "the authoritarian temptation," a hunger "not for bread but for ethnic, tribal and nationalist validation."[9] Instead of fighting against our own decadence, the democracies might well scratch the bleeding itch of resentment by passing measures to empower the government to control the media, to limit the franchise, to abolish parties, even to restrict elections. We might dispense with the annoying guarantees of free speech and assembly and personal liberty, and instead impose new constitutions based on "the common good" instead of vaporous notions of individual rights. If the goal is order, equality, and tranquility, perhaps we should dispense with democracy itself.

Such measures have been tried in plenty of other places. There are even Americans and other democratic citizens—people who should know better—who believe in at least some of them. They have had enough of the secular freedom that allows other human beings to make choices they find dangerous, morally suspect, or even repulsive. Some of them want to replace liberty with the authority of a god; others with a committee of the learned; a few with powerful technocratic managers; still others with the voice of the mob.[10] We might even learn to like abandoning our liberties, as the Harvard Law School professor Adrian Vermeule assures us:

> Just authority in rulers can be exercised for the good of subjects, if necessary even against the subjects' own perceptions of what is best for them—perceptions that may change over time anyway, as the law teaches, habituates, and re-forms them. *Subjects will come to thank the ruler* whose legal strictures, possibly experienced at first as coercive, encourage subjects to form more authentic desires for the individual and common goods, better habits, and beliefs that better track and promote communal well-being. (emphasis added)[11]

This isn't even the pretense of democracy. It is a school of thought that represents a bold leap into the Middle Ages, and its proponents barely bother to disguise their intentions. As the law professor Randy Barnett said in a rejoinder to Vermeule's authoritarianism: "This wolf comes as a wolf."[12]

We have more choices, however, than autocracy or collapse. Citizens of the democracies are the authors of their own destinies, and what they have made they can also change and improve. Liberal democracy is not a set of arrangements frozen in amber, pretty to look at but untouchable and unchangeable. Some problems can be remedied with policy fixes. Deeper crises require structural changes, such as amendments to a basic law or constitution.

Any solution of any size, however, must rely on a human commitment to freedom. We cannot ask machines or algorithms—to whom we have already delegated too much authority—to make our choices for us or solve our problems. Nor can we simply pass rafts of laws demanding that we do the things that we should do anyway. Indeed, if we must be told under penalty of law that we must be better citizens, then we have already failed. Laws are important codifications of norms. They have many roles and functions. They can guide us in our communal endeavors, they can protect us from each other (and from the government), they can instruct us in specific duties as citizens, and they can deter us from doing wrong and punish us if we transgress. They are indispensable if we are going to live with each other. But laws, by their existence, cannot make us *believe* in their principles if they were passed without such belief in the first place.

If we treat democracy solely as a transactional relationship, a "social contract" in the very narrowest sense, then we are already lost. Marriage, for example, is a contractual relationship. It carries certain obligations imposed by the state once two people enter into an agreement to be married. The state can pass laws to recognize the privileges and property rights of marital relationships, and it can force us to provide money for the care of our children. But laws about marriage cannot make us into good husbands and wives or loving parents. If we must pass laws requiring us to give our spouses a kind word now and then, or to be supportive and share our mate's burdens and joys as we would our own, then the institution of marriage means nothing. A relationship solely governed by such laws is not a "marriage," and a state thickly forested with similar regulations is not a society so much as it is a carefully supervised and legally patrolled adult version of a kindergarten.[13] As Samuel Johnson wisely put it: "How small, of all that human hearts endure, that part which laws or kings can cause or cure."

THREE MODEST PROPOSALS

As much as my instincts lie with the path of moral hectoring, I will offer here three very brief recommendations in areas where the United States and the other democracies should think about changes that go behind mere policy choices such as hiking tax rates on the richest among us (which is a good idea) or trying to impose government control over the internet and social media (a very bad idea). I could write about the redistribution of income or the restructuring of social media, but these are subjects better covered by others with more expertise and in more depth than I can offer here. And my main worry, in any event, is not in the details of such legislation, but that such measures, if enacted rashly, are unlikely to succeed, or even worse, they might only succeed in the short term as some sort of punitive reflex enacted by a temporary majority while leaving intact the social dysfunction at the core of our democratic decline.

My recommendations here are related to political, military, and structural changes in modern liberal democracy. One is to make political parties stronger. Another is to reform both the culture and obligations of military service. The last is to think about how to enable representative institutions of the past to better handle the additional demands of larger and more diverse societies. I am choosing these not because they are the most important or the most far-reaching possibilities, but because I think they are attainable. They would have significant effects for relatively modest efforts. I offer them as suggestions for future discussion—and, mostly, for consideration only after we have thought about how to approach such remedies as better and more virtuous citizens.

1. The Party Should Decide

To extol the importance of political parties in the early twenty-first seems counterintuitive to the point of lunacy. Political parties fall into the category of things "we all know" are broken. Their dysfunction, their capture as vehicles for political charlatans, their blind commitment to winning at all costs—all of these are how we got here, aren't they? Ironically, Americans have for years thought of parties as too strong, particularly when it comes to choosing presidential candidates.[14] Would that it were true.

For example, the 2020 Democratic Party primaries were, as Jonathan Rauch and Ray La Raja described them, "a spectacle that would have struck earlier generations as ludicrous," because the Democrats had "decided to let small donors and opinion polls determine who deserved the precious national exposure of the debate stage." The Democrats should have learned from the disaster of the 2016 Republican primaries, "a 17-candidate circus," in which the GOP

> stood by helplessly as it was hijacked by an unstable reality-TV star who was not, by any meaningful standard, a Republican. The Democrats in 2016 faced their own insurgency, by a candidate who was not, by any meaningful standard, a Democrat. And yet, after the election, the Democrats changed their rules to reduce the power of the party establishment. . . . Then, as the 2020 race began, the party deferred to measures of popular sentiment to determine who should make the cut for the debates, all but ensuring runs by publicity-hungry outsiders.[15]

After this early and chaotic casting call, the Democrats finally swerved toward an establishment candidate. Joe Biden was buoyed by a surge of African American support, but also by the growing unease among Democrats that anyone other than Biden—who served as Obama's vice president and was a known quantity to his party and the American people—might actually lose to Donald Trump.[16]

The problem for both American parties is one that plagues party organization in other nations: political parties are no longer "parties" so much as they are merely vessels or brands for political entrepreneurs and interest groups. Americans, in particular, have come to think of parties not as private associations of like-minded citizens who believe in similar things, but as public utilities, something no one owns and anyone can use at will. The idea that a "party" is an entity owned and funded by a free association of citizens—one that can decide who is allowed to join, what its core tenets are, and who may run under its banner—is alien to Americans in the two-party system and, to judge from outcomes in other nations, a concept many democratic citizens find difficult to comprehend.

Indeed, I am struck when teaching and giving public lectures by how many Americans believe that parties are actually some sort of constitutional requirement, or that these organizations have some codified existence in the law. In fairness to the voters, some of these views are understandable given the dominance and longevity of established American political parties (and the effective barriers to entry for new parties in the U.S. and many other countries). But it is unhealthy when voters regard parties merely as the equivalent of battleships whose goal is to win brute-force turnout contests. Parties, when they exercise control over the candidates and platforms, are safeguards against elections devolving into temporary coalitions of angry citizens who only stick together long enough to defeat some other temporary coalition of angry citizens before breaking apart again.

Parties should return to being organizations that are welcoming to all comers but remain grounded in identifiable principles. (The U.S. Republican Party bottomed out in this regard in 2020 when it did not even bother to create a platform, and instead affirmed that whatever Donald Trump wanted constituted the party program.) Parties can and should remind voters that they are not just names or letters next to a name; they are organizations that require at least a general adherence to common positions and that will, on occasion, protect the meaning of that party from the shifting opinion of the majority. In some cases, they might deny a place on their stage or their funding to a candidate rather than allow their name to be used as a flag of convenience.

Perhaps I feel this particular issue more keenly as a former Republican. The GOP that I joined in 1979, and on whose bench I sat as a U.S. Senate aide to a moderate Republican (the late John Heinz of Pennsylvania) in 1990 and 1991, bears almost no resemblance to the party I left after the ascent of Donald Trump. But all parties are now under pressure merely to be megaphones for the most vocal activists within them, leaving them vulnerable not only to celebrity takeovers but to platforms—if they even bother to write any—that are meaningless. Parties once meant something. They can mean something again.

2. Military Service and the Culture of Spartanism

I have spent over twenty-five years in the service of the United States, most of it teaching military officers at the Naval War College, a graduate school where civilians and the professional military work side by side to enhance both U.S. national security and international peace. I am proud of this work and the opportunity it has given me both to observe and, I hope, strengthen the American civil-military relationship.

The stability of American civilian control over one of the most powerful militaries in the history of the planet is, to me, something of a miracle. The civil-military relationship in the United States has remained a triumph of balancing a first-rate and powerful military with the norms of an open and democratic society, and the U.S. military today is still one of the most trusted institutions in American society. The situation in the United States is one of the few exceptions in which an immensely powerful state has managed for centuries to keep armed forces that are a danger only to its enemies.

Unfortunately, changes over the past thirty years have endangered this exemplary relationship. While Donald Trump engaged in egregious attempts to politicize the U.S. military (especially once he was turned out of office), the reality is that American civil-military culture has been drifting away from the ideal of a nation of citizen-soldiers for decades. The American public, now accustomed to a very small but highly potent force of volunteers, is creating a privileged class of Spartans who agree to conduct the nation's tough assignments overseas in return for a privileged place in society. This is corrosive to a liberal democracy not only because it threatens the civil-military balance, but because it elevates martial virtues over democratic values.

There are many manifestations of this social deference to the military, from ritual incantations of "thank you for your service," to special discounts on even ordinary goods for veterans, to license plates that advertise which war the driver fought in and what medals were awarded. This is a public culture of militarization that approaches the old Soviet Union, in which veterans of the Great Patriotic War were seated first at restaurants and grandfathers wore their medals on their civilian clothes while doing their daily activities. It is also a change in public norms about military service that was unthinkable just a few generations ago. (My father's best friend, for example, won the Silver Star for a harrowing act of courage in Europe in World War II, and few people beyond his closest friends and family knew about it until it was displayed at his funeral thirty-five years later.)

This new Spartanism has multiple deforming effects not only on foreign policy but on democracy itself. For one thing, it allows civilians who have never served and never been touched by a military conflict to stake their complaints about democracy at large on cheap slogans about "forever wars" without ever experiencing any of the sacrifices and deprivations that actual wars levy on society. This reduces debates about "war" to a kind of political kabuki in which people who have never been in danger even of being mildly inconvenienced seek to cloak themselves in either militaristic patriotism or showy pacifism. The people who serve, meanwhile, become a source of political power, a voting bloc that has lived apart from society for too long because of too many deployments. This leads military personnel to become convinced of their own status both as superior to civilian society (which is always a risk with every military) and as victims, taken advantage of by those same weak civilians.[17]

As is almost always the case when there are troubles in democratic civil-military relations, the civilians are the source of the problem. Most Americans are unwilling to serve in the military—and increasingly, younger people are too unhealthy to induct even if they wanted to join—but this has not stopped American voters from supporting the repeated deployment and use of military force.[18] Shamefully, this has not led to paying these warriors more, or improving the services they should be offered as veterans; those things are hard, while rote incantations of gratitude are easy.

This imbalance in the civil-military relationship in turn leads to military excursions that are judged on the metrics of operational excellence valued by the military itself but are detached from any kind of strategic evaluation of success. When the civilians outsource security to volunteers, the military will report back about its own effectiveness, including things like efficiency and costs, enemy targets destroyed, the safety and security of U.S. and Allied personnel, and so on. This looks like winning, because the result is an ongoing situation characterized by highly professional military performance and low threats to U.S. citizens. Unfortunately, it is also how missions and deployments can go on for years with the U.S. armed forces essentially acting as an overseas constabulary force while hardly anyone asks, as U.S. Army Lt. General Douglas Lute did about Afghanistan in 2015 after years of engagements: "What are we trying to do here?"[19]

The draft is not an answer, but America in particular needs something in between a draft and the make-believe programs of civilian "national service" that too often are little more than paid internships. One option might be a "summer of service," in which youths spend perhaps six weeks in uniform and learn basic military skills—from making a bed to firing a weapon—and then return to society. Some might want to stay; others will find a way to opt out, as they always do. But there is no longer any common experience related to national defense, and the Spartanism that has come from volunteers fighting overseas engagements is not only unsustainable, it is planting dangerous seeds in a democracy that increasingly sees "citizens" and "soldiers" as two distinct classes of people.

3. Constitutional Reform

As an American, I am loath to amend a constitution that has survived over 240 years with only twenty-seven amendments—some of which, such as the Bill of Rights, are essential, and others, such as Prohibition, were stupid ideas in the first place. But the American system of government, as David Frum wrote in 2019, is now "ineffective and crisis-prone."

The point of elections is to produce effective governments generally regarded as legitimate by most citizens. Over the past two decades, the U.S. system of government has failed that test again and again. Elections now systematically disfavor voting majorities. From 1892 through 1996, the person who won the most votes became president, every time. In 2000, the U.S. got its first minority-rule president since the aftermath of the Civil War. That outcome was seen as a freak at the time. Four elections later, it happened again.... It should not take the largest voter turnout in U.S. history to guarantee that a president rejected by the majority of the American people actually stops being president.[20]

Trump, of course, was finally driven from office, but not before a mob at his command tried to overrun the Capitol and kill both the Speaker of the House and the vice president of the United States. Literally hours after that attack was repulsed, members of Trump's own party tried to overrule the Electoral College anyway on the floor of the House and Senate.

The American nation has been sorted into various camps—urban and rural, northern and southern, educated and uneducated —that are now so polarized that they represent a structural challenge to U.S. democracy. Despite the diversity of the American electorate, there is no leavening effect from this diverseness because voters have repelled each other into physically and politically distant enclaves, ensuring that people who hate each other can, in every way, avoid associating with each other.

Unfortunately, this structural problem, when combined with the authoritarian experience of the Trump years, has led to proposals that range from intemperate to harebrained.[21] Some of these include functionally obliterating American federalism and reverting to pure majoritarianism, compacts among states to thwart the constitutional mechanism of voting, computer-drawing of electoral districts, and schemes of requirements for political candidates (such as examination by boards of psychiatrists) that are unconstitutional at best and dangerous at worst.

I will not here pick and choose among these ideas, but will instead argue that it is time for citizens of good will to take up the responsibility of electoral and constitutional reform while facing down the most extreme elements to their right and left. The U.S. House, for example, has not increased in size since 1913. Such an increase is long overdue, would increase communication and accessibility between the voters and their elected representatives, and is easily within the power of a consensus of American citizens.[22] Likewise, there is nothing magical about fifty states. Changing this number would have immense partisan implications in the short term, but the District of Columbia and Puerto Rico could be added not only in the name of just representation but also to balance the problem that small populations on millions of sparsely populated acres of land in Vermont and Wyoming have two senators while nearly 700,000 Washingtonians have none.[23] States, if their citizens demand it, can redraw districts for representation that do not look like a messy plate of pasta or an experiment in abstract art. Here again, the problem is willpower; someone will win and someone will lose in all of these proposals, and the one thing democratic citizens no longer seem able to tolerate is losing, no matter how small the issue or how large the gain to be realized later.

I will not presume to advise America's sister democracies, particularly those with parliamentary systems, on how best to cope with increased demands for participation. I will only suggest that, as a principle, "more democracy" is not always the right answer. Instead, I will follow the advice of the founders of my own nation and suggest that for America, as well as for other nations, change should mean more participation—but by informed voters through institutions that are not constantly and immediately at the mercy of a majority. (This means, at the least, measures and processes that require more deliberation and thought than a one-shot national plebiscite of the sort that created Britain's shambolic exit from the European Union.)

Measures to increase informed participation and structural reform are not populism. They are the very opposite of populism, in that they require intelligent and considered constitutional design by political elites, the limiting of options by those same elites to goals that are achievable (and if they turn out to be mistakes, reversible) before turning to the masses for a vote, and an understanding before undertaking the course of reform that the object is greater unity and inclusion and not electoral revenge. Above all, changing our basic laws should always be done with the understanding that the authoritarian temptation and the populist temptation are more alike, and always closer to us, than we realize.

THREE NIGHTMARES

Rather than continue to provide moral exhortations to civic excellence, I will close by presenting three alternatives that might face the democracies should we in the United States and the other republics fail to defend our own systems of government. Images of goodness and prosperity and virtue can only take us so far, and so I admit that I will try to move you, here at the end, with fear, by presenting three nightmares that could emerge as our alternative futures. Each of these is from the imagination, and yet each of them is already a part of our reality in the twenty-first century more than we might want to admit.

"Proles and Animals Are Free"

Readers of George Orwell's *1984* always envision themselves as Winston Smith, the brave but tormented bureaucrat who, for just one idyllic moment before he is broken, dares to live his own life, love the woman of his choice, and think his own thoughts, before he is ground into nothingness by Big Brother. This is very much a compliment to ourselves. Very few of us are in danger of becoming Winston, because to do so requires character, nobility, and introspection. Modern society in the wake of a democratic collapse will not be made of sorrowful Smiths laboring under the yoke of a totalitarian state. Rather, we will become like the other denizens of Orwell's Oceania: the proles.

Orwell derived the name of the "proles" from the *lumpenproletariat*. In the modern usage of the term, derived originally from the writings of Karl Marx, this is the lowest order of society, the group that is merely a mindless rabble and not even developed enough economically or socially to be members of the working classes above them. They care nothing for politics; for that matter, they care about almost nothing at all. In *1984*, the regime largely ignores them. They are no threat to anyone in power because they are incapable of forming the kinds of thoughts that would allow them to rise to the level of awareness that would make them dangerous.

Winston Smith envies the proles because, as the underclass, they are allowed to mill about like animals, unmolested by the authorities. "Left to themselves," Orwell wrote, "like cattle turned loose upon the plains of Argentina, they had reverted to a style of life that appeared to be natural to them, a sort of ancestral pattern."

Heavy physical work, the care of home and children, petty quarrels with neighbors, films, football, beer, and, above all, gambling filled up the horizon of their minds. To keep them in control was not difficult.

All that was required of them was a primitive patriotism which could be appealed to whenever it was necessary to make them accept longer working-hours or shorter rations. And even when they became discontented, as they sometimes did, their discontent led nowhere, because being without general ideas, they could only focus it on petty specific grievances. The larger evils invariably escaped their notice.

Even the civil police interfered with them very little. There was a vast amount of criminality in London, a whole world-within-a-world of thieves, bandits, prostitutes, drug-peddlers, and racketeers of every description; but since it all happened among the proles themselves, it was of no importance.

If you live in the United States, or in any of the other advanced democracies, the idea that this could one day be a depiction of a majority of your fellow citizens might unsettle you, and well it should. It is a stratum of society that existed when Orwell wrote the book in the late 1940s, and it is a scene easily found anywhere, from the crowded cities to the sparse towns to the quiet countryside, in any country on Earth today. In *1984*, Smith sees the proles as the only hope for the future because they outnumber the tiny number of elites who control the terrifying Inner Party. But the Party itself knows better: the proles are harmless. They are not *above* suspicion, Orwell noted, they are *beneath* suspicion. Their numbers and their crowded impoverishment are their weakness, not their strength. They are, in the French writer Honore de Balzac's cold formulation, "the insignificant folk" who are not worth crushing because they already "lie too flat beneath the foot."[24] Or as the Party slogan in *1984* put it: "Proles and animals are free."

You may find it odd, in a book that began with a nod to Aldous Huxley's *Brave New World* and the repeated invocation of Neil Postman's warning about "amusing ourselves to death," that I do not overly worry about Huxley's world of sex and drugs and plenty as our future. That is because I think we live in that world now. It is already here. We have already failed to push back against Huxley's world by becoming a collection of democracies whose politics are decadent, hedonistic, and, most of all, *unserious*. As Postman said with obvious exasperation back in 1985, we cannot take up arms against a sea of troubles if we do not feel real anguish: "Who is prepared to take up arms against a sea of amusements? To whom do we complain, and when, and in what tone of voice, when serious discourse dissolves into giggles?"[25]

But if we continue on this path, we will continue the slide that has already begun from a sated middle class to a lumpen-bourgeoisie, and over successive generations we will cascade through a free fall of class divisions to becoming the proles, governed not by an Inner Party but by a combination of physical distance from others, arguments among ourselves, and cheap but plentiful amusements. The future will not be one of noble but defeated Winston Smiths having their teeth pulled from their mouths, but of a numb, quarrelsome swarm of drones kept in line with calories, intoxicants, pornography, and two hundred sports channels. We will not have time to rebel, and even should we wish to do so, we will not be able to move our bulky bodies off our couches and away from our televisions. We will truly be a "silent majority," in that we will be politically harmless to anyone who rules over us. Democracy will continue to be the name of our system of government, but it will be remembered only by those who practice it among themselves while living far from the proles and their bars and casinos and sports arenas.

This is already happening. The distance between the governors and the governed has become a gulf not just because of widening disparities in education and income, but because poverty and indolence are no longer as unbearable, at least in the advanced democracies, as they once were. Marx counted on the misery of working-class life and the alienation of industrial work to generate a revolutionary consciousness. But what happens if life isn't miserable *enough*? What if borderline poverty is merely tolerable, and even has real pleasures and distractions in it? The Inner Party of *1984* doesn't fear the proles, and modern authoritarians may not have to fear their twenty-first-century equivalent, either.

Perhaps we will not descend into this kind of anomic, brainless poverty. Perhaps the future will look something like the present, but with a firm, if tacit, compact between the rulers and the ruled to keep the lights on, the cars gassed up, the Wi-Fi strong, and the televisions bright, all in exchange for obedience and comity. A technologically advanced, consumer-driven imitation of democracy—again, we already see this happening today—can last quite a long time if the governing elites keep delivering the goods. This is not *Brave New World* with massage chairs and helicopter rides to amusement parks, nor is it the terrifying squalor of *1984*. It is instead a society based on a principle of "Good Enough."

"Just Get It for Them"

In 1975, Hollywood foreshadowed the world of "good enough" when the writers Lorenzo Sempel and David Rayfield adapted a novel about a low-level CIA analyst who stumbles onto an unauthorized operation within the CIA to invade the Middle East and take its oil. The film, *Three Days of the Condor*, featured Robert Redford as Joe Turner, the nerdy bookworm analyst who becomes a hunted whistleblower. (Redford even wore glasses for the role to tone down his too-perfect looks.) Veteran actor Cliff Robertson played Higgins, an honest and dedicated CIA official trying to help Turner unravel the plot.

The film's relevance to our time is in its very last scene. *Three Days of the Condor* is a violent political thriller, but at the end, the film turns away from its spy chase plot and delivers a chilling warning about the future of democracy in an age of decadence and citizen indifference.

After the CIA finds and kills the rogue executive at the center of the mad scheme, Higgins tells Turner that it's time to come in from the cold. He approaches Turner on a busy Manhattan street with a reassuring smile and a car door left open. Turner, knowing that the Agency has no choice but to eliminate him as an embarrassing loose end, instead tells Higgins he has a gun, and that they should take a walk and have a conversation.

With Turner's pistol in his back as they stroll, Higgins admits that the CIA and the U.S. government had no idea what was going on, and that the plan to invade was a war game that got out of control. Turner presses for more.

"Suppose I hadn't stumbled on their plan? Say nobody had?"

"Different ballgame," Higgins says with a shrug. "Fact is, there was nothing wrong with the plan." He turns to face the stunned Turner. "Oh, the plan was all right. The plan would've worked."

Turner is appalled at this unremarkable, poorly-dressed civil servant, a man with a bad haircut who works in drywalled offices and brightly lit cubicles, blithely admitting that a plan to subjugate millions of people might have worked. "Boy, what is it with you people? You think not getting caught in a lie is the same thing as telling the truth?"

Higgins then coldly explains the facts of life to Turner. "No. It's simple economics. Today it's oil, right? In ten or fifteen years? Food. Plutonium. And maybe even sooner. Now what do you think the people are going to want us to do then?"

Turner, indignant, says, "Ask them."

Higgins narrows his eyes at Turner's naïve self-righteousness. "Not *now*. *Then*. Ask them when they're running out. Ask them when there's no heat and they're cold. Ask them when their engines stop. Ask them when people who have never known hunger start going hungry. Want to know something? They won't *want* us to ask them. They'll just want us to *get* it for them."

In a classic 1970s trope, Turner then reveals that he's given everything he knows to the *New York Times*. Journalists in this period were still, to some Americans, heroes after the Watergate story forced Richard Nixon to resign. (Redford even played reporter Bob Woodward in *All the President's Men* the same year he starred in *Condor*.) But director Sidney Lumet wasn't going to allow even that much light at the end of *Three Days of the Condor*. As Turner walks away to lose himself in a busy New York holiday shopping crowd, Higgins calls out to him. "Hey Turner," he says. "How do you know they'll print it?"

"They'll print it," Turner answers, but with a new wariness in his eyes. Higgins gets the last line of the movie, as he allows himself a slight smirk. "*How do you know?*" The viewer is left to conclude that Higgins and the CIA will be just fine, but Joe Turner will forever be on the run.

This is the future I personally fear more than any other for the United States and other postindustrial democracies. It is one that is already being created around us. The end of democracy will come not with mobs burning the Capitol, or food riots, or juntas of national salvation, or demagogues leading the peasants to burn the castles of the rich. It will end, instead, with highly educated, technically proficient, otherwise decent men and women with families and children and mortgages and car payments who will decide that uninformed, spoiled, irascible voters simply can't produce coherent demands other than "just get it for us," and they will act accordingly.

This will not happen after a revolution, or a disaster, or a landmark court case—or even after a pandemic. It will happen as part of a million small decisions made every day without the input of the common citizen, as the fulfillment of an unspoken agreement between technocratic elites and the working and middle classes. Rights and participation and transparency will be shelved—as they too often were during the Cold War in the name of national security—as luxuries simply too expensive to indulge. The population will not be impoverished proles, but reasonably educated, comfortable people who have decided that "democracy" means a certain standard of living.

The proles, however, will still make their appearance in this future, living far from these working and middle classes, and visible from the gleaming spires of the cities if one looks far enough out past the rings of the suburbs. The elites and the middle classes will know that the regular circus of elections are meaningless; the working classes and especially the proles will view them as entertainment. Life will go on, but the ideals of a liberal democracy will have been long discarded in the name of comfort and expediency. The bright future of the twenty-first century will end up as merely a more technologically advanced version of a dystopian world we could already imagine in the 1970s.

We are perilously close to this now, by our own hand, with an elite that has mastered the art of getting things for billions of people who will have long ago ceased to care very much, if at all, where those things come from, and about how the power of the state is exercised in their name.[26] The technocrats and other elites will rule not because they have seized power, but because the bored and dissipated citizens of the democracies, seeing no real threats around them other than to their own comfort and living standards, will hand them power. The elites will rule not by deception, but by default.

The Glory That Was Greece

Is there any hope in all this? Perhaps we can find answers in antiquity, but even the ancient world hides one more nightmare in its honored past.

Americans and other democratic citizens (particularly in Western Europe) have long imagined themselves as the heirs to the Athens of Pericles, the great Greek democracy of the fifth century BCE.[27] Athens was a magnificent city-state, as rich in culture as it was in cash. It was the acknowledged master of the seas, a formidable military power whose alliance with other Greeks defeated the gigantic Persian Empire and saved what would come to be called Western Civilization. The United States and its allies saw in the twentieth-century Cold War with the Soviet Union an irresistible parallel with the long Athenian war against the other military superpower of ancient Greece, the slave-owning dictatorship of Sparta. Like the Cold War, this was a clash of competing systems. Athens, the leader of a democratic (at first) alliance, fought by sea and instituted democracies among its defeated foes; Sparta, the dogmatic and fading oligarchy, fought by land and likewise imposed dictatorships similar to its own at the point of its spears.

In the first year of this Peloponnesian War with Sparta, Pericles rallied the dispirited citizens of the city with an oration for the war dead that has stood for centuries as one of the great defenses of democracy.

Our constitution does not copy the laws of neighboring states; we are in fact a pattern to others rather than imitators ourselves. Its administration favors the many instead of the few; this is why it is called a democracy.

If we look to the laws, they afford equal justice to all in their private differences; if to social standing, advancement in public life falls to reputation for capacity, class considerations not being allowed to interfere with merit; nor again does poverty bar the way, if a man is able to serve the state, he is not hindered by the obscurity of his condition.

The freedom which we enjoy in our government extends also to our ordinary life. There, far from exercising a jealous surveillance over each other, we do not feel called upon to be angry with our neighbor for doing what he likes, or even to indulge in those injurious looks which cannot fail to be offensive, although they inflict no real harm.

But all this ease in our private relations does not make us lawless as citizens.

Against this fear is our chief safeguard, teaching us to obey the magistrates and the laws, particularly such as regard the protection of the injured, whether they are actually on the statute book, or belong to that code which, although unwritten, yet cannot be broken without acknowledged disgrace.

As he stood over those killed by the enemy, Pericles called on his fellow citizens to hold fast to their love of the city, and to remember that Athenian glory was a product of cultural self-confidence as well as physical courage. He reminded them that Athens was an open, bold, and questing society that embraced all visitors—even those who might later pose risks to the city itself.

We throw open our city to the world, and never by alien acts exclude foreigners from any opportunity of learning or observing, although the eyes of an enemy may occasionally profit by our liberality; trusting less in system and policy than to the native spirit of our citizens; while in education, where our rivals from their very cradles by a painful discipline seek after manliness, at Athens we live exactly as we please, and yet are just as ready to encounter every legitimate danger.

As he readied his farewell to the crowd, Pericles demanded that his fellow citizens remember that honor, above all, binds the generations to each other, living or dead. "For it is only the love of honor that never grows old; and honor it is, not gain, as some would have it, that rejoices the heart of age and helplessness."[28]

Can we regain this Athenian sense of honor, civic pride, love of community, self-sacrifice, and deep confidence in our way of life? Or are these virtues now to be lost in a dark sea of grievance, resentment, and envy?

I want to be optimistic. I believe in the strength and resilience of liberal democracy because I have seen it survive and triumph over estimable and dedicated enemies around the world. I do not believe that other human beings crave slavery, even if they are sometimes led to it by their own fears. I believe that liberal democracy—the system of open, tolerant, and cooperative self-rule, is, in every sense of the word, a *natural* preference of human beings. This is perhaps just an overly long way of saying that I, in my own small way, agree with Thomas Jefferson that men and women are endowed with unalienable rights—and that they know that they are endowed with these rights, no matter what arguments states or sovereigns might make against them.

Nor do I fear the overthrow of my democracy or any other by foreign conquest. Jefferson was right and so was Abraham Lincoln. "All the armies of Europe, Asia and Africa combined," Lincoln said in an 1838 speech that echoed the boasts of Pericles, "could not by force, take a drink from the Ohio, or make a track on the Blue Ridge, in a trial of a thousand years." Lincoln knew that if America were to end, its demise—like that of every democracy—would originate from a sickness within itself. "It cannot come from abroad," Lincoln warned. "If destruction be our lot, we must ourselves be its author and finisher. As a nation of freemen, we must live through all time, or die by suicide."[29]

This is the warning we should take as well from Athens. If we are to admire the spirit of Pericles's oration, we must also think about how Athens in the end betrayed its own ideals and became the agent of its own collapse. After fighting Sparta for over two decades, the Athenians became as cruel an empire as the Spartans they opposed. Many of the best Athenian military forces died in misbegotten attempts at foreign conquests. The city itself was betrayed by one of its most prominent leaders, who defected to the enemy. The Athenians and their navy were finally defeated not in a majestic sea battle, but in a humiliating miscalculation where most of their ships were captured or destroyed on a beach far from home. With the city facing starvation, Athens surrendered; its great defensive walls were torn down and its democracy was dissolved.

Pericles, however, did not live to see the defeat of the city. He did not see Athens become more savage and violent and less democratic. He had already died in the second year of the war—from a plague.

NOTES

Introduction

1. See Richard Wike, Katie Simmons, Bruce Stokes, and Janell Fetterolf, *Globally, Broad Support for Representative and Direct Democracy: But Many Also Endorse Nondemocratic Alternatives*, Pew Research Center, October 2017, https://www.pewresearch.org/global/2017/10/16/globally-broad-support-for-representative-and-direct-democracy/.
2. Larry Diamond, Lee Drutman, Tod Lindber, Nathan Kalmoe, and Lilliana Mason, "Americans Increasingly Believe Violence is Justified If the Other Side Wins," *Politico*, October 10, 2020, https://www.politico.com/news/magazine/2020/10/01/political-violence-424157.
3. Roberto Stefan Foa and Yascha Mounk, "The Democratic Disconnect," *Journal of Democracy* 27(3), July 2016, 7.
4. Dalibor Rohac, "The Problems with Populism Go Well beyond Donald Trump," *The Dispatch*, February 2, 2021.
5. Ian Bremmer, *Us vs. Them: The Failure of Globalism* (New York: Portfolio, 2018), 2.
6. Anne Applebaum, *The Twilight of Democracy* (New York: Doubleday, 2020), 19–21.
7. "Transcript and Analysis: President Trump's Inaugural Address, Annotated," National Public Radio, January 20, 2017, https://www.npr.org/2017/01/20/510629447/watch-live-president-trumps-inauguration-ceremony.
8. "Viktor Orbán's Full Speech for the Beginning of His Fourth Mandate," *Visegrád Post*, May 12, 2018, https://visegradpost.com/en/2018/05/12/viktor-orbans-full-speech-for-the-beginning-of-his-fourth-mandate/.

9. Dom Phillips, "Bolsonaro Declares Brazil's 'Liberation from Socialism' as He Is Sworn In," *The Guardian*, January 1, 2019, https://www.theguardian.com/world/2019/jan/01/jair-bolsonaro-inauguration-brazil-president.

10. For the panel as it appeared in 1971, see Jamie Weinman, "Earth Day Greetings from a Possum and a Porcupine," *Macleans*, April 22, 2009, https://www.macleans.ca/uncategorized/earth-day-greetings-from-a-possum-and-a-porcupine/.

11. Peggy Noonan, "Burn the Republican Party Down?" *Wall Street Journal*, July 30, 2020.

12. Peggy Noonan, "Bring the Insurrectionists to Justice," *Wall Street Journal*, January 7, 2021.

13. Annie Grayer, "Capitol Police Investigating after Congressman Discovered Carrying a Gun When Attempting to Go on the House Floor," CNN, January 22, 2021, https://www.cnn.com/2021/01/22/politics/congressman-gun-capitol/index.html.

14. See George Packer, "Trump's Legacy of Lies," *The Atlantic*, January/February 2021.

15. For an entertaining compendium of baffled responses two years after the vote, see Henry Mance, "One Thing about Brexit Is Certain—No One Knows Anything," *Financial Times*, December 20, 2018, https://www.ft.com/content/b2064c74-0460-11e9-99df-6183d3002ee1.

16. Quoted in David Frum, "The Great Realignment of Britain," *The Atlantic*, March 14, 2019.

17. Pamela Falk, "News Got You Down? Fear Not, Harvard Professor Tells U.N., The World Really Is Getting Better," CBS News, May 22, 2019, https://www.cbsnews.com/news/harvard-steven-pinker-says-world-getting-better-in-spite-authoritarian-populism-un/.

18. Darren Loucaides, "What Happens When Techno-Utopians Actually Run a Country," *Wired*, February 12, 2019, https://www.wired.com/story/italy-five-star-movement-techno-utopians/.

19. Robyn Dixon and David L. Stern, "How Ukraine's Zelensky Lost the Anti-Corruption Movement," *Washington Post*, March 17, 2020.

20. David Hesse, "'Ich glaube nicht an die direkte Demokratie," *Tages-Anzeiger*, March 30, 2019, 45.

21. Stuart Thompson, "'Canada Is Broken,' Say Majority of Canadians in Poll Taken in Wake of Rail Blockades," *National Post*, February 28, 2020.

22. Zselyke Csaky, *Dropping the Democratic Façade* (Washington, DC: Freedom House, 2020), 1.

23. Nicole Goodkind, "Inside Trump's War on the Postal Service," *Fortune*, August 14, 2020, https://fortune.com/2020/08/14/usps-trump-mail-in-voting-postal-service-2020-election-stamps-post-office/.

24. Steven Levitsky and Daniel Ziblatt, *How Democracies Die* (New York: Broadway Books, 2018), 5.

Chapter 1

1. "Remarks by President Obama in Address to the People of Europe," April 25, 2016, https://obamawhitehouse.archives.gov/the-press-office/2016/04/25/remarks-president-obama-address-people-europe.

2. See, for example, Michael Strain, *The American Dream Is Not Dead: (But Populism Could Kill It)* (West Conshohocken, PA: Templeton Press, 2020); Gregg Easterbrook, *It's Better Than It Looks: Reasons for Optimism in an Age of Fear* (New York: Public Affairs, 2018); Michael Cohen and Micah Zenko, *Clear and Present Safety: The World Has Never Been Better and Why That Matters to Americans* (New Haven, CT: Yale University Press, 2019).

3. William Davies, *Nervous States: Democracy and the Decline of Reason* (New York: W. W. Norton, 2019), xvi–xvii.

4. Eric Hoffer, *The True Believer* (New York: Harper & Row, 1951), 51–52.

5. George Will, "Crises and the Collectivist Temptation," *Washington Post*, April 3, 2020.

6. Experts disagree on why crime dropped over a 25-year period, but the reality of the decline is unarguable. For a quick survey of theories, see Matt Ford, "What Caused the Great Crime Decline in the U.S.?," *The Atlantic*, April 16, 2016.

7. Daniel W. Drezner, "This Time Is Different: Why U.S. Foreign Policy Will Never Recover," *Foreign Affairs*, May/June 2019.

8. Andrew J. Bacevich, *The Age of Illusions* (New York: Henry Holt, 2020), 2.

9. Trump launched a military attack on Iranian general Qasem Soleimani in early 2020, and just days after his defeat in the November 2020 election asked for options to strike Iran's nuclear facilities. He was, according to reports in the press, talked out of this by his advisers. I was among the observers who were concerned that Trump would try to use military action as a last-ditch effort to stay in office, or to saddle incoming president Joe Biden with a war. See Eric Schmitt, Maggie Haberman, David E. Sanger, Helene Cooper, and Lara Jakes, "Trump Sought Options for Attacking Iran to Stop Its Growing Nuclear Program," *New York Times*, December 2, 2020, and Tom Nichols, "Trump Could Still Start a Last-Ditch War with Iran," *The Atlantic*, December 30, 2020.

10. Pete Echells, "Declinism: Is the World Actually Getting Worse?" *The Guardian*, January 16, 2015.

11. Even nonhuman primates resent inequality, which suggests it might be a hard-wired evolutionary adaptation related to cooperation. See Sarah F. Brosnan and Frans B. M. de Waal, "Monkeys Reject Unequal Pay," *Nature* 425, September

2003, 297–299. One common finding (among humans, of course) is that people will reject improvement in their own situation if it means a fall in their own relative standing. As one study found, a majority of the respondents told the researchers that "a policy that increased their absolute income but lowered their relative income did not make them feel better off." See Sara Solnick and David Hemenway, "Is More Always Better? A Survey on Positional Concerns," *Journal of Economic Behavior & Organization* 37(3), November 1998, 381.

12. Hoffer, *True Believer*, 29.

13. E. J. Dionne, "Populism Isn't the Problem: It's a Response to Inequality," in Strain, *The American Dream Is Not Dead*, 115.

14. Toomas Hendrik Ilves, "Laughter as Medicine," *The American Interest*, November 12, 2019.

15. Quoted in Isabel Wilkerson, "Paradox of '94: Gloomy Voters in Good Times," *New York Times*, October 31, 1994, A1.

16. Charles Schwab Corporation, "2019 Modern Wealth Survey," https://www.aboutschwab.com/modernwealth2019.

17. Bruce Bartlett, "The Whiners Who Earn $200,000 and Complain They're Broke," *New Republic*, July 20, 2020.

18. The debate, "Is Middle Class Stagnation a Myth?," was hosted by the website Pairagraph in September 2020, from which both Boudreaux's and Milanovic's responses are taken. See https://www.pairagraph.com/dialogue/320a8c4b776b4214a24f7633e9b67795?1100.

19. Strain, *The American Dream Is Not Dead*, 59, 132–135.

20. See Strain, *The American Dream Is Not Dead*, 59–60.

21. Colin Woodard, "Half of Americans Don't Vote: What Are They Thinking?" *Politico*, February 19, 2019.

22. Simon Kuper, "The Revenge of the Middle-Class Anti-elitist: Why the Comfortably Well-Off Voted for Trump, Brexit and Italy's Lega," *Financial Times*, February 13, 2020.

23. Charles Kenny, "The Bogus Backlash to Globalization," *Foreign Affairs*, November 9, 2018.

24. Jake Tapper tells this story and its relation to *A Face in the Crowd* in "Why Americans Fall for Grifters," *The Atlantic*, November 2020.

25. Maria Recio, "These Texans Have Been Charged in the Capitol Riot—So Far," *Austin American-Statesman*, January 16, 2021; Ben Feuerherd, "Capitol Rioter Seeks OK to Travel to Mexico's Spring Break Haven," *New York Post*, February 1, 2021.

26. Strain, *The American Dream Is Not Dead*, 87.

27. Edward Luce, *The Retreat of Western Liberalism* (New York: Grove Press, 2017), 34.

28. Luce, *Retreat of Western Liberalism*, 32.

29. Charlie Warzel, "I Talked to the Cassandra of the Internet Age," *New York Times*, February 4, 2021.

30. See Tom Nichols, *The Death of Expertise* (New York: Oxford University Press, 2017), 140.

31. I was on Bill Maher's HBO show, *Real Time*, in August 2019, for example, when he said that he was hoping for an economic downturn that would then sweep Trump from office, a position with which I did not agree and for which Maher took great criticism. Others, such as some of the critics of Brexit, hoped that economic ruin, as awful as it would be, would also force people to their senses. See John Bowden, "Bill Maher Roots for Recession So That Trump Loses in 2020," *The Hill*, August 10, 2019, https://thehill.com/blogs/in-the-know/in-the-know/456942-bill-maher-roots-for-recession-so-that-trump-loses-in-2020. I argued in 2018 that Trump supporters should be given the trade war they voted for, so that they could experience its effects. Tom Nichols, "Trump Promised a Trade War. Should We Let His Voters Get What They Asked For?" *USA Today*, June 6, 2018.

32. Neil Postman, *Amusing Ourselves to Death* (New York: Penguin, 1985).

Chapter 2

1. For a review of Banfield's life and work, see James Q. Wilson, "The Independent Mind of Edward Banfield," *The Public Interest*, Winter 2003, 63–88.

2. For examples of work on social capital, see Robert Putnam, *Bowling Alone: The Collapse and Revival of American Community* (New York: Simon & Schuster, 2000), and Francis Fukuyama, *Trust* (New York: Free Press, 1996).

3. This and all other excepts from Banfield are from Edward C. Banfield, *The Moral Basis of a Backward Society* (New York: Free Press, 1958).

4. See Putnam, *Bowling Alone.*

5. See Drew Desilver, "In Past Elections, U.S. Trailed Most Developed Countries in Voter Turnout," Pew Research Center, November 3, 2020, https://www.pewresearch.org/fact-tank/2020/11/03/in-past-elections-u-s-trailed-most-developed-countries-in-voter-turnout/. The hotly contested 2020 election was the exception to this trend; U.S. election turnout in 2020 reached its highest level since 1908, cresting at nearly 67 percent of the eligible public.

6. Wilson, "The Independent of Mind of Edward Banfield."

7. See Robert Putnam, *Making Democracy Work* (Princeton, NJ: Princeton University Press, 1993).

8. Maurizio Viroli, *The Liberty of Servants: Berlusconi's Italy* (Princeton, NJ: Princeton University Press, 2012), xiii.

9. Viroli, *The Liberty of Servants*, xiii.

10. John R. Hibbing and Elizabeth Theiss-Morse, *Stealth Democracy: Americans' Beliefs about How Government Should Work* (Cambridge, UK: Cambridge University Press, 2002) 112–115

11. Jonathan Rauch, "How American Politics Went Insane," *The Atlantic*, July/August 2016.

12. Rauch, "How American Politics Went Insane."

13. Yamiche Alcindor, "Die-Hard Bernie Sanders Backers See F.B.I. as Answer to Their Prayers," *New York Times*, May 27, 2016.

14. See Philip Converse, "The Nature of Belief Systems in Mass Publics," in David Apter, ed., *Ideology and Discontent* (New York: The Free Press, 1964).

15. See Ezra Klein, "No One's Less Moderate Than Moderates," *Vox*, February 26, 2015, https://www.vox.com/2014/7/8/5878293/lets-stop-using-the-word-moderate.

16. Lee Drutman, "The Moderate Middle Is a Myth," FiveThirtyEight, September 24, 2019, https://fivethirtyeight.com/features/the-moderate-middle-is-a-myth/.

17. Jonathan Rauch, "How American Politics Went Insane," *The Atlantic*, July/August 2016.

18. Pearce tweeted some of his interviews; see https://twitter.com/mattdpearce/status/1217864280126775297?s=20.

19. Quoted in Dave Wasserman, "The One County in America That Voted in a Landslide for Both Trump and Obama," FiveThirtyEight, November 9, 2017, https://fivethirtyeight.com/features/the-one-county-in-america-that-voted-in-a-landslide-for-both-trump-and-obama/.

20. This and following quotes are from Tim Alberta, "Trump's Biggest Problem Isn't Wealthy Suburbanites. It's the White Working Class," *Politico*, July 28, 2020, https://www.politico.com/news/magazine/2020/07/28/letter-to-washington-scranton-white-working-class-381320.

21. J. V. Last, "Your VP Derby Hot Sheet," *The Bulwark*, July 29, 2020, https://thebulwark.com/your-vp-derby-hot-sheet/.

22. For a good explanation of "negative partisanship" and its electoral effects, see Lee Drutman, "How Hatred Came to Dominate American Politics," FiveThirtyEight, October 5, 2020, https://fivethirtyeight.com/features/how-hatred-negative-partisanship-came-to-dominate-american-politics/.

23. Jonathan Rauch, "Rethinking Polarization," *National Affairs*, Winter 2021.

24. George Packer, "We Are Living in a Failed State," *The Atlantic*, June 2020.

25. Mallory Simon, "Over 1,000 Health Professionals Sign a Letter Saying, Don't Shut Down Protests Using Coronavirus Concerns as an Excuse," CNN, June 5, 2020, https://www.cnn.com/2020/06/05/health/health-care-open-letter-protests-coronavirus-trnd/index.html.

26. The excerpts of the tape are available online at numerous sites, including Jamie Gangel, Jeremy Herb, and Elizabeth Stuart, " 'Play It Down': Trump Admits to Concealing the True Threat of Coronavirus in New Woodward Book," CNN, September 9, 2020, https://www.cnn.com/2020/09/09/politics/bob-woodward-rage-book-trump-coronavirus/index.html.

27. Damon Linker, "Coronavirus Is Revealing a Shattered Country," *The Week*, July 1, 2020.

28. Franklin Foer, "The Good Son," *The Atlantic*, August 13, 2020.

29. Eugene Scott, Natalie Jennings, and Amber Phillips, "Barack Obama's Full Democratic Convention Speech, Annotated," *Washington Post*, August 20, 2020, https://www.washingtonpost.com/politics/2020/08/20/obama-convention-speech-annotated/.

30. Russell Berman, "Barack Obama Is Scared," *The Atlantic*, August 20, 2020.

Chapter 3

1. See "John Adams to Mercy Warren, 16 April 1776," and "Samuel Adams to James Warren, 4 November 1775," both available from the University of Chicago Press at "The Founders Constitution," https://press-pubs.uchicago.edu/founders/.

2. The National Archive of the United States, Founders Online, "Judicial Powers of the National Government, [20 June] 1788," https://founders.archives.gov/documents/Madison/01-11-02-0101.

3. Christopher Lasch, *The Culture of Narcissism* (New York: W. W. Norton, 1979), xvi.

4. Lasch, *Culture of Narcissism*, 90.

5. See David Frum, *How We Got Here: The 70s: The Decade That Brought You Modern Live (For Better or For Worse)* (New York: Basic Books), 2, and Mark Lilla, *The Once and Future Liberal: After Identity Politics* (New York: HarperCollins, 2017), 21..

6. Jean Twenge and W. Keith Campbell, *The Narcissism Epidemic* (New York: Atria, 2009), x.

7. See Robert Putnam, *Bowling Alone: The Collapse and Revival of American Community* (New York: Simon & Schuster, 2000). For a brief review of some of the arguments about students, college age and younger (and some questions about Twenge and Campbell's methods), see Sadie Dingfelder, "Reflecting on Narcissism: Are Young People More Self-Obsessed Than Ever Before?" *Monitor on Psychology* 42(2), February 2011. For a more optimistic view of younger people, see Nick Roll, "The Kids Are Alright," *Inside Higher Ed*, October 13, 2017.

8. Joan Didion, "Eye on the Prize," *New York Review of Books*, September 24, 1992.

9. See, for example, Alex Shephard, "Mary Trump Diagnoses the President," *New Republic*, July 10, 2020.

10. Quoted in Chris Cillizza, "The Single Most Amazing Sentence from a Focus Group of Trump Supporters," *Washington Post*, July 30, 2015. This was one

of many such examples from focus groups and interviews with Trump voters throughout his time as a politician.

11. Eliot Cohen, "The Age of Trump," *American Interest*, February 26, 2016.

12. "Newsweek Editor Evan Thomas: Obama Is 'Sort Of God,'" Real Clear Politics, June 5, 2009, https://www.realclearpolitics.com/video/2009/06/05/newsweek_editor_evan_thomas_obama_is_sort_of_god.html.

13. Twenge and Campbell, *Narcissism Epidemic*, 259–260.

14. Laura Wronski, "Axios|SurveyMonkey Poll: Anger at the News," SurveyMonkey, October 2019, https://www.surveymonkey.com/curiosity/axios-hbo-poll-october-2019/; see also Scott Hensley, Poll: "Americans Say We're Angrier Than a Generation Ago," National Public Radio, June 26, 2019, https://www.npr.org/sections/health-shots/2019/06/26/735757156/poll-americans-say-were-angrier-than-a-generation-ago.

15. Rick Noack, "Nope, It's Not Just You: The World Around You Really Is Getting Angrier," *Washington Post*, April 26, 2019.

16. Julie Ray, "Americans' Stress, Worry and Anger Intensified in 2018," Gallup, April 25, 2019, https://news.gallup.com/poll/249098/americans-stress-worry-anger-intensified-2018.aspx.

17. Justin McCarthy, "New High of 90% of Americans Satisfied with Personal Life," Gallup, February 6, 2020, https://news.gallup.com/poll/284285/new-high-americans-satisfied-personal-life.aspx.

18. Michael Grunwald, "GOP Delegates Say the Economy Is Terrible—Except Where They Live," *Politico*, July 19, 2016, https://www.politico.com/magazine/story/2016/07/rnc-convention-gop-delegates-economy-is-great-214068/.

19. "Since Obama was elected," Pew researchers wrote in 2010, "Democrats have become more optimistic than Republicans about the state of the national economy. For most of the time that George W. Bush was in office, the reverse was true: Republicans were more upbeat—often, much more upbeat—than Democrats." Pew Research Center, "How the Great Recession Has Changed Life in America," June 30, 2010.

20. Arthur Brooks, "Our Culture of Contempt," *New York Times*, March 2, 2019.

21. Lilla, *Once and Future Liberal*, 105.

22. In case readers were in doubt that Anton aimed for both offensiveness and pretension, he decked his article out with a faux Roman pseudonym, as if it were a colonial era call to arms. See Publius Decius Mus, "The Flight 93 Election," *Claremont Review of Books*, September 5, 2016.

23. Erickson made these points in his *Substack* newsletter, in an article titled "Yep, I Did Change," in August 2020, and in subsequent responses to my questions to him.

24. Avi Selk, "Do You Really Believe This Is the Most Important Election of Our Lives? Because We've Heard That Before," *Washington Post*, August 29, 2019.

25. David French, "The Hate at the Heart of Conspiracy Theory," *Persuasion*, September 23, 2020, https://www.persuasion.community/p/the-hate-at-the-heart-of-conspiracy.

26. Eric Hoffer, *The True Believer* (New York: Harper Perennial, 1951), 14

27. Joseph Epstein, *Envy* (New York: Oxford University Press, 2003), 75.

28. Epstein, *Envy*, 81.

29. See Ian Buchanan, "Ressentiment," *The Oxford Dictionary of Critical Theory* (Oxford UK: Oxford University Press, 2010).

30. Epstein might have had a point that most holders of doctorates usually do not use their titles, but his article went on about his own lack of a doctorate, how he finished his education while on active duty in the military, and how doctorates are no longer prestigious in any case due to "the erosion of seriousness and the relaxation of standards in university education generally"—in sum, a series of complaints that amounted to a master class in exactly the unconscious *ressentiment* Epstein otherwise understands so well. Joseph Epstein, "Is There a Doctor in the White House? Not If You Need an M.D.," *Wall Street Journal*, December 11, 2020.

31. Quoted in Pankaj Mishra, *Age of Anger* (New York: Farrar, Straus and Giroux, 2017), 333.

32. Jonah Goldberg, "The Nietzschean Concept That Explains Today's PC Culture," *National Review*, June 19, 2015; Alan Wolfe, *The Politics of Petulance: America in an Age of Immaturity* (Chicago: University of Chicago Press, 2018), 34.

33. Jonathan Metzl, *Dying of Whiteness* (New York: Basic Books, 2019), 3.

34. Metzl, *Dying of Whiteness*, 3.

35. Vanessa Williamson, Theda Skocpol, and John Coggin, "The Tea Party and the Remaking of Republican Conservatism," *Perspectives on Politics* 9(1), March 2011, 26–27

36. Quoted in Patricia Mazzei, "'It's Just Too Much': A Florida Town Grapples with a Shutdown after a Hurricane," *New York Times*, January 7, 2019.

37. Quoted in Andrew McCormick, "Madness on Capitol Hill," *The Nation*, January 7, 2021.

38. Thomas Frank, *What's the Matter with Kansas?* (New York: Picador, 2004), 248.

39. Frank, *What's the Matter with Kansas?*, 62.

40. Frank, *What's the Matter with Kansas?*, 168.

41. Frank, *What's the Matter with Kansas?*, 141.

42. Edward Luce, *The Retreat of Western Liberalism* (New York: Grove Press, 2017), 47.

43. Lilla, *Once and Future Liberal*, 93.

44. See Anne Applebaum, *Twilight of Democracy: The Seductive Lure of Authoritarianism* (New York: Doubleday, 2020), 73–75.

45. Serling penned episodes for his *Twilight Zone* television series in the early 1960s that foreshadowed "Tim Riley's Bar." One of them, "Walking Distance,"

is about an advertising man who stumbles into the past, where he visits his own peaceful childhood; he is told by his father than he must return to his own time. In "A Stop at Willoughby," another overworked, underappreciated executive falls asleep on his commuter train home each evening and imagines himself getting off at an early twentieth-century town called "Willoughby." In the end, he finally leaves the train to stay in the antique world of Willoughby—because he has died, presumably of stress from life in rat-race New York. See Marc Zicree, *The Twilight Zone Companion* (West Hollywood, CA: Silman-James Press, 1992), 119.

46. There is some disagreement over the original ending of "Tim Riley's Bar." Serling biographer Joel Engel claims that series producer Jack Laird tacked on the feel-good ending. Windom and costar Susannah Darrow later confirmed that they were given scripts with the bleaker ending. Director Don Taylor and others, however, say there was only the one ending. While there is evidence that Serling (who died in 1975) vacillated on the ending, there are no alternate scripts or treatments in Serling's archives. See Joel Engel, *Rod Serling: The Dreams and Nightmares of Life in the Twilight Zone* (Chicago: Contemporary Books, 1989), 327, and Scott Skelton and Jim Benson, *Rod Serling's Night Gallery: An After-Hours Tour* (Syracuse, NY: Syracuse University Press, 1999), 87–88.

47. Quoted in Joseph Barbato, "Student Protesters, Angry Construction Workers and a Violent Confrontation," *Washington Post*, August 14, 2020. For a full account of the riots and an argument that they marked the beginning of the great divide between the educated elite and the working class in the United States, see David Paul Kuhn, *The Hardhat Riot: Nixon, New York City, and the Dawn of the White Working-Class Revolution* (New York: Oxford University Press, 2020).

48. Edoardo Campanella and Marta Dassù, *Anglo Nostalgia: The Politics of Emotion in a Fractured West* (New York: Oxford University Press, 2019), 3.

Chapter 4

1. Mark Arsenault, "Is Death the Great Equalizer?" *Sunday Boston Globe*, September 26, 2020, 1.

2. Brooks made the comment on Bill Maher's show *Real Time* on HBO, November 16, 2020.

3. The German director Fritz Lang's 1927 classic silent film *Metropolis* is a perfect depiction of this notion, with the workers living underground in an almost literal Hell while the elites romp in an Elysian paradise above them.

4. Patrick Buchanan, *Right from the Beginning* (Washington, DC: Regnery, 1990), 90.

5. Charles Krauthammer, "Buchanan Explained," *Washington Post*, March 1, 1992.

6. See Thomas Frank, "How the Democrats Lost Touch on Trade," *Politico*, September/October 2016, https://www.politico.com/magazine/story/2016/09/2016-election-working-class-trade-tpp-trade-democrats-214219/; Thomas Frank, *The People, No!* (New York: Henry Holt, 2020), 17.

7. Frank, *The People, No!*, 254.

8. Victor Davis Hanson, "The Origins of Our Second Civil War," *National Review Online*, July 31, 2018, https://www.nationalreview.com/2018/07/origins-of-second-civil-war-globalism-tech-boom-immigration campus-radicalism/.

9. Various, "Against the Dead Consensus," *First Things*, March 21, 2019, https://www.firstthings.com/web-exclusives/2019/03/against-the-dead-consensus.

10. Frank makes the point that this is exactly why "elites" are allergic to any form of populism: because it is a powerful movement that transcends partisanship. See Frank, *The People, No!*, 252–253.

11. Jack Snyder, "The Broken Bargain: How Nationalism Came Back," *Foreign Affairs* 98(2), March/April 2019, 58–59.

12. David Frum, "If Liberals Won't Enforce Borders, Fascists Will," *The Atlantic*, April 2019.

13. See Ian Bremmer, *Us vs. Them: The Failure of Globalism* (New York: Portfolio/Penguin, 2018), 8–9.

14. My colleague Jonathan Cristol notes that "neoliberalism" is often a way of saying "international market capitalism," and is often little more than an "amorphous political pejorative."

15. Noah Smith, "The Dark Side of Globalization: Why Seattle's 1999 Protesters Were Right," *The Atlantic*, January 6, 2014.

16. Shadi Hamid, "Left Populism and the Rediscovery of Agonistic Politics," *American Affairs* 2(4), Winter 2018.

17. The phrase "It's the economy, stupid" is usually attributed to Clinton campaign guru James Carville. Hamid, "Left Populism."

18. See Francis Fukuyama, "E Pluribus Unum? The Fight over Identity Politics," *Foreign Affairs* 98(2), March/April 2019, 168.

19. See David Autor, David Dorn, and Gordon Hanson, "The China Syndrome: Local Labor Market Effects of Import Competition in the United States," *American Economic Review* 103(6), October 2013, 2121–2168.

20. Scott Lincicome, "Testing the "China Shock": Was Normalizing Trade with China a Mistake?," CATO Institute Policy Analysis 895, July 8, 2020, https://www.cato.org/policy-analysis/testing-china-shock-was-normalizing-trade-china-mistake.

21. See, for example, James Q. Wilson, *The Marriage Problem: How Our Culture Has Weakened Families* (New York: Harper, 2003).

22. Noah Smith, "The Late '10s Were Better for Incomes Than the '90s," *Bloomberg Opinion*, September 23, 2020, https://www.bloombergquint.com/gadfly/median-household-income-grew-more-in-the-10s-than-the-90s.

23. Kevin Williamson, "Trumpism Expanded the GOP Tent," *Washington Post*, November 9, 2020.

24. Warren Brown, "The Day of the 7-Year Car Loan," *Washington Post*, April 13, 1986.

25. "People can get into very expensive cars," a business school professor told the *Journal*. "Households are taking on, on average, more risk." Ben Eisen and Adrienne Roberts, "The Seven-Year Auto Loan: America's Middle Class Can't Afford Its Cars," *Wall Street Journal*, October 1, 2019.

26. See, for example, Michael J. Hicks and Srikant Devaraj, *The Myth and the Reality of Manufacturing in America* (Muncie, IN: Ball State University, Center for Business and Economic Research, April 2017), 6, https://conexus.cber-data.org/files/MfgReality.pdf.

27. Christopher Lasch, *The Culture of Narcissism* (New York: W. W. Norton, 1979), xiii.

28. I wrote of the utter hypocrisy of this approach in 2016. See Tom Nichols, "Whitewashing Working-Class Woes," *New York Daily News*, June 27, 2016.

29. Cupp made the comment to Andrew Sullivan in a discussion on Bill Maher's *Real Time* on HBO, April 1, 2019.

30. Julian Borger, " 'Trump Thought I Was a Secretary': Fiona Hill on the President, Putin and Populism," *The Guardian*, June 12, 2020.

31. Bremmer, *Us vs. Them*, 5–6.

32. Kevin Williamson, "If Your Town Is Failing, Just Go," *National Review Online*, October 6, 2015.

33. Kevin Williamson, "Chaos in the Family, Chaos in the State: The White Working Class's Dysfunction," *National Review Online*, March 17, 2016, https://www.nationalreview.com/2015/10/mobility-globalization-poverty-solution/.

34. Andre Dubus, *Townie: A Memoir* (New York: W. W. Norton, 2011), 9.

35. The first version, according to an interview with Joel aired on XM Radio, was about the boredom of life in Levittown, New York, and then the tune returned to him when he played the Lehigh Valley in Pennsylvania. He settled on Allentown as a better rhyme for the lyrics, although the factories were in nearby Bethlehem.

36. Protest songs like "Eve of Destruction" were mostly relegated to folk music and would not dent the pop charts until the late 1960s; even the 1966 Vietnam-related "The Ballad of the Green Berets" was a patriotic song that had to settle for coming in behind Frank Sinatra and "Strangers in the Night" for the year.

37. Daniel McGraw, " 'The Craziness Is Exhausting People': How Trump Could Lose the Ohio-Pennsylvania Border," The Bulwark, August 3, 2020,

https://thebulwark.com/the-craziness-is-exhausting-people/. "Most people 65 and over still remember 'Black Monday' in September 1977," McGraw notes, "when a Youngstown giant steel mill closed its doors without warning and 5,000 workers instantly lost their jobs." The closing might be within memory for people who were children, but the experience of working in the mill for any appreciable amount of time would be limited to the elderly.

38. Williamson, "The White Working-Class's Dysfunction."
39. See Jennifer Taub, *Other People's Houses* (New Haven, CT: Yale University Press, 2014) 4–5.
40. Gretchen Morgenson and Joshua Rosner, *Reckless Endangerment* (New York: St. Martin's, 2012), 181.
41. As the scholar Michael Sandel wrote later: "His moral voice muted, Obama placated rather than articulated the seething public anger toward Wall Street." Michael J. Sandel, *The Tyranny of Merit* (New York: Farrar, Straus and Giroux, 2020), 21.
42. See Jeremy Peters, "The Tea Party Didn't Get What It Wanted, but It Did Unleash the Politics of Anger," *New York Times*, August 30, 2019.
43. This is known as "Fenno's paradox," named for Richard Fenno, the political scientist who first documented it. As the pollster Harry Enten notes, incumbents are not immune to low views of Congress, but they always run ahead of it in approval as individuals with their own voters. Harry Enten, "Disliking Congress, as a Whole and as Individuals," FiveThirtyEight, July 1, 2014, https://fivethirtyeight.com/features/disliking-congress-as-a-whole-and-as-individuals/.

Chapter 5

1. For links to all these reactions, see Tom Nichols, "I Tweeted That I Couldn't Stand Indian Cuisine and Started an International Food Fight," *USA Today*, November 26, 2019.
2. See, for example, my presentation to the Macdonald-Laurier Institute in Ottawa, Canada: Tom Nichols, "Russia's Actions Are a Direct Attack on US and Allied Democracies," *MLI Commentary*, October 5, 2018.
3. Tom Nichols, *The Death of Expertise* (New York: Oxford University Press, 2017), Chapter 4.
4. Michael S. Schmidt and Luke Broadwater, "Officers' Injuries, Including Concussions, Show Scope of Violence at Capitol Riot," *The New York Times*, April 2, 2021.
5. Robert A. Pape and Keven Ruby, "The Capitol Rioters Aren't Like Other Extremists," *The Atlantic*, February 2, 2021.

6. This term, borrowing from Marx's "lumpenproletariat" (the working class that cares about nothing and is too docile for elites even to bother with repressing them) was brought into the modern political science discourse by C. Wright Mills to describe not the poor, but a *middle* class that is "bored at work, restless at play"; other works have pointed out how this sense of unfulfillment creates a relatively prosperous class that is nonetheless antagonistic to democratic values. C. Wright Mills, *White Collar* (New York: Oxford University Press, 1951), 58–59. For a similar view of the January insurrection, see Michael Weiss, "Little Man, What Now?" *Newlines Magazine*, January 20, 2021.

7. See Pilar Menendez, "Texas Real Estate Agent Who Took Private Jet to Capitol Riot Is Arrested," *Daily Beast*, January 15, 2021, and Brittany Shammas, "The Woman Involved in the Capitol Riot Has Not Been Granted Permission to Vacation in Mexico (Yet)," *Washington Post*, February 3, 2021.

8. Rhiannon Lucy Cosslett, "Watching Porn in Public Is Not OK. It's Harassment," *The Guardian*, January 16, 2017.

9. Adrienne LaFrance, "Facebook Is a Doomsday Machine," *The Atlantic*, December 15, 2020.

10. Pew Research Center, "Mobile Fact Sheet," June 12, 2019, https://www.pewresearch.org/internet/fact-sheet/mobile/.

11. Pornhub has successfully created an image as just another service on the internet by donating to organizations fighting for racial equality, claiming it plowed Bostonians out of a snowstorm, and offering free pornography to help people cope with COVID-19 shutdowns—even as the company angrily denied charges that it monetizes child abuse and sexual assault. See Nicholas Kristof, "The Children of Pornhub," *New York Times*, December 4, 2020. *Boston* magazine suspects no plowing was done, but that Pornhub pulled off a "genius marketing stunt." See Spencer Buell, "Did Pornhub Actually Plow Snow in Boston?" *Boston*, March 29, 2017.

12. Maeve Duggan and Aaron Smith, "The Political Environment on Social Media," Pew Research Center, October 25, 2016, https://www.pewresearch.org/internet/2016/10/25/the-political-environment-on-social-media/.

13. Yevgeny Simpkin, "Social Media Is the Problem," The Bulwark, July 31, 2020, https://thebulwark.com/social-media-is-the-problem/.

14. Quoted in Zack Stanton, "How 2020 Killed Off Democrats' Demographic Hopes," *Politico*, November 12, 2020, https://www.politico.com/news/magazine/2020/11/12/2020-election-analysis-democrats-future-david-shor-interview-436334.

15. "Shitposting" is the injection of irrelevant or silly memes, images, and videos into an online discussion in order to be annoying and derail conversation. See Cordelia Jenkins, "Year in a Word: Shitposting," *Financial Times*, December 30, 2019.

16. A 2018 study by two scholars from Northeastern University found that schools were safer but that cable news and social media defeated the public's willingness to accept this statistical reality. See Martin Kaste, "Despite Heightened Fear of School Shootings, It's Not a Growing Epidemic," National Public Radio, March 15, 2018, https://www.npr.org/transcripts/593831564. A year later, a University of Chicago poll found that American anxieties about safety in schools have only increased in the two decades since the Columbine High School massacre despite the reality that "school is still among the safest places an American child can be." See Dana Goldstein, "20 Years after Columbine, Schools Have Gotten Safer. But Fears Have Only Grown," *New York Times*, April 20, 2019.

17. Timothy Snyder, "The American Abyss," *New York Times Magazine*, January 9, 2021.

18. Nellie Bowles, "A Dark Consensus about Screens and Kids Begins to Emerge in Silicon Valley," *New York Times*, October 26, 2018.

19. This and subsequent citations from Twenge are from Jean M. Twenge, "Have Smartphones Destroyed a Generation?," *The Atlantic*, September 2017.

20. Brian Primack et al., "Use of Multiple Social Media Platforms and Symptoms of Depression and Anxiety: A Nationally-Representative Study among U.S. Young Adults," *Computers in Human Behavior* 69, April 2017, 1–9. Platforms studied included Facebook, YouTube, Twitter, Google Plus, Instagram, Snapchat, Reddit, Tumblr, Pinterest, Vine, and LinkedIn. Likewise, Greg Lukianoff and Jonathan Haidt have pursued the impact both on the mental health and on the political views of a generation of younger people who were the first group to grow up "with smartphones in their pockets" and who were "plugged into social media" at an early age, arguing that this exposure to hyper-connectedness increases emotional fragility and anxiety. See Jonathan Haidt and Greg Lukianoff, *The Coddling of the American Mind* (New York: Penguin, 2018), 146–160; Greg Lukianoff, "Catching up with 'Coddling' Part One: Introduction," Foundation for Individual Rights in Education (FIRE), April 29, 2020, https://www.thefire.org/catching-up-with-coddling-part-one-introduction/

21. Amanda Carpenter, "The GOP Is a Propaganda Party," The Bulwark, November 30, 2020, https://thebulwark.com/the-gop-is-a-propaganda-party/.

22. Ben Smith, "We Worked Together on the Internet. Last Week, He Stormed the Capitol," *New York Times*, January 10, 2021.

23. Michael I. Norton, Jeana H. Frost, and Dan Ariely, "Less Is More: The Lure of Ambiguity, or Why Familiarity Breeds Contempt," *Journal of Personality and Social Psychology* 92(1), February 2007, 97–105.

24. Jeff Horwitz and Deepa Seetharaman, "Facebook Executives Shut Down Efforts to Make the Site Less Divisive," *Wall Street Journal*, May 26, 2020.

25. Jonathan Haidt and Tobias Rose-Stockwell, "The Dark Psychology of Social Networks," *The Atlantic*, December 2019. This also creates a market for what a veteran national journalist once privately described to me as the "dunk-five" culture he thinks rules aspiring younger writers who seek to promote themselves through social media. "Dunk" on your enemies—that is, find something negative to say about people you don't like or with whom you disagree—and then "high-five" your friends, building social solidarity among like-minded consumers while contributing very little to the public conversation.

26. Anyone who has ever tangled with Taleb online will have to smile at this description: "The blast radius around his twitter feed is not a safe space for anyone besides members of his own cult of Mesopotamian personality." Venkatesh Rao, "The Internet of Beefs," ribbonfarm.com, January 16, 2020, https://www.ribbonfarm.com/2020/01/16/the-internet-of-beefs/.

27. Robert Putnam, "Tuning In, Tuning Out: The Strange Disappearance of Social Capital in America," *PS: Political Science and Politics* 28(4), December 1995, 678.

28. Ronda Kaysen, "Why Zillow Addicts Can't Look Away," *New York Times*, September 14, 2018.

29. See, for example, Brenna Donovan, "Why Realtors Hate HGTV," *Boston Globe*, April 19, 2018.

30. Quoted in Joseph Epstein, *Envy* (New York: Oxford University Press, 2003), 32.

31. One of the earliest studies on this was Hui-Tzu Grace Chou and Nicholas Edge, " 'They Are Happier and Having Better Lives Than I Am': The Impact of Using Facebook on Perceptions of Others' Lives," *Cyberpsychology, Behavior, and Social Networking* 15(2), 2012. Subsequent studies confirmed this effect not as an inevitable result of Facebook use, but among those who engage in "surveillance use" of Facebook "to see how their friends are doing compared with their own lives." See Edson C. Tandoc, Patrick Ferrucci, and Margaret Duffy, "Facebook Use, Envy, and Depression among College Students: Is Facebooking Depressing?" *Computers in Human Behavior* 43 (February 2015).

32. Hamza Shaban, "Deactivating Facebook Leaves People Less Informed but Happier, Study Finds," *Washington Post*, January 31, 2019.

33. Yoni Appelbaum, "How America Ends," *The Atlantic*, December 2019.

34. See, for example, Robert P. Jones, *The End of White Christian America* (New York: Simon & Schuster, 2016), 199–240.

35. Quoted in Stanton, "How 2020 Killed Off Democrats' Demographic Hopes."

36. Among them was Missouri Republican Todd Akin's assertion, when fending off a question about whether abortion should be allowed in the case of rape, that abortion wouldn't be necessary because "if it's a legitimate rape, the female body has ways to try to shut the whole thing down." Democrats across the U.S. seized on this statement immediately and made it into a national issue.

See Lori Moore, "Rep. Todd Akin: The Statement and the Reaction," *New York Times*, August 20, 2012, and Anna Palmer, "Dems Nationwide Run against Akin," *Politico*, October 8, 2012, https://www.politico.com/story/2012/10/dems-nationwide-run-against-akin-082125.

37. David Samuels, "The Rap on Rap: The 'Black Music' That Isn't Either," *New Republic*, November 11, 1991.

38. Ice Cube, who formed the group NWA (which stood for Niggaz With Attitude) later starred in dozens of movies and television shows, including several comedies. Ice-T, an artist whose band Body Count created a national uproar with a song called "Cop Killer," later became a mainstay—playing a police officer—on the U.S. television series *Law and Order: SVU*, and by 2020 was selling extended auto warranties in commercials. Flavor Flav, a founder of the group Public Enemy, became a reality TV star and appeared in a Pepsi commercial with Elton John during the Super Bowl in 2012.

39. Taryn Finley and Oliver Noble, "67 Times Rappers Name Dropped 'Donald Trump,'" *Huffington Post*, August 21, 2015, https://www.huffpost.com/entry/hip-hops-25-year-obsession-with-donald-trump_n_55d61727e4b055a6dab3524a.

40. Yevgeny Simkin notes that this is also how internet cults form: every town has someone walking around saying "The End Is Near," but the internet allows "all these guys to find each other so that now they think they're just as normal as everyone else." Simkin, "Social Media is the Problem."

41. The writer Will Wilkinson, for one, has made a compelling argument for the importance of population density in cultural conflict and polarization. See Will Wilkinson, "The Density Divide: Urbanization, Polarization, and Populist Backlash," Niskanen Center, June 2019, https://www.niskanen-center.org/the-density-divide-urbanization-polarization-and-populist-backlash/.

42. Damon Linker, "How Right-Wing Populism Overcame Distance," *The Week*, December 1, 2020.

43. Pankaj Mishra, *Age of Anger: A History of the Present* (New York: Farrar, Straus and Giroux, 2017), 6.

44. Dani Alexis Ryskamp, "The Life in *The Simpsons* Is No Longer Attainable," *The Atlantic*, December 29, 2020.

Conclusion

1. Jonathan Metzl, *Dying of Whiteness* (New York: Basic Books, 2019), 3–5.

2. Republican presidential candidate Ron Paul was visibly shocked when he asked an audience at a South Carolina primary debate in 2011 if he, as a physician, should let someone die if they were uninsured and many in the crowd

yelled "Yeah!" See Michael Muskal, "Support at GOP Debate for Letting the Uninsured Die," *Los Angeles Times*, September 13, 2011.

3. Kyle Dropp and Brendan Nyhan, "One-Third Don't Know Obamacare and Affordable Care Act Are the Same," *New York Times*, February 7, 2017.

4. "This confusion," Dropp and Nyhan, noted gently, "may affect the public debate over health care policy." Dropp and Nyhan, "One-Third Don't Know."

5. I discussed examples of this in *The Death of Expertise*, including the wildly wrong guesses of average Americans about everything from the location of North Korea to the size of the foreign aid budget. To ask Americans about foreign policy is to reenact comedian Jimmy Kimmel's regular feature where he stops citizens on the streets and lures them into very serious but ludicrous answers to nonsensical questions because they cannot bear to admit they know absolutely nothing about the issues.

6. Brink Lindsey, "In Search of Civic Virtue," Niskanen Center, February 2021, https://www.niskanencenter.org/in-search-of-civic-virtue/.

7. Alan Wolfe, *The Politics of Petulance* (Chicago: University of Chicago Press, 2018), 18.

8. Wolfe, *Politics of Petulance*, 163.

9. Charles Krauthammer, "The Authoritarian Temptation," *Washington Post*, November 8, 2019.

10. Jason Brennan calls for an "epistocracy" of rule by the intelligent, while Garrett Jones argues for more independence for certain kinds of government agencies, among other measures. See Jason Brennan, *Against Democracy* (Princeton, NJ: Princeton University Press, 2016), and Garrett Jones, *10% Less Democracy* (Stanford, CA: Stanford University Press, 2020).

11. Adrian Vermeule, "Beyond Originalism," *The Atlantic*, March 31, 2020. Perhaps I am too much a child of the television age, but Vermeule's creepy assurances reminded me of a classic science fiction television movie titled *Colossus: The Forbin Project*, in which a supercomputer entrusted with national defense becomes—as they always do—a sentient being who puts an end to the arms race by enslaving humanity. "In time," Colossus says at the end, "you will come to regard me not only with respect and awe, but with love."

12. Randy Barnett, "Common-Good Constitutionalism Reveals the Dangers of Any Non-originalist Approach to the Constitution," *The Atlantic*, April 3, 2020.

13. I first heard this example in a classroom at Boston University in 1983. For some reason, I was short a required course for graduation, and I filled it by taking an introductory course in philosophy with the late Erazim Kohak. With the usual arrogance of a graduating senior, I didn't think a freshman course would have much to offer me. And yet his description of a marriage governed by laws (part of his lecture on the notion of "the social contract") has stayed with me for nearly forty years.

14. A group of scholars even produced a book in 2008 with the title *The Party Decides*, arguing that party elites have too much influence over the process. Rather than choosing nominees in the "smoke-filled rooms" of an earlier time, filled with men and cigars making decisions in secret, *The Party Decides* made a persuasive case that "invisible primaries" among influential insiders and donors limited choices ahead of time, long before the actual voting. Marty Cohen, David Karol, Hans Noel, and John Zaller, *The Party Decides* (Chicago: University of Chicago Press, 2008).

15. Jonathan Rauch and Ray La Raja, "Too Much Democracy Is Bad for Democracy," *The Atlantic*, December 2019.

16. Counterfactuals are impossible to prove, but the Democrats were probably right to be worried about the electability of any of the other 2020 candidates, a point made by *Boston Globe* political reporter James Pindell a week after the election. James Pindell, "No, Bernie Sanders Wouldn't Have Won," *Boston Globe*, November 12, 2020.

17. See, for example, Thomas E. Ricks, *Making the Corps: 10th Anniversary Edition* (New York: Scribner, 2007); for the classic examination of how military nationalism leads officers to the "politics of wanting to be above politics," see Bengt Abrahamsson, *Military Professionalization and Political Power* (Beverly Hills, CA: SAGE, 1972).

18. I have argued at length that the prohibition against the use of military force in international affairs has dropped dramatically since the end of the Cold War, in part because of the willingness to use volunteers to intervene in humanitarian disasters. See Thomas Nichols, *Eve of Destruction* (Philadelphia: University of Pennsylvania Press, 2008), Chapter 2.

19. Craig Whitlock, "At War with the Truth," *Washington Post*, December 9, 2019.

20. David Frum, "The American System Is Broken," *The Atlantic*, November 4, 2020.

21. Ben Sasse, a U.S. senator from Nebraska, offered a package of reforms that ranged from turning off the cameras in the chamber—which might not matter much except to political junkies who watch C-SPAN2—to repealing the Seventeenth Amendment and abolishing the direct election of senators, which is purely wishful thinking about a bad idea. Ben Sasse, "Make the Senate Great Again," *Wall Street Journal*, September 8, 2020.

22. The average House district is now about twice as large as it was in 1950. See Sarah J. Eckman, "Apportionment and Redistricting Following the 2020 Census," Congressional Research Service, December 9, 2020, https://crsreports.congress.gov/product/pdf/IN/IN11360.

23. See Andrew Duehren, "Q&A: How Washington, D.C., Would Become a State," *Wall Street Journal*, June 26, 2020, and Jill Lawrence, "Wyoming, Monaco, Voting Rights and Taxes: All the Reasons Washington, DC Should Be a State," *USA Today*, September 18, 2019.

24. C. Wright Mills invoked this line by Balzac in his description of the modern lumpenproletariat. C. Wright Mills, *White Collar* (New York: Oxford University Press, 1951), 28.

25. Neil Postman, *Amusing Ourselves to Death* (New York: Penguin, 1985), 156.

26. When I mentioned this idea to my colleague Nick Gvosdev, he immediately said: "Vaccine nationalism," the demand by citizens that their governments hoard COVID-19 vaccines and "just get it for them," with no questions asked about how they got it, rather than disperse the vaccines in some sort of orderly or rational pattern. I am indebted to Nick for this insight. See, for example, the alarm raised by the head of World Health Organization on this subject: Tedros Adhanom Ghebreyesus, "Vaccine Nationalism Harms Everyone and Protects No One," *Foreign Policy*, February 2, 2021.

27. British prime minister Harold Macmillan once noted in a famous comment in 1943 that Britain was to America much as the Greeks were to the Romans—teachers and civilizers of a new empire. Christopher Hitchens wrote about this relationship in *Blood, Class and Empire: Anglo-American Ironies* (New York: Farrar, Straus and Giroux, 1990).

28. Robert Strassler, ed., *The Landmark Thucydides* (New York: Free Press, 1996), 112–118.

29. Abraham Lincoln, "Address to the Young Men's Lyceum of Springfield, Illinois," In *Speeches and Writings 1832–1858* (New York: Library of America, 1989), 28–29.

INDEX